Ted Barris divides his time between teaching at Toronto's Centennial College in the journalism department and writing/broadcasting professionally. His work on CBC and TVO is well known (he has earned a Billboard Radio Documentary Award and numerous ACTRA Award nominations) and his bylines appear in such publications as the *National Post* and *Globe and Mail*, and the *Legion, Beaver,* and *Air Force* magazines. He has published 16 non-fiction books. In 1993, he received the Canada 125 Medal "for service to Canada and community." In 2004, the Remembrance Service Association of Halifax recognized Ted Barris and his military history writing with its annual Patriot Award. In 2006, the 78th Fraser Highlander regiment awarded Barris its annual excellence award, the Bear Hackle Award, to recognize his "contribution to the awareness and preservation of Canadian military history and traditions."

Since January 1997, **David Bercuson** has been the Director of the Centre for Military and Strategic Studies at the University of Calgary and is also the Director of Programs of the Canadian Defence and Foreign Affairs Institute, based in Calgary. He has published on a wide range of topics, specializing in modern Canadian politics, Canadian defence and foreign policy, and Canadian military history. His most recent book is *The Fighting Canadians; Our Regimental History from New France to Afghanistan.*

Books of Merit

Deadlock in Korea

MILITARY HISTORY

Behind the Glory: Canada's Role in the Allied Air War
(1st edition, 1992)

Juno: Canadians at D-Day, June 6, 1944

Days of Victory: Canadians Remember, 1939–1945
(with Alex Barris, 1st edition, 1995)

Deadlock in Korea: Canadians at War, 1950–1953
(1st edition, 1999)

Canada and Korea: Perspectives 2000 (contributor)

Days of Victory: Canadians Remember, 1939–1945
(Sixtieth Anniversary edition, 2005)

Victory at Vimy: Canada Comes of Age, April 9–12, 1917

Breaking the Silence: Veterans' Untold Stories
from the Great War to Afghanistan

OTHER NON-FICTION

Fire Canoe: Prairie Steamboat Days Revisited

Rodeo Cowboys: The Last Heroes

Positive Power: The Story of the Edmonton Oilers Hockey Club

Spirit of the West: The Beginnings, the Land, the Life

Playing Overtime: A Celebration of Oldtimers' Hockey

Carved in Granite: 125 Years of Granite Club History

Making Music: Profiles from a Century of Canadian Music
(with Alex Barris)

101 Things Canadians Should Know About Canada (contributor)

DEADLOCK IN
KOREA

CANADIANS
AT WAR,
1950–1953

TED BARRIS

THOMAS ALLEN PUBLISHERS
TORONTO

Library and Archives Canada Cataloguing in Publication

Barris, Ted
    Deadlock in Korea : Canadians at war, 1950-1953 / Ted Barris.

Includes bibliographical references and index.
ISBN 978-0-88762-528-2

1. Canada—Armed Forces—History—Korean War, 1950–1953. 2. Canada—Canadian
Army—History—Korean War, 1950–1953. 3. Korean War, 1950–1953—Participation,
Canadian. I. Title.

DS919.2.B37   2010   951.904'240971   C2009-907223-8

Jacket image: Stefano Rellandini

Published by Thomas Allen Publishers,
a division of Thomas Allen & Son Limited,
145 Front Street East, Suite 209,
Toronto, Ontario M5A 1E3 Canada

www.thomas-allen.com

This book was originally published in hardcover by Macmillan Canada in 1999.

 ONTARIO ARTS COUNCIL
CONSEIL DES ARTS DE L'ONTARIO

 Canada Council
for the Arts

The publisher gratefully acknowledges the support of
the Ontario Arts Council for its publishing program.

We acknowledge the support of the Canada Council for the Arts, which
last year invested $20.1 million in writing and publishing throughout Canada.

We acknowledge the Government of Ontario through the
Ontario Media Development Corporation's Ontario Book Initiative.

We acknowledge the financial support of the Government of Canada through the Book
Publishing Industry Development Program (BPIDP) for our publishing activities.

14 13 12 11 10 5 4 3 2 1

Printed and bound in Canada

For Don Stickland and all Korea veterans like him. They volunteered to restore peace in a war zone and battled in peacetime to get these stories told.

CONTENTS

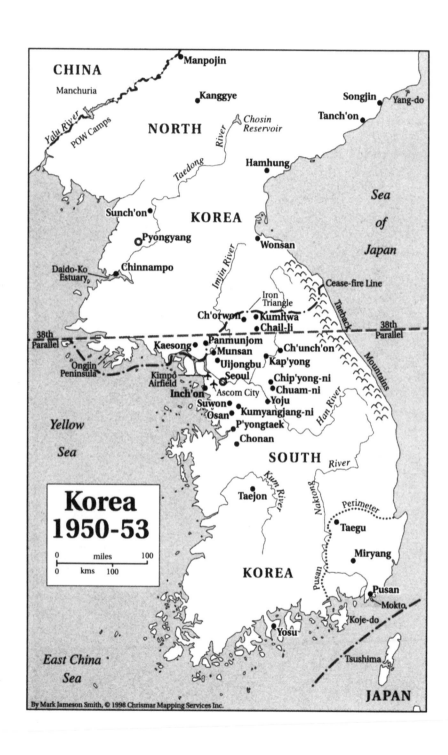

CHINA

Manchuria

Manpojin

Kanggye

Songjin

Yang-do

Tanch'on

Yalu River

POW Camps

NORTH

Chosin
Reservoir

Taedong River

River

Hamhung

Sea
of
Japan

Sunch'on

KOREA

Pyongyang

Wonsan

Chinnampo

Daido-Ko
Estuary

Imjin River

Cease-fire Line

Iron
Triangle

Ch'orwon

Kumhwa

Chail-ji

Taeback

38th
Parallel

38th
Parallel

Panmunjom

Kaesong

Munsan

Ch'unch'on

Ongjin
Peninsula

Uijongbu

Kap'yong

Kimpo
Airfield

Seoul

Chip'yong-ni

Mountains

Inch'on

Ascom City

Chuam-ni

Suwon

Yoju

Osan

Kumyangjang-ni

Han River

Yellow

Sea

P'yongtaek

Chonan

SOUTH

River

Kum River

Naktong

Taejon

Perimeter

Korea
1950-53

0   miles   100

0   kms   100

Taegu

Miryang

KOREA

Pusan

Pusan

Mokto

Koje-do

Yosu

Tsushima

East China
Sea

JAPAN

By Mark Jameson Smith, © 1998 Chrismar Mapping Services Inc.

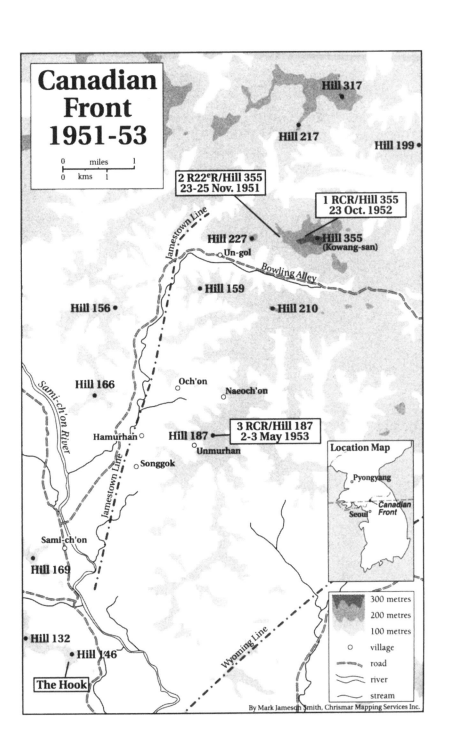

Canadian Front 1951-53

0   miles   1
0   kms   1

Hill 317

Hill 217

Hill 199 •

2 R22°R/Hill 355
23-25 Nov. 1951

1 RCR/Hill 355
23 Oct. 1952

Hill 227 •
Un-gol

Hill 355
(Kowang-san)

Bowling Alley

• Hill 159

Hill 156 •

• Hill 210

Hill 166
•

Och'on
○

Naeoch'on
○

Jamestown Line

3 RCR/Hill 187
2-3 May 1953

Hamurhan ○

Hill 187 •

Unmurhan

○ Songgok

Sami-ch'on River

Location Map

Pyongyang
○

Canadian
Front

Seoul ○

Jamestown Line

Sami-ch'on
•
○

Hill 169
•

300 metres
200 metres
100 metres
○   village
road
river
stream

• Hill 132

• Hill 146

Wyoming Line

The Hook

By Mark Jamesch Smith, Chrismar Mapping Services Inc.

Acknowledgments

The completion of this volume is the result of much energy and cooperation from friends, professionals and many veterans of the Korean War. But the book could never have happened without the initial efforts of the Korea Veterans Association of Canada, in particular, the KVA book committee in London, Ontario. Its assembly of veterans' diaries, memoirs, anecdotes, clippings, and photographs constitutes the genesis of this book.

Many others, individually and collectively, offered assistance when, as usual, the end seemed so distant from the beginning.

Fellow journalists, reporters and authors offered their help. Author John Melady allowed me to quote from his library of Korea veterans' interviews. Terry Scott, of Broadcast News, helped open the doors of the Canadian Press archives to the files of war correspondent Bill Boss. Author Carl Christie offered documentary support. Senior Writer D'Arcy Jenish assisted at the *Maclean's* magazine archives. Korea veteran Les Peate provided material from his *esprit de corps* columns. And former North Korean Young Sik Kim permitted the publication of excerpts from his personal memoirs.

Others loaned the author original materials: Dal Richards offered files on his wife, entertainer Lorraine McAllister. Terri O'Connor and her mother, Vera, allowed the publication of Pat O'Connor's poem "Blood on the Hills." Jack LaChance and the KVA permitted the publication of the poem "The Korea Veterans' Wall." Terry

(Dale) Millar and Lew Lewis contributed "Wayne and Shuster" photos and clippings. Tom Boutillier gave access to files on the Canoe River train crash. Ken and Belle Charlton sent original material on the sports junket to Korea. Ken McOrmond passed along binders of pictures and memoirs. Neil Goodwill contributed navy diaries. And Col. Deuk-Hwan Kim, at the Republic of Korea embassy in Ottawa, sent original data. For additional archive recordings, the author thanks Ron MacDonald and the RCAF Memorial Museum at CFB Trenton, Ontario, and Barbara Clarke at the CBC Radio archives. The author is also grateful to Bill Allan and Unit 57 of the KVA in Mississauga, Ontario, for their assistance in the compilation of the Wall of Remembrance story.

Several professional photographers readily offered stills from their own portfolios: Dick Loek, of the *Toronto Star*, Laura Salverda, of the *Brampton Guardian* and Jim Lynch Jr. For their photo expertise, the author thanks Peter Robertson at the National Archives of Canada, and John Bradley of the Canadian Forces Photographic Unit. For his personal photo collection from the Canoe River accident, thanks to John Stables. And for their creative expertise, mapmakers Mark Smith and Christine Kennedy deserve much thanks.

The author thanks several Korea veterans who took the time to read portions of the manuscript before publication—Scotty Martin, Don Hibbs, Ron Trider, Herb Pitts, Ted Zuber, Geoff Magee and Don Flieger. Also thanks to another friend currently in the military—Patrick Warren.

The author is indebted to a platoon of reliable transcribers: Marlene Lumley, Michelle Williams, Quenby and Whitney Barris and especially Braunda Bodger.

Closer to home, much gratitude is owed those who gave support in less tangible, but equally vital ways. To Ronnie for her lunches, to Norie for her interest, to Keenan for his dogged regimen, to Katy for her writer's empathy, to Kay and Alex for their life-giving enthusiasm and to Jayne for her eternal faith . . . the author's heart-felt thanks.

— Ted Barris, 1999

Introduction

Canadians celebrated as never before when Japan formally surrendered aboard the U.S. battleship USS *Missouri* in Tokyo Bay on September 2, 1945. The Second World War had been the greatest and costliest war in history and Canada had played a full part from the very beginning. More than one million Canadians had fought on land, at sea, and in the air over six years to defeat the Axis and for that same six years the nation at home had focused on organizing its people, its factories, and its resources for the sole purpose of victory. Canadians were tired of war. They looked forward to the return of their servicemen and women and to post-war reconstruction. With families to start, homes to establish, and new lives to be lived after a decade and a half of economic depression followed by war, Canadians anticipated what one Oscar-winning Hollywood movie called "the best years of their lives." They did not look forward to another war.

Neither did the Canadian government. Prime Minister William Lyon Mackenzie King led his Liberal Party to a smashing majority victory in the federal election of June 1945, promising jobs, prosperity, reconstruction, and social justice. The government had laid the foundations of its 1945 election platform with the introduction of universal Mothers' Allowances in 1944 and a comprehensive program of veterans' benefits from free education to generous pensions for the wounded. Planning for the new post-war Canada was based on the notion that government had a major role to play in ensuring

xvi | Deadlock in Korea

equality of opportunity for all Canadians, income redistribution through welfare and taxation measures, and job creation by economic pump-priming. At the same time, however, Canada was deeper in debt in 1945 than it had ever been. Not only did the government need the funds to pay for the new promises, it also had to pay off that massive debt. As Mackenzie King put it, it was time to shut down military spending and ramp up social spending.

The defence budget and the three armed services were cut to the bone between 1945 and 1947. From over 400,000 men and women at the end the war, Canada's military shrank to 34,000 by mid-1948 with a budget of less than $400 million. But although war was the last thing on the minds of Canadians at the end of 1940s, the Communist leader of North Korea, Kim-il Sung had conquest on his mind, and with the blessing and active help of the Soviet Union and the new Communist government in China, he launched his Russian-trained and -equipped armed forces to grab South Korea on June 25, 1950.

It is doubtful if many Canadians on that early summer day even knew where South Korea was, and even less likely that any might have guessed that within eight months, Canadian soldiers would be fighting a war in the frozen hills of central Korea. And yet that is exactly what happened. The Communist attack on South Korea was considered a wake-up call by many Western leaders, especially U.S. president Harry S. Truman and the Secretary General of the United Nations, Trygve Lie. Both men strongly suspected that North Korea was acting on behalf of Russia and China and that, left unchecked, Communism might win only a small material victory in Korea, but a huge moral and political one. Just a year earlier, the North Atlantic Treaty Organization had been created to guard against a Communist military attack against western Europe. Though Korea was far from western Europe, a successful snatch and grab by the Communists there could encourage them to try again—in Europe.

In short order, the UN condemned the attack and called upon UN members to defend South Korea. The United States, Britain, Australia, and most of the NATO nations pledged fighting forces.

Once Canadians recognized the threat, they too wanted to send military forces to Korea while Washington, London, and the UN put great pressure on Canada to join in. By late August 1950 Canada had joined. Ottawa sent three ships and a transport squadron to aid the UN effort in Korea and began mobilizing a brigade group of some 8,000 men, mostly Second World War veterans to fight there. By the time the war ended with a ceasefire agreement on July 27, 1953, almost 27,000 Canadians had served in Korea, with 516 dead on active service and over a thousand wounded. South Korea was saved; today it is a prosperous, free, and democratic state.

Wars may be about politics, as the noted Prussian military analyst Carl von Clausewitz wrote in the 1830s, but they are fought by people—individuals who must bear the extreme physical hardships of war, the cruelty of the enemy, the harshness of the elements, their own deep-seated fear of death or mutilation. Some historians write of brigades, divisions, corps, and armies as if they were single organisms with thousands of parts rather than collections of individuals, each with his (and now her) own story. Ted Barris has never written his histories that way and his *Deadlock in Korea*, first published in 1999, follows the pattern of his many other books on Canadians at war.

The raw material of this book is the interviews that Ted Barris conducted with Canadian veterans of the Korean War and the personal accounts—written anecdotes, diaries, letters, interviews—left behind by others in newspapers, magazines, or personal papers. His style puts the reader in with the soldiers, sharing a desperate moment in combat, slogging through a long and dangerous night patrol near Chinese positions, hurriedly digging slit trenches and firing pits, or stringing barbed wire, as the sound of battle nearby tells the Canadians that they will soon be hit by their relentless enemy. Ted Barris's intent is not to explain the complex geo-politics that lay behind almost two years of deadlock in the ceasefire talks between the UN and the Communists, but to tell his readers what the soldiers who waited for death on the hilltops during that deadlock thought of the whole thing and what they experienced.

The Korean conflict was Canada's third largest war, a war largely forgotten by Canadians today. *Deadlock in Korea* is arguably the best place for Canadians to begin to re-learn the experiences and the lessons of that war from the perspective of the soldiers who fought it.

— David J. Bercuson

THE WAR
THAT WASN'T

T HEY KNEW that throwing stones at the Chinese was ludicrous, but it served a purpose. On otherwise quiet nights, when two or three Canadian soldiers manned forward listening posts in no-man's-land, they sometimes lobbed stones into the darkness to provoke the communist reconnaissance patrols to open fire. The flashes of their guns would reveal their location, and within seconds the Canadians could bring down an artillery barrage on the Chinese intruders and chase them back to their own lines.

By the fall of 1952, warfare between the communist forces of North Korea and China, on one side, and the combined armies of South Korea and fifteen member countries of the United Nations, on the other, had been raging for more than two years. Strangely, combat up and down the Korean peninsula had not included the thousand-plane sorties that were a regular feature of the Allied carpet-bombing campaign against Germany just half a decade earlier. There had not been the epic tank battles of El Alamein, nor the critical naval encounters of Midway or the Battle of the Atlantic, nor the massive infantry engagements of Normandy or Stalingrad. Nor had warfare in Korea unleashed anything like the two atomic bombs that had levelled the Japanese cities of Hiroshima and Nagasaki only a few hundred kilometres away. Instead, the fighting in Korea harked back to the First World War and sometimes came down to throwing stones at the enemy across the 38th parallel during lulls in the fighting.

The night of October 23, 1952, was not to be one of those lulls. Thirty-four men in "B" Company of the Royal Canadian Regiment (RCR) had moved into one of the forward defensive positions in front of a mountain the Koreans called Kowang-san. But continuous Chinese artillery bombardment of Hill 355, as the Canadians referred to it, had left few or none of the RCR's field defences intact. Minefields and protective barbed wire had been destroyed. Weapon pits that held ammunition had been nearly buried by the shelling. Bunkers that the troops used for shelter had caved in. And ground-laid telephone lines linking the forward positions to the company command post had been chopped to pieces.

As the Canadians took up their positions, stones were not the weapons of choice for either side. In fact, Canadian army records report that after dark on the twenty-third, all the company of RCR soldiers could do was try to remain alert with "one of the occupants of each weapon pit watching while the other rested at the bottom of the pit, huddled in his poncho." A rifleman with No. 5 Platoon, Private George Griffiths, was one of those occupants, posted to a forward trench to protect a 30-calibre machine gun weapon pit in the "B" Company area. Then a twenty-two-year-old infantryman, he remembered "it was just like the movies where we're ducking every time an enemy shell comes in . . . the dirt hitting our helmets. Bang, rattle, rattle . . . And all I could think of was that I had left a good job on Bay Street in Toronto to come to this."

At 6:20 p.m., about an hour after sunset, Chinese gunners put down a tremendous concentration of artillery fire on "B" Company's position for eight or ten minutes. Then it focused fire on positions to the left and right of the Canadian position for another forty-five minutes. In what had been known as a "box barrage" during the First World War, the Chinese bombardment effectively cut off "B" Company on both flanks and the rear. Every RCR soldier in those forward positions knew that an infantry attack was imminent.

Even before the last of the Chinese artillery shells exploded around their weapon pit, George Griffiths and his trench mate, Art Bates, heard the bugles of the charging Chinese infantry. The Chinese sometimes sent a first wave of assault troops through their own artillery barrage to overwhelm defenders before they had a chance to react. This time the manoeuvre worked. Several Canadian weapon pits were soon facing heavy small-arms and mortar fire, and casualties were high as the defenders fell back. Griffiths and Bates were instantly cut off as the rest of their company retreated. With the Chinese controlling the surface, they began to run for their lives through the decimated trench system.

At a crossroads in the trenches, the two Canadians made a fateful mistake. Unknowingly, they chose a trench that led deeper into the Chinese advance. A shell exploded close by and sent shrapnel into Griffiths's right foot. He put his head down and kept running, but soon lagged behind Bates.

A Chinese soldier jumped from the parapet above the trench and threw a grenade into Griffiths's path. The Canadian ducked into an intersecting trench before the grenade exploded, but the concussion still caught him in the face and chest and knocked him down. From his hands and knees he managed to return a round from his .303 rifle. The shot caught the Chinese soldier in the belly and likely killed him, because he disappeared into the shadows of the trench. By now, Griffiths was running out of time and space. The new trenchway led to a bunker and a dead end. He could hear the Chinese troops all around him on the ground above the trenches, so one by one he tossed his remaining four hand grenades into their midst. This brought down another Chinese concussion grenade which caught him in the shoulder and left knee.

"I knew I was beat," Griffiths said. "I pulled aside the blanket in the doorway of the bunker and fell inside. There were three or four bodies there. Didn't know who they were. But I lay down and reloaded my rifle . . . when two Chinese came in. One had a flashlight and a rifle, the other a burp-gun which fires 450 rounds a minute. My single-shot Lee-Enfield was good for nothing.

"Now in the heat of battle, when it comes to taking prisoners, they don't take your pulse to see if you're dead or alive. They stab you with a bayonet . . . So they stabbed these other guys and they were dead. When they came to me, I went, 'Uh-uh!'"

Behind the bunker in which George Griffiths surrendered, about a dozen members of his "B" Company had made it safely to "A" Company lines. A counterattack was being planned. Commonwealth Brigade artillery had already begun a heavy bombardment of the area that Griffiths and his comrades had tried to defend. By 3:30 on the morning of October 24, Hill 355 was back in United Nations hands. The action had cost the Royal Canadian Regiment eighteen killed, thirty-five wounded and fourteen prisoners of war, including Pte. George Griffiths.

The next few hours Griffiths thought might be his last. It was no secret that in October 1950 the bodies of sixty-eight soldiers of the Eighth US Army were discovered in a railway tunnel near Sunchon, North Korea; the POWs had been machine-gunned to death on their way to supper. As the Chinese brought Griffiths and thirteen other Canadian prisoners to a gathering point that night, Pte. Don Orson asked to retrieve a fellow RCR soldier who lay wounded in the field. The Chinese refused and a guard went out and killed the man with a burst from his burp-gun.

Thus began George Griffiths's ten-month incarceration in communist prisoner-of-war camps. He credits Orson and Pte. Ken Dawe for keeping him from being shot; they dragged and propped him up on the long trek behind enemy lines. He endured countless forced marches on his wounded foot through the mountains of North Korea. Early on, he and his fellow POWs received a strafing from a US Air Force jet fighter. One night, in a mountain cave, under threat of execution, he was forced to remain still as cold water dripped across his neck and down his back. He attempted several escapes and narrowly missed confinement in "the hole," a two-foot-wide space between two buildings with no toilet and no shelter from the elements. His diet consisted of soya beans and burnt rice tea. And then there were the numerous interrogation sessions, designed not so much to glean military information as to provide his Chinese captors with propaganda opportunities.

"Were you on Koje Island?" demanded Griffiths's interrogator in remarkably fluent English. Earlier in 1952, at Koje, an island off the coast of South Korea, "B" Company of the Royal Canadian Regiment had guarded communist POWs; during a camp uprising, thirty-one Chinese and North Korean prisoners were killed. The interrogator knew Griffiths served with "B" Company.

"No," said Griffiths, "I wasn't on Koje."

"You *were* in 'B' Company and you *were* at the Koje Island massacre."

Griffiths was amazed they knew so much about his outfit. He realized that he couldn't lie to them, but he wasn't with "B" Company on Koje, and insisted, "I wasn't on Koje. I wasn't."

Griffiths was offered a cigarette. He refused. All he could think of was: *And this I can't forget/A man who turns traitor for just one cigarette.*

Then later, "Why did you come to Korea?"

"To kill Chinese," Griffiths said bluntly.

"You have blood on your hands," fumed the interrogator. "Get out!"

For nearly ten months, Griffiths and 171 other UN POWs—men from Greece, Turkey, France, Australia, the US and Canada—sat through the daily interrogation and indoctrination, which the Chinese called "social studies." The prisoners were not given a change of clothes. They were not given medical attention. The mud and straw huts they ate and slept in had no tables, no chairs, no beds, no blankets and no lights. Just dirt floors. The occupants called themselves "the Throwbacks" because they rejected the Chinese version of the truth. They signed nothing. They refused to give the communists the answers they wanted.

Not surprisingly, the letters POWs were allowed to write home had to reflect the correct attitude. Griffiths tried numerous times to write to his wife, Barbara; as far as she knew, George was "Missing In Action" and presumed dead. He tried desperately to write prose that would pass the camp censors. When he described the clothing he wore as "a uniform that looked like a quilted blanket," the Chinese forced him to rewrite the statement countless times because he appeared to be complaining that all he had for warmth was a blanket. The letters never reached his wife. One he wrote in December 1952 did reach his friend Dick Ogden in Brighton, Ontario, in May 1953. In it he offered enough small talk about a Thanksgiving supper served by the Chinese Volunteer Army and the winter weather being "similar to home" that the letter passed both the Chinese and UN censors. And that's how Barbara Griffiths discovered that her husband was still alive half a year after his capture.

In June 1953, treatment of prisoners improved in the camps. (Griffiths found out later that the peace talks at Panmunjom had taken a positive turn as the negotiators agreed to the mechanics of exchanging POWs.) The Chinese gave each POW a hat, a pair of pants, socks, a pair of running shoes and even a tube of toothpaste. Griffiths, who had not received medical attention since his capture, suddenly became a priority. To prepare him for an operation, Chinese doctors fed him five opium seeds to act as a general anaesthetic. They put a pillowcase over his head because Chinese culture discourages watching surgery on the body. Griffiths removed the hood and watched as they cut out the shrapnel that had been blown into his foot the night of the attack on Hill 355. When Griffiths was mobile again, the Chinese transported him and other POWs by truck to the rail terminus at Manpojin, North Korea, then by train to Freedom Village, at Panmunjom, and across the Bridge of No Return to the South.

On August 23, 1953, during his first hours of freedom, George Griffiths was deloused, given a new set of Australian-made clothes and fed a big meal with Coca-Cola and beer. The food was so rich, he got sick. In hospital, doctors operated on his wounds again, and examined his eyes and teeth. He flew home aboard a Canadian Pacific passenger plane. Aside from the bits of shrapnel he still carried in his body, the only mementoes of his imprisonment were a crucifix he had fashioned from the tube of toothpaste he'd been issued and a tiny booklet. Made from cigarette papers he'd hidden under his belt, the booklet contained all the names and addresses of the POWs with whom he had been imprisoned. The Canadian government confiscated it.

When Pte. George Griffiths finally stepped off the train in Toronto, his anxious wife, Barbara, his younger brother, Verdon (also a Korean War veteran) and his parents awaited him, as did a rude reception at the Kingston Veterans Affairs office a short time later. There he requested a veterans' allowance of $700 for a down payment on a house where he and Barbara could have a family and forget about the war and his imprisonment.

"You have no benefits," the civil servant told him.

"What do you mean?" Griffiths said.

"No benefits. It wasn't a war . . . Not officially, anyway."

"You don't think Korea was a war?" shouted Griffiths, pounding the official's table. "You'll have one here before I leave!"

SPECIAL FORCE

THE ROAD to the Korean War began in Cairo. In late November 1943, while the Second World War was still raging, British prime minister Winston Churchill debarked the battlecruiser *Renown* at the Egyptian port of Alexandria. When two of his wartime allies—American president Franklin D. Roosevelt and Generalissimo Chiang Kai-shek of the Republic of China—arrived by air, Churchill met them at a villa near the pyramids. The Cairo Conference, code-named Sextant, would be a tense four-day discussion focused on redrawing the world map in anticipation of the end of the war. The British wanted to define the various Allies' roles as occupying powers; the Americans were suspicious of British intentions in the Balkans; and both Churchill and Roosevelt wondered how they could spur the Chinese to take positive military action against the Japanese in Southeast Asia without sparking Chinese expansionism in the region.

Their joint declaration at the conclusion of the Cairo Conference announced, among other things, that following victory over Japan, "Korea shall become free and independent in due course." Roosevelt admitted later it might take forty to fifty years before Korea would be ready for complete independence, but this was a diplomatic attempt to keep China and Russia out of Korea. It was doomed to failure.

President Roosevelt died in April 1945. In August of that year, as the war in the Pacific drew to a close, his successor, Harry Truman, suggested that in Korea the Soviets receive the surrender of Japanese forces north of the 38th parallel, and that the Americans receive the surrender of Japanese troops to the south. That seemingly innocuous agreement sealed Korea's fate. The Soviets took the surrender arrangement as a granting of territorial rights, which touched off a battle for the hearts and minds of Koreans and turned a previously homogenous people on both sides of that parallel into mortal enemies.

Dividing the peninsula roughly in half—at 38 degrees north latitude—may have made sense for administering a surrender, but it was not a natural boundary. It cut across several north-south mountain ranges, at right angles to at least two major river systems, and right through Kaesong, ancient capital of Korea's early Koryo dynasty. The American zone, to the south, encompassed about 42 percent of the territory but two-thirds of the population; it also contained most of the arable land that fed both north and south. The Soviet zone, north of 38 degrees, held most of the peninsula's minerals and the country's only petroleum and cement production plants; its hydroelectric works served both north and south.

Traditionally known as "The Hermit Kingdom," Korea had been a unified nation since the 7th century. Weakened regimes had fallen under Chinese or Japanese sway from time to time. Japan occupied it in 1905 and annexed it five years later, but the kingdom had never been divided. Suddenly in 1945, there were two Koreas. The split angered Koreans on both sides.

The Soviets clearly had ideas as to how their neighbour should develop. They cut off nearly all traffic into and out of the northern part of the peninsula. Meanwhile, the Americans moved 25,000 members of the US 24th Infantry Division, recently victorious over the Japanese on Okinawa, to the southern part for occupation duty, because in Truman's words, Korea was now "an ideological battleground on which our entire success in Asia depends." As the two sides established their spheres of influence, Koreans in the south began to stage protests.

As early as December 1945, the foreign ministers of the United States, Great Britain, China and the Soviet Union met essentially to discuss the same principle as the one raised in Cairo in 1943—the establishment of an independent Korea. In the meantime, the "trusteeship" of Korea remained in the hands of a US-USSR Joint Commission, led by an American general and a Soviet general. No joint conference—in December 1945, in March 1946, or May 1947—moved Korea any closer to independence, nor did the election of a provisional government. When a further attempt to negotiate Korean independence failed, the American secretary of state took the issue to the United Nations (in just its second general assembly). On November 14, 1947, despite Soviet opposition, the UN adopted the US-sponsored motion to establish Korean independence, withdraw all occupying forces and stage free elections in 1948. The UN General Assembly named a nine-nation UN Temporary Commission on Korea (UNTCOK) to supervise the electoral process. Australia, China, El Salvador, France, India, the Philippines, Syria, Ukraine and Canada provided representatives for the commission.

There was at least one Canadian already ashore in Korea before the UN assigned Canada to the mission in Korea. At age eighteen, Prince Edward Islander Bentley MacLeod seemed destined to follow his father into the Baptist ministry. During his father's stint at a church in West Buxton, Maine, however, Bentley jumped at the chance to join the US Army. A one-year tour, he felt, would give him some freedom and tuition for a university education. It also got him into the 31st Infantry, which was posted to Korea.

"I landed at Inch'on [in 1946] and joined the regiment in Seoul," MacLeod remembers. "We spent three months at the 38th parallel staring at the Russian troops opposite us. We were the occupational force. We took over the former Japanese barracks in Seoul and guarded railways, railheads and airports from domestic riots that were becoming more frequent and more violent across South Korea."

As the debate over the future of Korea intensified, both the American and the Soviet military commands sponsored returning exiles they saw as potential leaders of their version of a unified Korea. In the north, the Soviets supported Kim Il Sung. At twenty-eight, Kim had been educated in Moscow during the Second World War. He had become a prominent partisan fighter in Manchuria against the Japanese and had emerged as a Korean patriot who embraced both Chinese and Soviet communism. In the south, the Americans heralded Syngman Rhee. As a champion of Korean autonomy, he had been tortured by the Japanese and exiled to the United States in 1904. There he completed his Ph.D. in international law at Princeton University, and at age seventy-five was returning to Korea as an uncompromising anti-communist and the Americans' favourite son.

While Rhee had the full support of American authorities in the forthcoming UN-supervised elections, he did not have the popular support of the Korean people. Absent for more than forty tumultuous years, he was out of touch with the mood of the public and lacked the vigour of a younger man. Furthermore, the communists were active not only in China and the Soviet Union, but also throughout the Korean peninsula. A pro-communist movement jelled around post-war political turmoil in the cities and peasant unrest in the countryside. The Central Intelligence Agency (CIA) estimated as many as 6,000 guerrillas were active in the south alone. An American journalist dispatched by the *New York Times* to cover guerrilla warfare in the region reported that large parts of southern Korea "are darkened today by a cloud of terror that is probably unparalleled in the world."

As Bentley MacLeod remembers it, "there was a very active communist party in [southern] Korea and they were always agitating . . . They would gather a hundred people with red flags at a street corner. And the police would rush in, arrest them and throw them in jail. I remember being in a police station when they were bringing people in. They'd interrogate them and throw them in a cell. They weren't concerned about such things as human rights."

Both the Soviet Union and the United States were committed to withdrawing their occupational forces. Both were active members of the UN, where each publicly accused the other of dragging its feet on withdrawal, while quietly training, fortifying and arming the Koreans on its side of the divide.

The UNTCOK representatives duly arrived in Seoul to supervise the prescribed elections. The Soviet Union refused to cooperate with the commission and refused it entry north of the 38th parallel. On May 19, 1948, an election took place in the south and two weeks later, 198 assemblymen arrived in Seoul to open the first National Assembly. As house speaker, Syngman Rhee addressed an assembly with 100 seats left vacant for the representatives from the north. By July, Rhee was president. August 15, 1948, he established his government and proclaimed the independent Republic of Korea, which became known as South Korea. Not to be upstaged by Seoul, during the same period, the north approved a communist constitution, staged elections and proclaimed the Democratic People's Republic, soon referred to as North Korea, with Kim Il Sung as its first premier. The Soviet Union completed its troop withdrawal by December 25, 1948. The last American troops withdrew to Japan on June 29, 1949, leaving behind a group of 500 military advisers.

The desire for a unified Korea remained strong. Within a year of Syngman Rhee taking office as president, he wrote: "I feel strongly that now is the most psychological moment when we should take an aggressive measure . . . to drive Kim Il Sung's men to the mountain region and there we will gradually starve them out. Then our line of defence must be strengthened along the Yalu River"; that is, driving the communists out of Korea and into China. Rhee had roughly 81,000 troops at his disposal; they were still being trained by the American advisers, the US Military Advisory Group to the Republic of Korea, or KMAG. Republic of Korea (ROK) Army combat troops were armed only with M-1 rifles, carbines, mortars, howitzers and ineffective bazookas. Unlike their northern counterparts, they had no medium artillery and no recoilless rifles. However, there seemed to be unlimited credit; South Korea was receiving more than $100 million a year in the form of US grants (the entire budget of Rhee's government was $120 million).

Despite Rhee's rhetoric, war did not break out in 1949, although there were certainly enough sparks to light the fires of a general war. Border fighting became nearly an everyday occurrence. In May 1949, a four-day engagement near Kaesong, at the 38th parallel, killed 400 North Korean and 22 South Korean soldiers. Another engagement saw 6,000 North Korean border guards bombard South Korean units that had occupied a small mountain north of the 38th parallel. That summer Rhee sent naval patrol boats up the Taedong River and they sank four North Korean ships. On June 26, 1949, heavy fighting on the Ongjin peninsula, at the 38th parallel, attracted UN officials who travelled to the area by naval vessel and reported that north and south could engage in major battles at any moment and that Korea had entered "a state of warfare."

In his New Year's message for 1950, Kim Il Sung vowed to liberate the south, entreating his "People's Army, the frontier defence troops and the police to complete preparedness for war . . . Let us pray that 1950 will become a year of unification; and may glory shine upon our people, who are marching forward toward victory. Long live unified Korea!" His bravado was justified. The departing Russians had left behind an arsenal of weapons, including mortars, howitzers and T-34 tanks. In addition, the Chinese communists had recently won the bloody civil war against Chiang Kai-shek's Nationalist Army; as repayment for communist Korea's support, Chinese leader Mao Tse-tung sent home some 100,000 Korean People's Army (KPA) troops and further augmented their numbers by sending 12,000 more veterans from the ranks of the Chinese People's Liberation Army (PLA). By early June 1950, Kim Il Sung was commander-in-chief of nearly ten full divisions, roughly 150,000 soldiers, of which 89,000 were trained combat troops.

The declaration of war came at 4 a.m. on Sunday, June 25, 1950. As in the year before, a skirmish began on the Ongjin peninsula between units of the Korean People's Army and the 17th Regiment of the Republic of Korea Army. East of Ongjin, monsoon rains were falling along much of the 38th parallel, but the thunder that morning was at ground level. Batteries of Soviet-made 122-mm howitzers and 76-mm artillery began pounding the South Korean approaches to Kaesong, just south of the parallel. Then two KPA regiments, some led by Soviet T-34 tanks, others transported in railway cars on secretly laid tracks, sped into the old capital. By 9:30 a.m. the town had fallen.

There was little or no resistance at Kaesong or elsewhere. The four divisions of ROK Army troops positioned along the parallel were understrength; as many as a third of its troops were on leave bringing in the harvest. Nor were there many of the 500 American advisers near the front. They had joined the American ambassador and South Korean army officers in Seoul on Saturday night to inaugurate the new officers' club at ROK Army headquarters. However, even if the KMAG advisers and the officers had been at Kaesong, little would have changed. Half the KPA force of 90,000 was already on the move along the Uijongbu Corridor, a natural invasion route through Kaesong south to Seoul. Southern forces were outnumbered five to one.

"The North Koreans, they've taken Kaesong!" an officer told a senior American military adviser in Seoul. "War has come!" The two men raced to the front to supervise a defence along the Imjin River and to blow up the only bridge across it.

The American ambassador, John Muccio, received word of hostilities along the 38th parallel and headed to the embassy to cable Washington. En route, Muccio encountered United Press correspondent Jack James, who proceeded to the embassy press room. James checked Muccio's report of "activities on the 38th parallel" with officers at ROK headquarters and with Muccio's assistant. He then cabled San Francisco the scoop of his life, which very closely paralleled Muccio's own message, that this attack "constitutes an all-out offensive against the Republic of Korea."

More than three million people would die in Korea between June 25, 1950, and July 27, 1953. More than half of those killed would be civilians. On the northern side, nearly 316,000 North Korean soldiers would be killed or missing-in-action. Their Chinese allies would lose 422,000. Another 400,000 Chinese and North Korean troops would die of disease. On the southern side, about 113,000 Republic of Korea soldiers would lose their lives. Among the fifteen members of the United Nations forces sent to defend South Korea, the United States would sustain nearly 64,000 killed or missing-in-action, while the rest (including Canada's 1,557 casualties) would experience nearly 5,900 killed or missing-in-action.

In Washington, Secretary of State Dean Acheson and his staff alerted the Pentagon to draft a plan of action. In New York, the UN was asked to call "a meeting of the Security Council . . . the following afternoon, Sunday, and obtain a resolution requesting or ordering all parties to return within their borders, to cease any aggression, and calling upon all members of the UN to assist in this endeavour."

The impact of the incursion from North Korea was not lost on the Secretary-General of the United Nations, Trygve Lie, who responded to an American official: "My God, that's war against the United Nations!"

Late Sunday afternoon, June 25, meeting at the UN's temporary headquarters at Lake Success, the Security Council voted nine to zero in favour of a US resolution recommending that "members of the United Nations furnish such assistance to the Republic of Korea as may be necessary to repel the armed attack and to restore international peace and security in the area." Notably absent to exercise a veto was Soviet ambassador Jacob Malik. Publicly, the word was that Malik was returning home for consultations; privately, Joseph Stalin had instructed his delegation to stay away from Security Council sessions.

To US president Harry Truman and his chiefs of staff the course was clear. They would reverse the American trend of withdrawal from Asia. In the president's words: "I wasn't going to let this attack on the Republic of Korea . . . go forward. Because if it wasn't stopped, it would lead to a third world war. And I wasn't going to let that happen . . . For the first time in history, an aggressor [was] opposed by an international police force [to] save the free world." Truman's "police force" initially consisted of air cover to protect the American evacuation of Seoul, dispatching the US 7th Fleet from the Philippines to prevent any attack on Formosa, and instructing Gen. Douglas MacArthur, supreme commander of the Far East Command, to provide air and naval support of South Korean forces, but only south of the 38th parallel. By June 29, with the North Korean armies breaking through South Korean defences, Truman authorized MacArthur to order ground forces (the US 24th Infantry Division on occupation duties in Japan) to bolster the ROK Army in Korea.

The next day—Friday, June 30, 1950—the date Canadian MPs had selected to prorogue Parliament for the summer, Prime Minister Louis St. Laurent rose in the House of Commons to declare that Canada would not participate in any war against another state, but it would take "part in collective police action under the control and authority of the United Nations for the purpose of restoring peace." While he waited for UN directives, St. Laurent announced that three Canadian destroyers, which had been preparing at Esquimalt, B.C., for a European cruise, would instead sail into the Pacific. The leaders of the opposition spoke. The House then passed the normal Government Appropriations Bill. Parliament recessed on the eve of the country's 83rd Dominion Day.

In South Korea the war was going all one way. The day the Security Council signed the assistance resolution, the first units of the North Korean 4th Division entered Seoul. By July 1, remnants of the ROK 1st and 7th Divisions pulled out of the South Korean capital. Almost half of the original 98,000 ROK troops had been killed, captured or were missing. By then the North Korean 6th Division had captured Kimpo Airfield, west of Seoul, and was en route to the west coast city of Inch'on.

Once across the Han River at Seoul, the North Koreans advanced steadily, taking Suwon, Osan and Chonan in the first week of July. Despite the addition of the US 1st Cavalry (actually infantry) and the 25th Infantry Divisions to the US 24th, the retreat south and east continued. In the battle of Taejon, American units not only felt the impact of frontal assaults from the North Koreans, they also had to contend with guerrillas; local peasants disguised as refugees would come running down the hillsides and "at a given signal, the refugees snatched rifles, machine guns and hand grenades from their bundles and brought down withering fire on the troops below."

By the end of July, the North Korean advance had boxed three American and five reorganized South Korean divisions into the southeastern corner of the country with their backs to the port of Pusan. Nearly surrounded in what was called the Pusan Perimeter, Truman's police force had very quickly become a retreating force.

Just as rapidly, the official Canadian response to the war was evolving from limited support to active participation. On June 27, Secretary of State for External Affairs Lester Pearson had commented that he did not expect American military response to the North Korean invasion. By July 15 he was suggesting greater Canadian involvement, because if "peace is endangered in Korea, it becomes a matter of immediate concern to the Canadian people; for Canada, in this jet-propelled, atomic interdependent age, cannot by itself remain secure and at peace in a warring world."

Pearson's passionate oratory revealed the true sentiment of the St. Laurent government. On July 21, the government announced that No. 426 RCAF (Thunderbird) Squadron would dedicate six North Star transport aircraft to a trans-Pacific airlift of supplies for the war effort. On July 27, the US government sent a message to the prime minister's office, requesting a Canadian brigade join UN forces in Korea. Britain, Australia, New Zealand and South Africa had already announced plans to send troops and equipment.

During the first week of August, the entire Eighth US Army withdrew across the Naktong River, the last natural barrier defending the UN-held Pusan Perimeter. Half a million refugees crossed the river with the soldiers retreating to Taegu. US military intelligence reports estimated that combined UN strength was now down to 160,000. Opposing them, along 300 kilometres of battle front were fifteen army divisions, or about 200,000 North Korean troops. That week the only good news for UN forces in Korea was the arrival of a convoy of ships in Pusan harbour; they delivered the first 6,500 US Marines.

On Monday, August 7, Prime Minister St. Laurent announced on CBC Radio that Canada would recruit an expeditionary brigade of 5,000 men for duty in Korea. Fit young men, preferably veterans, between the ages of nineteen and thirty-five, would be recruited for a temporary eighteen-month service. The brigade would become part of Canada's active regular army (not reserve) and would be known as the Canadian Army Special Force. The next night, Minister of National Defence Brooke Claxton provided more details and announced that recruiting depots would open for the Special Force the following day.

"That's it! I'm gone!" That was Mel Canfield's reaction to the radio broadcast. For Canfield, the government's invitation to join the Special Force was a prayer answered. Army regulations allowed boys who were at least seventeen and a half to join, if they had their parents' permission. In March 1945, Mel was eligible, but his family in New Westminster, B.C., had no intention of permitting him to fight in Europe or the Pacific. Undaunted, young Canfield announced that on his eighteenth birthday he could and would join on his own. He turned eighteen in September 1945, just days after the Japanese surrendered. Disappointed, he turned to a series of jobs in the forestry service and the lumber business.

"The night St. Laurent came on the radio announcing the expeditionary brigade, I was on a lunch break at the mill," Canfield recalled. "I was among the first in line at the No. 11 Personnel Depot in Vancouver the next morning."

Another who heard the broadcast was a militiaman about to celebrate his nineteenth birthday. In August 1950, Art "Chip" Evoy was spending yet another summer beating up the parade square with the Lanark and Renfrew Scottish Regiment near Picton, Ontario. When the Korean War broke out, he said, "I decided to follow in my cousin Chip's footsteps. He was Chip, Sr. I was Chip, Jr." His namesake had blazed quite a path, having won two Military Medals for acts of bravery during the Second World War.

"After the war, cousin Chip's job on the railway wasn't working out," Evoy remembered. "So when they were forming the Special Force, he decided to join up again. I thought that wasn't a bad idea for me either. But I didn't tell him I was going in. He just about died when I showed up at Camp Shilo, Manitoba," in the Royal Canadian Horse Artillery.

Pat O'Connor and his wife of two years sat at the kitchen table many hours that summer. They discussed Pat's decision to enlist. Vera was supportive of her husband, but pointed out that they had two small children and only one income; Pat was the operator of a horse-drawn bread delivery wagon in Sarnia, Ontario. She also reminded her husband he'd served four years as a stoker aboard RCN corvettes escorting North Atlantic convoys during the last war, and maybe it was up to someone else this time, but Pat insisted that "somebody had to stop the communists." A short time later, O'Connor packed up, said his goodbyes at home (the family didn't have the cab fare to get everybody to the train station) and joined the Royal Canadian Regiment.

Lesley Pike had only been a Canadian for a year when he heard news of the Special Force. The previous spring, Pike had left high school to find work and had witnessed the Dominion of Newfoundland become the tenth province of Canada. After doing several odd jobs—butchering cattle, selling wood chaff in brin bags and delivering groceries—Pike felt the urge to leave his home town of Carbonear, Newfoundland, in search of a different life.

"I'd always wanted to go St. John's," Pike admitted. "I'd never been outside Newfoundland. And partly because I became a Canadian on April 1, 1949, I decided to volunteer for the Canadian army."

"I hopped on my Harley 45 motorcycle when I heard the call," Larry Moore said. At the time, he was working for a tire manufacturing firm in Kitchener, Ontario, but that weekend he'd been visiting friends at a resort lodge in the Muskoka Lakes region of Ontario. Moore was a bit of a bookworm and always read *Time* magazine, so he knew more than most about Korea, communism and the fledgling United Nations. But there wasn't enough money in the family to send Larry to university. Suddenly all the pieces came together and his path seemed clear.

"I felt that if I joined the army, I'd serve a couple of years, mature a little bit and have the government pay part of my way through university," Moore said. "But just as important, I thought the United Nations was a marvellous idea, to get a group of volunteer countries to actually become policemen for the world. And I wanted to be part of it. So I raced to Chorley Park to join up."

Moore couldn't have chosen a busier destination that first week of August. No. 6 Personnel Depot at Chorley Park in east end Toronto was alive with some of the same excitement it had known in 1939 when the Second World War broke out. There was also an awful lot of confusion. "Lotus" was the code word that was supposed to initiate the very specific instructions for recruiting the Special Force across the country. When officials at each of the army personnel depots received the code word (presumably on Monday, August 7, the day the prime minister spoke), they were to open recruiting documents and not begin processing volunteers until Wednesday, August 9. However, in many parts of Canada, including Ontario, a civic holiday on that Monday delayed delivery of the "Lotus" code.

Consequently, when No. 6 Personnel Depot opened in Toronto on Tuesday morning, the commanding officer, who had not heard the Special Force broadcast, nor read the morning newspaper, was amazed to find several hundred volunteers on his doorstep. He immediately sent out an emergency call for typists, doctors and clerks to deal with the sudden rush of recruits. In the middle of the confusion, the mobilization instructions and the "Lotus" envelope arrived, but the obvious backlog of volunteers at Chorley Park hit the press. The evening *Toronto Daily Star* reported that hundreds of men had enlisted, while official papers to Ottawa from No. 6 Personnel Depot showed nowhere near that number because of the lengthy enlistment process. Politicians were left with the impression that military red tape was hampering the recruitment effort. This state of affairs didn't stem the flow or the enthusiasm of volunteers; by the end of August, the Toronto depot had enlisted 2,075 men.

On August 12, the front page of the Saturday *Sudbury Daily Star* featured a photograph of five smiling, young Sudburians and a caption that read: "They're off to enlist in Canada's Korea Army Brigade." The *Star* photographer had evidently found twenty-year-old Ray

Morgan, nineteen-year-old Red Butler, brothers Vern and Roland Roy, who were twenty-four and twenty-two, and the old man of the group, twenty-seven-year-old Ken McOrmond, and had asked them to pose for the shot. Immediately afterwards, the five piled into McOrmond's Meteor bound for Toronto's army recruiting office. "They said they did not want to wait until recruiting for the Special Force began in Sudbury," the newspaper reported, "in case the brigade had its full complement by that time."

"If it had been an enlistment for a hundred years," remembered McOrmond, who had finished the Second World War building bridges in Belgium with the 18th Field Company, "we'd have signed up for a hundred years." McOrmond, like so many, got out of the army in 1946, returned to Sudbury, took a job in a department store, then a menswear shop, but admits "civilian street seemed so bland. But as soon as you went back into uniform for Korea, things started to get exciting again."

At age eighteen, prairie farm boy Jim McKinny was afraid he wouldn't pass grade ten, let alone get a job. The McKinny family had not fared well on the land near Gladstone, Manitoba, so taking over the family farm wasn't an option. Korea seemed like a perfect out. Besides, Jim, his younger brother, Jack, and two friends in neighbouring Neepawa had also heard "as long as you could walk and breathe, you had no problem getting into the army . . . So we jumped on the bus and joined the army," McKinny said. "I had my sights set on the armoured corps. Maybe I figured travelling by tanks was better than walking through a war. We were told we all couldn't get in the armoured corps, but there was room for all of us in artillery. I asked where we would be trained and found out it was Shilo, Manitoba. And I figured, 'Super. I could walk home on leave.'"

Another potential Korea volunteer eager to get off the farm was Muriel White. Her family operated a mixed farm just up from the Lake Ontario shoreline, near the town of Elizabethville, "population thirty-two. If you blink you miss it.

"A cousin of father's suggested I might work for the Red Cross," she recalled. "That's what happened. After working for them a year, I was transferred to a veterans' hospital in Toronto, working in the arts and crafts department. Then, one day, my supervisor asked if I'd like to go to the Far East. I guess I had a sense of adventure. I said, 'Yes.'"

Seeking adventure. Seeing the world. Securing work. Making up for missing out on the previous war. Feeling patriotic and a need to prove oneself. Escaping small-town life. Fleeing debts, family or the law. Many of the traditional motives for joining the forces were at play in Canada that summer of 1950. One francophone from Quebec joined the Royal Canadian Navy and volunteered for Korea, not to fight the communists, not to join the United Nations policing action, not even to get away from home. At seventeen, Jean Pleau, from L'Épiphanie, just outside Montreal, joined the service to learn Canada's other official language.

"My mother had to sign for me," Pleau remembered. "I couldn't speak a word of English. Every place I had gone in Montreal to find a job, you had to speak both languages. And a relative had always told me, 'Join the navy and you'll learn English.' So I did, and not long after I was on my way to Korea aboard a destroyer."

In the small fishing village of Buctouche, on New Brunswick's east coast, young people grew up in large families and knew very little about the world outside their Acadian culture. Leo Gallant was the eldest of eight children. Economic conditions forced Leo to leave school and assist his father in the blacksmith trade. And there he might have stayed but for the Second World War. That's when he began dreaming of becoming a soldier, because "I can still remember the first people who came back on leave in December 1939. They were wearing . . . uniforms with puttees and hats. It fascinated me and stayed in my mind. I tried the air force in 1948, but didn't have enough schooling. But when they were recruiting for the Special Force, schooling didn't matter.

"I enlisted in Moncton, and from there went to Valcartier. I was a francophone and didn't know the Vandoos [R22eR] from the RCR or the PPCLI [Princess Patricia's Canadian Light Infantry]. They could have sent me anywhere as long as I was in the service."

Jean-Paul St-Aubin was the youngest of eight children living in Ottawa. An older brother had joined the Cameron Highlanders of Ottawa during the Second World War and was killed a month after D-Day in Normandy. Jean-Paul's earliest connection to the military came as a post-war employee of the Department of Veterans Affairs. For a while, he was responsible for packaging and shipping veterans their medals. Handling such military awards as the Africa Star, the Burma Star, the 1939–45 Star and other volunteer medals, must have left an impression, because "when war broke out in 1950, I got talking with friends and we decided, 'What the heck, let's enlist.'

"The next day we were at No. 13 Depot in Ottawa signing up," St-Aubin said. "They didn't ask us where we wanted to go. They saw we were French so they shipped us to the Royal 22e Régiment in Quebec."

While recruitment of the Canadian Army Special Force received most of the attention, the Regular or Active Force responded to the mobilization as well. The Minister of National Defence had given responsibility of training the Special Force to the existing permanent force regiments. "On-the-job training," Brooke Claxton had described it, so that "the men who join the Special Force will absorb the customs and the characteristics of the parent unit . . . and become rapidly ready for action." In other words, Claxton was calling all soldiers—Regular Force, reserve officers and even retirees—to heed a general call-to-arms.

Among those who came forward was Scottish-born Canadian Jim "Scotty" Martin. Having turned twenty-four in June 1950, the Second World War veteran was waiting for the Department of National Defence to make him an offer in the peacetime army. Toward the end of the 1939–45 war he had volunteered for a combined US/Canadian special service force, in which he'd learned to navigate, read maps, interpret field and terrain intelligence and speak Japanese. The war ended before he could be posted to the Pacific to apply his training. Now he was seriously considering leaving the army for a civilian job with the Pinkerton's National Detective Agency. That's when his brigadier called and offered him a transfer to the Royal Canadian

Regiment to train members of the Special Force, or newly formed 2nd Battalion of the RCR. He took it.

Another Second World War veteran from New Brunswick, Hal Merrithew had come home from European occupation duty in 1946 to pursue an accounting career at a business college in Saint John. Money for tuition and living expenses ran out, so Merrithew rejoined the army, becoming an instructor at Camp Borden, Ontario. When the government announced the Special Force, Merrithew began training the Service Corps—all the behind-the-lines soldiers, from cooks to clerks—for Korea.

J. R. Stone had already served his country with distinction. During the Second World War, he landed in Sicily with the 1st Canadian Division. Later, in the critical battle for Ortona, on the east coast of Italy, he earned the Military Cross. By the end of the battle for the Hitler Line, he was promoted to lieutenant colonel. After the war, he disappeared into civilian life to build a lakeside summer resort in British Columbia, until a friend convinced him to rejoin the army in the summer of 1950.

In Korea, Scotty Martin would command his own platoon with the RCR in the battle of Kowang-san. Hal Merrithew would lead his own platoon with the R22eR and win a Military Cross. And "Big Jim" Stone would command the 2nd Battalion of the PPCLI to international recognition at Kap'yong.

Col. Stone's old regiment, the Princess Patricias, had been busy that year. In mid-winter, the 1st Battalion had joined American forces in Yukon and Alaska during an Arctic training exercise known as Sweetbriar. The objective was to gauge the regiment's performance under harsh conditions. In temperatures of minus 50 degrees, the Patricias were dropped from Dakota aircraft to seize an airport. A few weeks later, the regiment was called out to save the suburbs of Winnipeg during the Red River flood of 1950.

In contrast, the Special Force recruits, who would soon be arriving at the PPCLI's home barracks to train in Calgary, were untrained, untested and, in some cases, out of touch. It seemed to Stone that the government was "in a hell of a hurry. They were recruiting off the streets, anybody who could breathe or walk . . . Claxton was pushing hard. He had recruited an army to fight . . . [but] they were recruiting off the streets."

That's exactly where Don Hibbs came from. Born in Galt, Ontario, Hibbs discovered early that he had more talent at the ice rink than in a classroom, and when given the choice in grade ten, he chose hockey. As a pretty solid defenceman, Hibbs pinballed around the game from Junior A to the Scottish Ice Hockey League, and finally, in 1948, to a western Ontario Intermediate A league made up of Second World War veterans "who drank a case of beer before the game, not after." The bottom line was less than satisfying—$35 a week, little chance of a shot at the NHL and, without an education, not much of a future.

By 1950, Don Hibbs was driving taxi for his friend Clad Essig's Seven-Eleven Cab Company in Galt. In those days and in Hibbs's economic state, he wasn't drawing much of a pay cheque. Whenever he needed a pair of pants, he'd go to the tailor's in town and charge it on Essig's account. If he needed money for a date or room and board at home, Essig would stake him the funds. Hibbs, the school drop-out, was living, but living hand-to-mouth at best. On August 7, 1950, the night Prime Minister St. Laurent announced the Special Force on radio, Hibbs was driving fares around Galt.

"I didn't have a clue about Korea," Hibbs admitted. "All I knew was, I'd missed out on the Second World War. And I wanted to be a soldier, you know, pulling pins out of grenades with my teeth, like I'd seen in those John Wayne war movies. I knew John Wayne had never been in the war, not a day in his life. But I thought it'd be great to be a real soldier. I wanted to be a hero."

A few days later, Hibbs the taxi driver was Hibbs the army volunteer, joining up at the Wolseley Barracks in London, Ontario. In fact, he arrived after hours and had to scale a wire fence around the encampment to get in. Once he signed his enlistment papers, Hibbs was ushered into a large room where an army officer invited him and about fifty other recruits to swear allegiance to king and country and sit down. Then the officer welcomed them all to their new home— life in the Canadian army.

"I know some of you guys are from the Second World War," the officer began. "I know some of you have been on the road trying to find work. I know it's been tough. And I know some of you here have even served a little time in jail. That doesn't matter. You're with a new family now. Your new family is the Canadian army. Don't be afraid, but now that I mention it, all those who have spent time in jail . . . stand up."

The entire room of men stood up, except Don Hibbs.

"I'd never spent a day in jail in my life," Hibbs remembered thinking. "Yet there I was, the only guy seated in a roomful of criminals!" So he stood up to make it unanimous.

3

A GALLON OF SWEAT

LATE IN THE AFTERNOON, on July 25, 1950, tourists and reporters on Parliament Hill snapped photographs of a formation of transport aircraft approaching from the east. The six North Stars, from No. 426 Transport Squadron at Dorval, were the first RCAF aircraft bound for overseas service in the Korean War. En route, they made one low-altitude pass over the Peace Tower with its flag at half mast in tribute to the country's tenth prime minister. William Lyon Mackenzie King had been lying in state in Ottawa since his death three days earlier.

The gesture was full of irony. King, for twenty-two years Canada's prime minister, had been a fierce nationalist and, particularly in military matters, a chief proponent of Canadian autonomy. Although Britain had declared the Commonwealth at war against Hitler's Germany on September 3, 1939, Prime Minister King had waited nearly a week, until September 9, when an emergency session of Parliament sent Canada to war against Germany too. Then, during the Second World War, it was King who had stubbornly delayed signing into law Canada's largest financial commitment to the war effort—the British Commonwealth Air Training Plan (which would school in Canada all aircrew for the war)—until he obtained assurance from Britain that the plan would be administered by Canadians and that its Canadian aircrew graduates would fly into battle in separate Canadian squadrons and under RCAF command.

Less than a week after King's death, RCAF airmen were entering a wartime airlift not under the Canadian flag, but under United Nations (principally American) command. King's successor, Prime Minister Louis St. Laurent, had now dispatched No. 426 Transport Squadron to airlift supplies in support of US and Republic of Korea troops hemmed into the Pusan Perimeter in the southeastern corner of Korea.

"We were standing on the tarmac in front of the six North Stars," Bill Tigges said. An RCAF instrument technician, recently transferred from Edmonton to No. 426 Transport Squadron, twenty-year-old Tigges was among the flying officers, aircrew and 185 ground crewmen lined up in Dorval before departure. "We were already assigned to our aircraft. Our equipment was all packed. The press was there. And Wing Commander [C. H.] Mussels said any of us who didn't want to go, didn't have to. We knew we were flying out of the country. We knew we'd be gone for a year. But that's it."

Also standing on the tarmac that day was Eric Glustien, a twenty-nine-year-old RCAF navigator. He too had just been transferred to Dorval. The previous day, Glustien had been flying at 20,000 feet over northern Canada as part of a mapping operation, "but when I came down at Norman Wells in the Northwest Territories, there was a signal from headquarters. They needed navigators. They flew us back East the same day."

"We arrived back in Dorval the day Mackenzie King died," pilot Rowly Lloyd said. Well travelled and also twenty-nine, Lloyd had flown Halifax bombers in the latter stages of the Second World War. He then worked at the Institute of Aviation Medicine in Toronto, and was on a South Atlantic training flight from Dorval to Bermuda to France to north Africa to Brazil to Trinidad, and "we arrived home on Sunday morning . . . Tuesday evening we flew out of Dorval as part of the Korean airlift."

The mission was code-named Operation Hawk. Orders to RCAF No. 426 Transport Squadron included a curtailment of all domestic transport operations, the integration into McChord Air Force Base at Tacoma, Washington, and placement under direct operational control of the US Military Air Transport Service (US MATS). As organized as that sounds, ten hours after their low-level formation tribute to Mackenzie King over Ottawa, the six North Stars landed at McChord amid "conditions that could best be described as chaotic."

That 426 Squadron diary is kinder to the base than Leading Aircraftman (LAC) Tigges, who recalls having all RCAF kit, tools, repair equipment and parts dumped in a "no-man's-land" at McChord. The gear was heaped in an open field, with no runways, no hangars, no workshops, no lights and a barracks with broken windows. Confusion reigned on the flightline too. Since there were few, if any, runways, US MATS crews found themselves building airstrips between aircraft takeoffs and landings. As Tigges remembered it, "This was not the driest place on Earth," so RCAF crews often worked fourteen-hour days under tarpaulins in the rain until the Americans repaired barracks and built nose hangars for their North Stars. Still, Tigges and the rest of the ground crew had no choice. For the next three years, rain or shine, they had to keep a dozen North Stars airborne, completing fifteen round trips between North America and Japan each month.

During the Korean airlift, No. 426 Transport Squadron flew approximately 600 round trips, carried 3,000,000 kilograms of freight and mail and ferried about 13,000 passengers, mostly soldiers en route to or coming home from Korea. One day, early in his year-long posting to McChord, Bill Tigges diverted his attention from work long enough to spot crews disembarking returning troops, soldiers that "were just eighteen- and nineteen-year-old American kids," Tigges said. "Some had bandages. Others were amputees. That's when I realized there was a war going on over there."

As responsive as Canadian airmen were to the call, for the third war in a row, Royal Canadian Navy ships and crew were first into action.

Three Tribal Class destroyers—named after Native Canadian tribes—were anchored at Esquimalt on the West coast. HMCS *Cayuga*, commanded by Captain Jeffry Brock, and sister ships in the Pacific Destroyer Command, HMCS *Athabaskan* and *Sioux*, had been slated to rendezvous with three ships in Halifax in late summer, 1950, and cross the Atlantic for manoeuvres in Europe. That plan changed on July 5, when the Canadian government placed its Pacific fleet under UN command for duty in the waters off Korea. Suddenly, *Cayuga* wasn't preparing for a leisurely cruise to Europe, but for action in a war zone.

"There was a great sense of urgency," recalled the ship's newly promoted supply officer Bill Davis. "We had to bring some of our electronic equipment and armament up to scratch. We had to get ammunitioned. And we had to get our crew up to wartime strength. . . from around 150 to 230 some odd . . . But one of the things I was particularly worried about was how we were going to pay for fuel oil, food and such things as dockage fees. Where was I going to get the coconuts for all that?"

Only a supply officer of a few weeks' standing, the twenty-two-year-old Davis couldn't answer that question, but by this time he'd learned the first rule of supply: You demand answers. He quizzed the ship's engineers about fuel, the ship's cooks about food and the ship's veterans about dockage. Then, to complicate matters, Captain Brock announced that Davis would have to determine future supply needs, not only for *Cayuga*, but for all three ships in the squadron. Shouldering the added responsibility, Davis soon determined that each destroyer would need about $300,000 for a total of $1 million US for the destroyers to operate between North America and Korea.

Not surprisingly, a million-dollar supply budget created a stir at naval headquarters. Eventually the estimate received official blessing and each destroyer placed in its vault $10,000 US in cash, some Canadian cash and bills of exchange for the rest, that is, blank cheques from the Bank of Montreal backed by the government of Canada in the sum of $290,000 US. All Davis had to do was find banks en route to and from Korea that would honour the bills. And there was one more hitch: the bills of exchange came in denominations of $10,000 and each had to be negotiated separately.

The test of Lt. Davis's floating economics occurred on July 12, when *Cayuga*, *Athabaskan* and *Sioux* pulled into Pearl Harbor. While in port, the ships' crews conducted anti-submarine exercises; one sailor was arrested by the United States Navy (USN) shore patrol and there was near mutiny on board *Cayuga* over orders to wear full uniform in the blistering Hawaiian sunshine. However, most important to the squadron's supply officer (after fuel, food and ammunition purchases) was that each ship had spent its US cash. It was time to see if those Bank of Montreal bills of exchange were legal tender at the Bank of Hawaii.

"Tell me your problem," the bank vice-president said sympathetically. Luckily he was a Canadian expatriate from Montreal. He looked at the lieutenant's bills of exchange worth $290,000 per ship. He listened as the supply officer explained the caveat that each bill of $10,000 had to be negotiated individually.

"Well," the bank VP said, "if you go in and out of that front door twenty-nine times, we have exchange. We have had twenty-nine transactions."

"Yes sir," agreed Davis, unable to believe his ears.

"You get your guys here," the banker said, "and we'll negotiate all the bills of exchange. And you'll get your $290,000 per ship."

Davis wanted to hug the man.

"One problem," he said. "In Hawaii we don't have anything bigger than a twenty-dollar bill."

The ramifications of that last detail didn't sink in until Davis was halfway back to *Cayuga*. When he realized that, next day, he'd be travelling through downtown Honolulu with nearly a million dollars in twenty-dollar bills, the thought almost overwhelmed him. Nevertheless, at the appointed time, Lt. Davis, and the other two supply officers and the ships' first lieutenants as co-signers boarded a bus operated by US Navy guards armed with machine guns. They were escorted by jeeps full of police outriders, with shotguns.

Inside the Bank of Hawaii, Davis handed over the bills of exchange, then sat in the vault with his fellow officers, nervously counting stacks of twenty-dollar bills. When that was done, the Canadian navymen filled mail sacks with the American cash, shook hands with the accommodating bank manager and filed out of the bank and onto the waiting bus and armed convoy. With sirens blaring and tires screeching, the entourage raced back to the shipyard.

"Talk about being panic-stricken," Davis said. "There I was making $212 a month, carrying a million bucks through the streets of Honolulu. And the ship's safe wasn't even big enough to hold it all; we put the ship's Canadian money in a locker in my cabin and the American bills in the safe. I was finally relieved. As far as I was concerned, we could go anywhere and buy anything. We had the universal medium of exchange—US dollars."

The Canadian destroyers sailed into the port of Sasebo, Japan, in mid-afternoon on July 30, 1950. Eight kilometres long and ringed by jagged peaks, Sasebo harbour lay on Japan's southwestern coast 100 nautical miles from Korean waters. The day HMCS *Cayuga*, *Athabaskan* and *Sioux* arrived, the harbour was jammed with navy vessels: warships two and three together riding buoys in the channel, huge bulk-supply ships moored at every available wharf and jetty, and merchant ships at anchor in the remaining space. The US and Royal Navies had organized the entire inlet according to repair, re-supply and, in the most distant reaches of the harbour, refuel and rearmament. This would be the RCN's home away from home for the next thirty-seven months of fighting and where Canadian seamen awaited their first assignments.

In early August, the RCN destroyers joined British, Australian and New Zealand warships in the Yellow Sea off the west coast of Korea, while US Navy vessels sailed up the east coast. The reason was that if a Commonwealth ship veered into Chinese territorial waters, Britain, which had recently established diplomatic relations with the People's Republic, could deal directly with Peking. The US had not recognized Red China, and the UN command did not want to draw the Chinese into the war.

Daylight operations for Canadian warships initially included convoy duty—escorting troopships and screening aircraft carriers—and at night RCN destroyers were released for coastal patrol. Easier said than done. Korea's west coast was jagged with coves, shifting channels, concealed shoals, extreme tides and innumerable small islands. The uncharted waters made navigation tricky, and the labyrinth of inlets up the coast provided ample cover for North Korean gunboats, raiding parties and strategically laid mines.

On her fifth day in Korean waters, August 15, *Cayuga* steamed to the southern port of Yosu, where North Korean forces were marshalling artillery for an anticipated assault against the Pusan Perimeter. *Cayuga* anchored offshore and, taking directions from spotter aircraft, began shelling the shore positions with her four-inch guns. It was *Cayuga*'s first-ever wartime action. It was the first time since 1945 that an RCN ship had fired guns in combat. To mark the occasion, crewmen saved the brass casing from the first shell, later shaped it into an ashtray and gave it to Prime Minister St. Laurent as a memento. The shell was also the first of 130,000 rounds that Canadian ships would hurl at their enemy over the next three years.

"I spent a lot of our first days in Korean waters deciphering messages," remembered *Athabaskan* radio operator Ernest Sargeant. "It was a different set of dots and dashes than I was used to, but I eventually learned to decode them . . . But most memorable on that tour was the Inch'on landing," for which the telegraphist had a front-row seat. On escort duty, on September 15, *Athabaskan* joined 260 warships in a lightning attack on the west coast port occupied by the North Koreans. Gen. Douglas MacArthur's tactically brilliant amphibious landing, the largest since D-Day in 1944, deposited 80,000 US Marines safely behind the Korean People's Army lines. Within twenty-four hours, Inch'on was seized from the North Koreans, thousands of KPA troops had become prisoners-of-war and across the peninsula along the Pusan Perimeter, the UN counter-offensive began. The collapse of North Korean forces came, as

Time magazine reported, "with avalanche swiftness." Fifteen days later, Republic of Korea (ROK) Army soldiers crossed the same 38th parallel from which they had retreated on June 25. It looked as if the war would be over by Christmas.

Aside from the indelible impression in the minds of RCN sailors like Ernest Sargeant, the action at Inch'on had "one other lasting impact on the Royal Canadian Navy," according to Bob Peers, operations officer aboard HMCS *Sioux*: "At the time, we had a red maple leaf painted on each side of our funnel. Early in the war, over our radios, we had heard US fighter pilots referring to it as a 'red star,' so we quickly repainted it green . . . and the green maple leaf has been standard ever since."

And while war diaries show no record of American planes mistakenly firing on RCN destroyers, they report that the Canadian naval squadron was battered by another enemy. After three months in Korean waters, *Sioux, Athabaskan* and *Cayuga* were dispatched to Hong Kong to lay up over Christmas. En route, the flotilla ran smack into Typhoon Clara in the East China Sea, where a year earlier a similar storm had capsized several US Navy destroyers.

"The rolling became worse than I had ever experienced," recalled R. L. Lane on board *Cayuga*. For two and a half days the typhoon tore motor boats, cutters and carley floats loose from the destroyer's decks, warped doors, and turned her crew and its belongings upside down. The severe rolling of the ship, once to a 52-degree angle, "brought the sea pretty well over the portholes, which meant the main deck was completely awash," Lane wrote. "We were getting light on fuel, so we began flooding our fuel tanks to maintain ballast. We were as stable as we could be, which wasn't saying much . . ."

Meanwhile, aboard *Athabaskan*, several crewmen were on deck where a huge wave caught them and washed sailor Robert Elvidge overboard and beyond the grasp of his shipmates. Elvidge wasn't a swimmer; he had failed swimming in basic training. A quick signal astern brought *Sioux* into the path of the floundering sailor, and in one quick manoeuvre a sailor on *Sioux* grabbed Elvidge from the crest of a wave as it swelled alongside the ship. Next day, Elvidge requested an addendum to his record noting he had passed his swimming test. His request was granted.

By Armistice Day, 1950, all Royal Canadian Navy seamen were safe and sound in Hong Kong. Four days later, an honour guard of sailors from the three destroyers made its way to Saiwon Cemetery to pay respects to the Royal Rifles of Canada and Winnipeg Grenadiers who had fought to defend Hong Kong against the Japanese in 1941. The ill-fated mission had cost 303 men killed on the island colony and 254 others who died in Japanese POW camps.

The shadow of the Hong Kong disaster extended further than Saiwon Cemetery. The memory of sending nearly 2,000 poorly trained Canadian troops into the front line against the Japanese army in 1941 haunted Canadians, even as the St. Laurent cabinet wrestled with its Korean commitment in the fall of 1950.

"I do not want to see another Hong Kong, where ill-trained and ill-equipped men were sent into battle," stated Victor Quelch, a Social Credit MP in the House of Commons. "I think it is extremely important that any men who are sent out of this country shall be properly trained and properly equipped, and that no man should be sent from the country until he has reached that degree of perfection."

At first the recruits for Canada's Special Force (a.k.a. the 25th Canadian Infantry Brigade) were a long way from perfection. Critics dismissed them as misfits and rascals or, at best, as soldier-of-fortune types. Even the Royal Canadian Regiment's war diaries reveal that "a fair percentage of the first enlistments consisted of . . . 'scruff,' men who had volunteered not out of patriotism but because they were unhappy or uncomfortable in civilian employment, or wished to leave home in search of adventure." If the recruits were short of the mark, so was the recruiting system. Recruiting stations that had been handling a dozen men a week were suddenly swamped with hundreds each day. When Minister of National Defence Brooke Claxton suggested that the military was too slow to enlist, attest and dispatch recruits, the resulting speed-up created more problems. Apocryphal or not, there were tales of enlisting a man of seventy-two, a boy of fourteen, one with an artificial leg and "a couple of hunch-backs," one officer said. "When the political heat is on, you can't reject anybody who's able to walk."

Reg McIlvenna was hastily signed up in Ottawa on August 7, the day Prime Minister St. Laurent announced the Special Force. In fact, he claims that his regimental number—C 850000—denotes the country's very first recruit in the brigade. However, that's when any special status or treatment ended. He was hustled outside the recruiting station and told to stand beside a line of waiting trucks. When they pulled out for the RCR's home base at Petawawa, McIlvenna was left standing there.

"How do I get to the camp?" he asked an officer.

Nonplussed, the officer asked who he was.

"I'm the only one on the draft."

The officer turned the air blue with curses, then laughed and drove McIlvenna to Camp Petawawa personally. At the camp he was interviewed again, issued an oversize bush uniform and boots, pho-tographed, fed and taken to an empty H-shaped barracks and left there alone. His first night in the Canadian Army Special Force, Pte. Reg McIlvenna, regimental number C 850000, slept on a bunk with a mattress beneath him and another pulled on top of him because there were no blankets.

As far as Don Flieger was concerned, "The enlisting procedures were atrocious." A former militiaman with the North Shore Regi-ment in New Brunswick, Flieger had also worked as a bank clerk and a semipro hockey player before he joined the permanent army early in 1950. His clerical skills (and probably his sports conditioning) made him an ideal clerk at Petawawa: "I spent two months getting rid of the riffraff we had enlisted. The medically unfit, the deserters, a lot of people who slipped through the cracks . . . they were on this X-List and had to be discharged. What a pile of paper. The 2nd Bat-talion RCR alone had 500 men who went AWL in September and October of 1950."

Compounding the chaos, during the early days of recruitment, the non-operating employees of Canada's two railways—Canadian

National and Canadian Pacific—went on strike in late August. The walkout prevented the equitable dispersion of recruits to their training stations at Chilliwack, Calgary, Shilo, Borden, Petawawa, Barriefield and Valcartier. Until the railway dispute could be resolved, Petawawa received the majority of central and eastern Canadian recruits by truck and bus convoy. However, using the roads meant stopping for rests. Every rest stop afforded another watering hole, which sparked more drunkenness and desertion, to a point that transport officers carried shackles, in case there was trouble. Of the 8,000 who enlisted in the first two months of the Special Force recruitment, more than 2,000 were discharged and more than 1,500 deserted.

Troops without transport and barracks without blankets were only part of the problem. In the earliest days of the Special Force, equipment, uniforms and boots were limited, much of it having been sold to friendly nations and army surplus stores after 1945. During basic training some recruits used sticks in place of rifles, overalls instead of battle dress and socks in lieu of gloves. Accommodations were equally substandard; the H-huts were cold, the showers were colder and the food was coldest. There was, of course, no privacy. There was plenty of theft, and there was plenty of bullying.

In Calgary, where the 2nd Battalion of the Princess Patricia's Canadian Light Infantry trained, it was no different. Currie Barracks faced the same shortages as Petawawa—no boots, no bullets, no breeches. First Battalion officers conducted parades and drills in smart-looking jump smocks, high-top boots and cherry berries (maroon berets), while their new keeps still had only civilian clothes and shoes. For recruit Don Hibbs, wearing street garb was embarrassing and degrading, particularly one day when he was stopped by an apparent peer.

"What's the dress?" scolded the soldier.

Hibbs paused a second to make sure the man wasn't an officer, then snapped back, "What you see is what you get, man."

"You're on charge, soldier," the man shouted, and Hibbs was confined to barracks for seven days, sweeping floors and washing latrines for talking back to a so-called senior private.

At Valcartier, Quebec, home of the Royal 22e Régiment, the Special Force recruits did basic training on the clock system—one hour on map reading, one hour on parade drill, next hour on first aid and one on weapons, then a repeat of the entire cycle, for the whole day, with the same instructors repeating the same lessons to each group. It was a process 2nd Battalion instructor Jim Boire called "roboticizing" the recruits. As monotonous and dehumanizing as the training seemed, Lt. Boire believed it was necessary because "in infantry, we have to order men to do what is against their nature, something that may cause death. Infantry must react regardless of danger or fear. It's the source of discipline."

Training, as far as PPCLI platoon commander Bob Peacock was concerned, was like learning—always unfinished and never complete. Peacock was convinced that Canadian army instruction was based on sound principles because they had been proven in combat. When training was prepared with a clear purpose, he said, not wasted or treated frivolously, it built excellent morale, confidence in leadership and in the soldier himself. "A gallon of sweat spent in training," claimed Peacock, "is better than a pint of blood in battle."

Pte. Harley Welsh's training regimen was never that inspiring. The night the Special Force was announced, Welsh decided to join, "because I felt I'd missed out on the Second World War." The next morning he was first in line at the Saskatoon Recruiting Office. They sent him to Regina to be processed, then to Calgary to train with the PPCLI. Welsh should have recognized a bad omen when his uniform didn't fit and when the Permanent Force instructors began picking on his group of recruits; the veterans were angry that the volunteers would be going to Korea first. Welsh felt the friction was just "a teething problem" at the station.

However, the Saskatoon recruit vividly remembers his gas mask exercises in September 1950. Sometimes forty or fifty of the trainees were told to put on their respirators for an outdoor exercise. Other times they were sealed in a room full of tear gas. Breathing was not difficult while their gas masks were in place, but then the instructors ordered the recruits to remove their masks with the tear gas still circulating.

"We had to sit there and take it," Welsh said bitterly. "Two minutes was one thing, but ten was unnecessary. And we suffered—eyes running, and coughing and wheezing for six or eight hours afterward . . . They called it just another test of discipline."

Special Force volunteers in the PPCLI and the R22eR received their advanced training on the eastern Alberta prairie, near the small town of Wainwright, population 5,000, although J. G. Tony Poulin, battalion commander of the R22eR, insisted "the census takers must have included the dogs." In ideal conditions, Camp Wainwright enjoyed the lush green of the Battle River basin in summer and the occasional chinook wind to ease the deep freeze in winter. Conditions, however, were usually far from ideal. PPCLI recruit John Carson's recollection is typical: "Brutal sun singed our hides by day. Coyotes mocked us by night. There were days when the dust would rise up and choke us. Others when the rain poured down and turned all to bogs."

The inhospitable climate played havoc with exercises too. One afternoon, the PPCLI training staff staged a mock frontal assault with covering artillery fire. The whole operation was nearly wiped out twice. Platoon commander E. Ray Knight suddenly recognized the first problem during the infantry charge when the so-called friendly shells began falling short. He quickly called off the manoeuvre. The man-made barrage was soon followed by a natural one.

"Few noticed what was brewing up around us," Knight wrote. "Clouds were rolling in. Breezes rapidly grew to moaning winds. Lightning flashed in earnest. I realized we were in grave danger. I had everyone hunker down in their holes as far beneath the surface of the ground as possible . . . Then the storm front hit. The ground shook as lightning struck. The smell of the disturbed grasses and soil was overcome by a more acrid, metallic stench as the air became electrified. Then hail came down. Within seconds the sandy soil was saturated, unable to absorb the flood washing over us. Our shallow holes filled up in seconds."

Somehow, though, rookie infantrymen found their way. They survived confinement to barracks or kitchen patrol. They endured endless drills with rifles that were relics of the First World War. They found pride in regimental badges presented to them in late fall. And camaraderie seeped into the ranks during needle parade, pay parade and first leave. Don Hibbs, still without a uniform, learned how to trim woollies off his dress pants with his shaver, how to keep his pant crease straight by putting weights in the cuffs and how spit and polish would make even his street shoes shine. Harley Welsh never once complained about being gassed by frustrated instructors, and he survived to go to Korea before they did. E. Ray Knight's platoon learned from Alberta gumbo how to fight in Korean mud. RCR Pte. Ron Trider also observed a burgeoning esprit de corps as "the soldier evolved. From the great gathering throng there was a coming together. The so-called Special Farce became the Special Force. Pride in platoon, company and battalion overcame provincial loyalties. Respect for one another's differences bound individuals together as they learned to drill, polish kit, practice weapons skills and fight together."

Above the rank and file, the officialdom of building a fighting force for Korea went on like clockwork. Minister of National Defence Brooke Claxton had successfully drawn back the superintendent of Pacific Stage Lines in B.C. to command Canada's Special Force. John M. Rockingham, like the men the government was recruiting for the Special Force, was a Second World War veteran. In addition to his distinguished service as a brigade commander in northwestern Europe (he'd received the Companion of the British Empire, Distinguished Service Order, the Belgian Order of Leopold and the Croix de Guerre), it was felt that "Rocky" could get along with the Americans and, most important, win the confidence of this new volunteer force—the 25th Canadian Infantry Brigade. Within weeks, Rockingham had the brigade well in hand. He had chosen officers and assigned artillery batteries, engineers, signals, ordnance, electrical and mechanical engineers, medical and dental corps and provosts to their respective infantry regiments. His command had also won praise for presenting the new recruits with regimental badges; at least now they had a sense of belonging.

Rocky, however, had no control over the onset of winter. November 1, 1950, had been accepted as the time to move Canadian troops overseas. But where? American authorities didn't think UN forces should train in Japan. A Canadian military official had checked out Okinawa and found it unsuitable. Still others recommended that the Special Force go directly to Korea. Meanwhile, the war in Korea had changed. By the end of October, UN ground forces had the North Korean army in full flight back across the 38th parallel. There was some speculation that no additional troops would be needed anyway and Gen. MacArthur was confident enough of victory to suggest that "Canada might prefer to send [a] small token force to show the flag." Nevertheless, Canadian officials made plans to move Special Force training to Fort Lewis, Washington, during the coming winter and, should they be needed, to embark on ships at Seattle for the Far East.

"The logistical problems were mammoth," Ron Trider wrote. The unofficial RCR diarist summed up the exodus to Fort Lewis as "a monumental task," and listed some of the items required by support companies, from vehicles to weapons to ordnance. But he couldn't resist throwing a few barbs at some members of the Special Force and their requirements, including the maintenance crews who would need "Blanco, Brasso and Silvo by the gallon [and] the provost corps [and their] motorcycles, jeeps and handcuffs by the hundreds . . . maybe even thousands!"

While packing up and heading west to Fort Lewis was relatively straightforward for infantry, it was a little more complicated for artillery. Since the prime minister's call for recruitment of the Special Force, the Royal Canadian Horse Artillery (RCHA) had been training at Camp Shilo. On the prairies, just west of Winnipeg, three new batteries (about 450 gunners who would back up the infantry in Korea) had been earning their $65 a month by pounding the parade square, grappling with logarithms and learning the finer points of firing 25-pounder field guns. Each gun crew consisted of a sergeant (or senior NCO), two drivers, a layer who sighted the gun, a loader who placed each shell in the breach block and a rammer to engage the shell in the barrel, insert the cartridge case and close the block.

"We did everything by hand," Lance Bombardier Tom Boutillier recalled. Because his grandfather, father, uncle and older brother had all served in artillery regiments, however, the workload was no surprise. "Up to the gun sheds first thing each morning, lug the gun out of a big hole, prepare to advance, set up and fire," Boutillier said. "And remember, the gun weighed about a thousand pounds!"

From the heat of mid-August through the freeze-up of early November 1950, the Special Force, or 2nd Field Regiment, of the RCHA, had learned day firing and night firing so that "by the time we reached Korea," bragged one gunner, "a good crew could have three rounds in the air at once." During that time, the three artillery units—"D," "E" and "F" Batteries—also found out which infantry unit they would protect in Korea. Dog Battery would support the Royal Canadian Regiment, Easy Battery the Princess Patricia's Canadian Light Infantry and Fox Battery the Royal 22e Régiment. By mid-November the RCHA gunners were loading all their gear aboard two troop trains at Shilo, to join the rest of the 25th Canadian Infantry Brigade in Fort Lewis, Washington.

The Canadian railways dubbed the huge transport mission Operation Sawhorse. On November 11, 1950, members of the 2nd Battalion of the R22eR boarded their train at Valcartier and headed west. On November 16, the 2nd Battalion of the RCR pulled out of Petawawa. And the train carrying the 2nd Battalion of the PPCLI arrived at Fort Lewis on November 21. In all, twenty-three troop trains were employed to transport 286 officers and 5,773 other soldiers to Fort Lewis. The total dollar cost was $436,534.11.

The human cost for some, however, was much higher.

When the first train steamed out of the Shilo siding on Monday, November 20, all of the RCHA's Dog Battery and half of Easy Battery were aboard. A few hours later, the rest of Easy Battery and Fox Battery—338 men—left on the second train. Because of the cold November air, the military passengers were glad to get under way;

somebody had chalked the lyrics "Good-night Irene" across the passenger-car wall. Accommodation aboard was rustic at best. The troop coaches were steel-clad on the outside but flimsy on the inside, with primitive seats and wooden berths that folded down from above. They were the same passenger cars that had carried immigrants on the CNR in western Canada half a century before.

By Tuesday morning the second troop train—seventeen cars long—was steaming its way west through the Rocky Mountains on one of the most remote sections of the CNR system, a little west of Canoe River, B.C. Hours behind the first train, a railway communications error had directed the westbound troop train on to the same track as the ten-car Transcontinental Flyer, eastbound from Vancouver.

Most of the RCHA gunners were up and had eaten breakfast in the dining cars at the rear of the troop train. They were settling in for a long, relaxing ride through the mountains. Gnr. Doug Walton, from Easy Battery, had just returned to his seat in Car 31, the first passenger coach behind the engine, coal tender and baggage car. He loved "dusters," so he pulled out the latest paperback he had and stretched out lengthwise on the seat to read. Above him on a fold-down berth, a fellow gunner did the same.

On the next coach back—Car 32—a porter was working his way up the aisle. "Mind moving, fellas?" the porter asked L/Bdr. Boutillier and some of his mates. "We've got to make the beds."

Boutillier and his friend, Gnr. Bob Craig, obliged. They had been playing cribbage on a fold-down table. Craig was from Foam Lake, Saskatchewan; Boutillier from Kingston, Ontario. For both these artillerymen, this was the first trip through the Rockies, so they got up to watch the passing mountain scenery. They made their way back one car to where a newsy sold magazines and cigarettes from a wicker basket in the washroom. Boutillier asked for some smokes and handed the newsy a five-dollar bill. It was 10:35 in the morning.

In the same coach—Car 33—Gnr. Art Evoy had returned from his shift in the dining cars and had set up a portable table to play some cards with three of his chums. He was "sitting facing the direction the train was going as we rounded a bend . . . And then there were two distinct crashes," Evoy said, as their westbound troop train collided head-on with the eastbound Transcontinental. "The first crash was when the two steam engines hit and everything seemed to kind of stop . . . but the passenger engine plowed through [our] baggage car and the first troop coach."

The initial impact killed both locomotives' engineers and firemen. Then the modern and much heavier steel passenger train kept smashing through the troop train, first knocking its baggage car off the rails and down the hillside, then chewing through the first wooden passenger car—Car 31—where Doug Walton and most of the Easy Battery men were seated. As the coach flew apart around him, Walton was catapulted through an opening and outside onto the mountainside. His mate from the berth above landed on top of him. Most of the rest of Easy Battery disappeared into the disintegrating coach.

The passenger locomotive kicked the second coach—Car 32—up in the air and on top of the third coach before it stopped. A city block's length of troop train had been compressed to less than a few storefronts. In Car 33, where the newsy had been selling magazines and cigarettes in the washroom, Tom Boutillier was alive but trapped beneath wreckage. Pressurized steam began escaping from ruptured pipes throughout the troop train, searing those trapped in the twisted debris.

"Boots!" cried out Bob Craig from inside a cloud of steam. "Help me, I'm stuck!"

"I'm stuck too," Boutillier shouted back as he struggled to get free to save his friend.

It was too late for Craig. And it was too late for eleven others. Gnr. Red McKeown had been among Boutillier's best chums at Shilo. Gnr. Bill Wright used to cut hair in camp. Gnr. Albert George was a Second World War vet getting back into action. Gnr. Jim Wenkert had got into trouble and lost his two stripes just before they left Shilo. And there was Gnr. Weldon Barkhouse, who'd been in Car 31 because alphabetically, they'd assigned the first men of Fox Battery to join the last of Easy Battery up there.

Just down the mountainside from what had been Car 31, Doug Walton was up to his armpits in snow. His elbow and ribcage had been smashed in, but most uncomfortable of all was that his buddy, from the berth above, was injured and lying on top of him. They were among the few from Easy Battery who survived the impact.

When they eventually removed Tom Boutillier from the wreckage, he saw how close he'd come to death. What was left of the Transcontinental engine had stopped just short of the newsy's washroom concession stand in Car 33. His rescuers put a tag around his neck indicating his injuries—steam burns and back injuries—and the dosage of morphine he'd been given. Of the rescue, Boutillier recalls that, despite being a "dry" train, somehow "a heck of a lot of booze showed up" to warm up coffee, calm some of the shock and sterilize what surgical instruments they had. There was, however, no medical officer with the RCHA troops.

On board the Transcontinental, Dr. Patrick Kimmitt and his wife were en route home to Edson, Alberta. Running a family practice in an isolated community, Dr. Kimmitt had basic surgical skills "doing such operations as hernias and amputations . . . but the biggest concern after the crash was for the burn victims . . . My wife, Beatrice, and a nurse from the passenger train, Mrs. [J. T.] Richardson, tore up sheets for bandages . . . But that's all we could do—keep the wounds clean and the patients warm."

For six hours, the three civilians worked up and down a sleeper car that had become a makeshift hospital. They consoled the injured men and rationed what little morphine and aspirin the troops could find to ease the victims' pain. Dr. Kimmitt remembered, "Amazingly, there was no panic. We went about our work, while the soldiers worked quickly bringing the injured to us for treatment [and] taking those who had been killed to the last car in the train which we used as a morgue."

"When I looked at them, the bodies of my friends who had been burned to death," said Gnr. Bill Carbray, one of four sentries on duty in the morgue car, "it made me sick."

Outside, the rescue effort continued non-stop. Gunners and bombardiers scrambled through the wreckage that teetered precariously atop the steep embankment. They improvised with what tools they could find to free trapped companions. They spliced the telegraph lines that had been broken by flying debris so that emergency crews could be called in. In frigid conditions they gave up their greatcoats to be used as blankets, stretchers and as covers for the dead.

In contrast to this heroism, there were some at the scene who failed to recognize the magnitude of the disaster. At one point, a group of RCHA stretcher-bearers, their hands bloody and freezing from carrying wounded through the snow to the rear of the troop train, asked to come aboard the passenger train to warm up. The conductor refused, saying they would panic his passengers. At another point, five RCHA gunners and a bombardier climbed onto the Transcontinental, where they were told they could find clean sheets and dry blankets. The group met a porter who refused to unlock the folded overhead berths to donate the linen. Moments later, a gunner returned with an ax.

"You've got just ten seconds to unlock those berths," fumed the bombardier, "or we'll chop them apart!"

The porter turned over the keys, but demanded to know the soldiers' names and numbers. They ignored him.

Later, when the relief train with the dead, the injured and many of the survivors pulled into Edmonton, the RCHA soldiers had trouble steering the stretchers through the coach stairs and doorways. An RCHA sergeant took a fire ax and smashed out one of the coach windows so that the injured could be lifted straight into waiting ambulances. A CNR official shouted at the soldier to "stop damaging CNR property."

"If you want to see damaged CNR property," retorted the sergeant, "go up the tracks a few miles."

What was left of Easy and Fox Batteries of the RCHA assembled at Camp Wainwright a few days later. Except for some instructing officers, few were there. Members of Dog and half of Easy Battery were already in Fort Lewis, Washington. In the Wainwright drill hall, the survivors of the train wreck—those who could travel on—were rekitted with greatcoats, boots, helmets and whatever other personal gear had been lost when the baggage car tumbled down the CNR embankment in B.C. The most eerie moment of all "was the roll call," Art Evoy said. "It was a very small group that answered the roll call that day." When Doug Walton recovered from his injuries and arrived at Fort Lewis two months later, they didn't know who he was. His records had been lost in the train wreck.

The crash that killed twelve artillerymen and four train crewmen—four of whose bodies were never found—claimed four more soldiers who died aboard the relief train en route to Edmonton, and one more in hospital. Fifty-two RCHA gunners and six CNR crew were injured. Canoe River was Canada's worst military train accident. Indeed, the RCHA suffered more casualties that day than it would during an entire year of action in Korea.

It wasn't until he got to Fort Lewis, Washington, ten days later, that RCHA gunner Art Evoy was able to start putting the crash out of his mind. And that's because on one of his first days there, he got drunk, and as a result got a full night's sleep. By that time, the rest of the 25th Canadian Infantry Brigade was already in the thick of its new training regimen (except for the PPCLI, which almost immediately sailed for Korea). RCR 2nd Battalion commander Lt.-Col. R. A. Keane let it be known that he was not impressed with the physical condition of his soldiers. He conducted battle inoculation drill—nearly 90 minutes of traversing a course covered in stones and obstacles—as well as night schemes, which included periodic flares, explosions, and tracer fire as the RCR troops and Col. Keane crawled through the course together.

Brigadier John Rockingham didn't stand on the sidelines either. Throughout the schemes, or war games, that followed around Fort Lewis, Rocky participated in the action. He rarely viewed the training exercises from afar. Instead, he often drove his own jeep, while driver and adjutant watched from the back seat; or Rocky observed manoeuvres while at the controls of a motorcycle. As he had shown in the Scheldt Estuary during the Second World War, he preferred to be at the front with his men where he "could get the feel of the battle . . . see how their morale was . . . The front line was where a brigade commander belonged." That's where he could inspire ordinary soldiers, no matter how bleak the military situation or climatic conditions.

Under other circumstances a visit to the base of Mt. Rainier might have been inviting. But during the early winter of 1950, advanced training exercises—code-named Kiwi, Shakedown and Ignes Bellum—sent the Special Force recruits into simulated battle conditions in the great outdoors. Raw gales and blankets of wet snow made survival difficult, let alone army exercises. Still, advanced training proceeded. After all, if they could operate in North American winter, certainly they could operate in Korea's which, the official Canadian handbook on Korea explained, "is a chilly version of British Columbia's." And so, various phases of mock attacks had the infantrymen sometimes attacking positions, sometimes defending them. All phases were "wet runs," using live ammunition controlled from observation towers along the attack routes.

Pte. Ken McOrmond roughed it through these exercises. He had just sent off his greatcoat and other heavy clothing to the cleaners. In addition, these schemes were staged without tents, so soldiers "slept outside in zero weather," McOrmond wrote in his diary. "Shaved in ice-encrusted water . . . Platoon attack assisted by flame-throwing carriers, called Wasps. Sure like to stay near Wasp flames where it's warm . . . I swear the cold, damp ground sucks all the warmth out of a person's body . . . Some have a lousy night without tents. One lad must have prayed all night, because he kept calling out 'Jesus Christ!'"

Fort Lewis was memorable for the frozen ground, the forced marches and the fist fights. Sometimes there were fisticuffs between mortar and rifle platoons quartered on different levels of the barracks. Other times fights broke out simply because a member of the R22eR spoke French and happened to look over at another group of non-francophone RCR soldiers. Some of the pushing matches became out-and-out brawls, but the fiercest mêlées were saved for encounters with American servicemen in Tacoma, just off the Fort Lewis site. One night at a Post Exchange (PX), for example, a tangle between some Vandoos (R22eR) soldiers and American Military Police (MPs) disintegrated into a full-fledged riot. Such events brought negative public response and criticism from the Tacoma press.

"What makes those men of yours so obstreperous?" a newspaper reporter asked Brigadier Rockingham.

"Well," Rocky answered, "they're fighting men. That's what they're trained to be."

Late in their stay at Fort Lewis, some members of the 2nd Battalion of the Royal Canadian Regiment and the Royal 22e Régiment began drinking heavily. The men got boisterous, then belligerent. Again someone called the MPs. They burst onto the scene with Colt automatic pistols drawn. In the ensuing fist fight, several of the MPs were knocked unconscious. When the MP riot squad arrived and stormed the premises, they were beaten back by a barrage of half-pint milk bottles. It was a massacre in which nobody fired a shot. Fortunately, it was the night before the RCR and the R22eR left Fort Lewis en route to Seattle harbour and embarkation for the Far East. The men, whom Brig. Rockingham had once called "my thugs," were about to become soldiers in the heat of a war zone.

In turn, as they marched up the gangplank in Seattle, Canada's Special Force soldiers could be heard singing a backhanded tribute to their commander:

Why don't you join up?
Why don't you join up?
Why don't you join old Rocky's Army?
If it wasn't for the war
We'd have fucked off long before
Rocky, you bastard!

The war that had looked as if it would be over by Christmas had changed direction dramatically. Originally, the United Nations had launched a policing action, or a so-called "war for containment," to halt the invasion of North Korean soldiers across the 38th parallel and into the south. However, with the successful landing of UN forces at Inch'on in September 1950, and the resulting retreat of Korean People's Army forces north, Gen. Douglas MacArthur clearly intended to push not only the North Koreans out of the south, but also the communists out of Korea. In fact, the commander-in-chief of UN forces had favoured a so-called "war for rollback" from as early as July 1950. The victories across the 38th parallel, however, were hollow. The battles for Wonsan, Hamhung and the North Korean capital, P'yongyang, were won remarkably easily. The trap that MacArthur appeared to have laid at Inch'on was coming up empty.

The North Koreans were employing a tactic perfected by the communist Chinese during their civil war—that of withdrawal and retreat. As quickly as the UN forces swept north, the KPA raced to fortified positions in mountains adjacent to the Yalu River (Sino-Korea border). While the world press documented what appeared to be the defeat of the North Korean Army, the KPA was simply carrying out a planned withdrawal to Kanggye, Kim Il Sung's old guerrilla lair in the north. A captured KPA officer described the strategy this way: "We withdrew because we knew that UN troops would follow us . . . and spread their troops thinly all over the vast area . . . the time came for us to envelop and annihilate them."

The third phase of the war began as the winter of 1950–51 began in Korea. Just as MacArthur had planned the rollback campaign from as early as July, Chinese leader Mao Tse-tung had considered sending Chinese troops into Korea as early as August, because of the sacrifice so many Koreans had made during the Chinese civil war. In fact, Mao told Soviet leader Joseph Stalin that the decision to join the war was made when MacArthur crossed the 38th parallel, not when American troops reached the banks of the Yalu River farther north.

Suddenly in October and November, there were reports of "fresh, newly equipped troops" striking at the UN front lines. Savage attacks on the ROK Army troops appeared to come from nowhere. It wasn't until MacArthur began a general offensive to trap the remaining KPA forces along the Yalu that American pilots began reporting long columns of enemy soldiers swarming through the countryside. When a few were captured, it was clear they were like nothing their United

Nations captors had ever seen before. The enemy troops wore home-made, quilted uniforms. Their officers showed no military ranking, save an extra pocket and sometimes a side arm. They appeared to be poorly armed with old Japanese or Russian Type-R rifles, both of First World War vintage and both bolt action. The soldiers travelled light, with cloth roll packs containing several days' rations of pow-dered rice and dried fish to chew on. They were young. They were fit. They were disciplined. And they were flooding from Manchuria across the Yalu into Korea. These were the first of Mao's army of Chinese volunteers committed to the North Korean cause. Within weeks they turned the tide of the war, forcing the UN troops as quickly down the peninsula as MacArthur's rollback campaign had moved them up.

In late November, when Canadian seamen returned to the Japanese port of Sasebo, they received word that they would not be going home in time for Christmas. Plans to recall the three RCN Tribal Class destroyers to Canada had been reversed and Capt. Jeffry Brock, aboard *Cayuga*, assumed command of a new task force consisting of six destroyers and several minesweepers. They were dispatched to prowl waters and islands off the west coast of Korea, between Inch'on and the Yalu River, to search out junks and sampans that might be transporting Chinese soldiers to the Korean peninsula. At sea and in the air, United Nations forces had supremacy. Not so on land. Facing upward of 300,000 Chinese troops, UN forces were now retreating pell-mell to the 38th parallel and beyond it. To the east, the US X Corps was falling back from the Chosin Reservoir. The ROK Army had collapsed in the centre of the front. And to the west, the Eighth US Army was in full flight back to P'yongyang. The withdrawal was known as "the Big Bug-Out."

Overnight, Capt. Brock's orders to blockade North Korean ports on the Yellow Sea were altered; he and his task force were to assist by all means in their power the evacuation of the Eighth US Army from Chinnampo, the port for the North Korean capital of P'yongyang. The UN naval squadron would now have to cover a fleet of US transport ships exiting the harbour, give gunfire support to the retreating army and make sure that the large stores of fuel and munitions in Chinnampo did not fall into Chinese hands.

The problem was that Chinnampo was about thirty kilometres up the Daido-Ko River, well beyond the range of Brock's naval guns. In addition, the Daido-Ko estuary was cluttered with a maze of low islands and shifting mudflats. The tides would be difficult to navigate, as would the floating mines left behind by the North Koreans. Complicating matters was the winter weather, which had closed in with drizzle that froze on contact; north winds effectively reduced the temperature to below zero. Late on December 4, 1950, as Brock assembled his armada, he received word that Chinnampo was bulging with soldiers, civilians and equipment and that the situation had reached "emergency" proportions. The RCN captain would have to launch his Dunkirk-like mission in the dead of night.

The minesweepers led the way upriver, clearing a channel 500 yards wide and marking its edges with unlit dan-buoys. The strong current kept pulling the markers loose, necessitating the use of ASDIC radar to monitor for mines every step of the way. Meanwhile, the tide had ebbed, so the flotilla advanced, HMCS *Cayuga* at the lead, "dead slow ahead" because at times the ships were operating in less than a metre of water. Despite all precautions, HMAS *Warramunga* grounded on a shoal. A half hour later, HMCS *Sioux* grounded on a sandbar and tangled a propeller shaft on a dan-buoy wire. The two destroyers eventually freed themselves but were forced to withdraw to make repairs. The other four pushed on up the estuary.

The drizzle became a blizzard. Visibility diminished until, as Capt. Brock later wrote, "it was as black as the inside of a cow." More lookouts were positioned in the bows and shells were stockpiled on deck to reduce the number of steps should the shooting start. Below decks the watch became a nightmare for ships' navigators as they dashed from radar screens to chart tables and back. In *Cayuga*'s plot room, Lt. Andrew Collier made 132 navigational fixes that night, which Lt. Bill Davis described as "a masterful piece of work . . . Nobody had confidence in the unlit buoys to get us through. We'd seen one mine blow a hole in a US destroyer . . . Meanwhile, there were pieces of dead people in the water, so we were pretty apprehensive about the mines." On the bridge, Brock conned the ship through the darkness, so that before dawn HMCS *Athabaskan*, USS *Forest Royal*, HMAS *Bataan* and HMCS *Cayuga* were safely anchored in Chinnampo harbour.

Throughout that day, December 5, Capt. Brock, now in charge of defending the port, supervised the evacuation. Troops and materiel were loaded aboard the US transports. A steady stream of sampans moved refugees out of the city. Brock ordered *Athabaskan* downriver to scrutinize the civilian vessels for mines and other weapons. Navy demolition and fire parties were dispatched to destroy what equipment couldn't be saved. As reports of a Chinese breakthrough north of the city reached the port, the transport vessels weighed anchor, leaving the last three destroyers alone in the harbour to complete the job.

At 1735 hours, Brock ordered all guns to open fire. Within minutes, explosions were rocking the railway marshalling yards, the city's cement factory, its shipyards and gasoline storage tanks. North Korea's key port city, which had once been home to 75,000 people, was now, from its industrial district to its waterfront, an inferno. A day later, when the entire flotilla was safely clear of the Daido-Ko River channel and back at sea, Chinnampo was still ablaze.

The mission was a complete success. The Eighth US Army had been safely withdrawn from western North Korea. Any booty the advancing Chinese armies hoped to find in Chinnampo had been destroyed. The entire naval task force under Jeffry Brock's command had returned virtually unscathed in what some call "the most important and most dangerous naval mission of the Korean War." *Cayuga*'s captain was awarded the Distinguished Service Order; its navigator, Andrew Collier, the Distinguished Service Cross; and its coxswain, D. J. Pearson, the British Empire Medal. However, even Capt. Jeffry Brock, whose destroyer would go on to earn a reputation as "the galloping ghost of the Korean coast," knew that the action at Chinnampo had been a successful retreat, not a victory.

LAND OF THE
MORNING CALM

I T WAS RAINING the day the Princess Patricia's Canadian Light
Infantry left for Korea, Saturday, November 25, 1950. A band
of musicians at the Seattle docks played "Hinky Dinky Parlay
Voo" and "It's a Long Way to Tipperary," tunes associated with the
First World War, not 1950. A thousand US Army troops and 927
2nd Battalion PPCLI soldiers, carrying full packs and rifles, moved
steadily up the gangplank aboard the grey-coloured troop transport
USNS *Private Joe P. Martinez.*

Just beyond the retaining fence on the pier stood Donna Deitzer,
who was looking for her fiancé, Fred Elvers, a private in the PPCLI.
The two twenty-year-olds were supposed to be getting married that
day. Instead, Pte. Elvers's regiment was leaving for Korea. So although
the troopship was about to set sail under sealed orders (secrecy surrounding its departure and destination), the young woman had been
given permission to see the ship cast off. Just as the gangplank was
about to be lifted, officers allowed Fred Elvers to go to his weeping
fiancée. The soldier embraced her and, with comrades cheering him
on, kissed her one last time. Then he sprinted back up the gangplank
and the *Martinez* pulled away from the wharf.

The *Martinez* and others like her—*General Edwin P. Patrick* and
General Simon B. Buckner—were Liberty-class ships built in the US

during the Second World War. They were welded bucket-cargo carriers, produced assembly-line style almost overnight and launched just as quickly to transport materiel, petroleum products, ammunition, mail, and sick or wounded military personnel. Many were constructed by Kaiser Industries, hence the moniker "Kaiser's coffins" bestowed on the ships by soldiers on board. At about 17,000 tons and with a top speed of twenty-two knots, if a Liberty ship reached its first voyage destination with cargo intact, it was generally felt that it had justified its cost.

Each Liberty ship had watertight bulkheads so that if it were struck by torpedo or shellfire, it could stay afloat. Each cargo hold was subdivided by walls, or minor bulkheads, which were further divided with floor levels called "tween decks." Accommodations included large tanks of fresh water for drinking and cooking, while water for washing was piped in from the ocean; salt-water soap was issued, but it would soon disappear down the drains with little trace of lather. Sleeping quarters consisted of bunks made of tubular steel with thin strips of canvas suspended by short chains attached to the frames. The bunks were layered four high, with a living space of about eighteen inches between each layer. The men slept head to head and foot to foot, and if a soldier on top got sick, everyone below him knew it first-hand.

Also sailing with the PPCLI aboard the *Martinez* that Saturday was Al Hill, from Smiths Falls, Ontario. Pte. Hill hoped that because his brother had survived service aboard an RCN corvette—HMCS *Mayflower*—on the North Atlantic during the Second World War, he too might have some innate ability to cope with ocean crossings. Like all men aboard, Hill received a tag that listed his name, hold, level and bunk number.

"It was so cramped in those bunks," Hill said, "you couldn't lay on your side. If you went in on your back, you had to come out on your back. But in the first rough seas, I didn't want to move, I was so sick. I think it was the seventh day when I was able to get up. So I went to get something to eat. I got a breakfast of macaroni and cheese. And all at once I see these little black beetles cooked in the food. That threw me off for another three days."

Other unappetizing meals for the enlisted men included soup with four crackers, sometimes a boiled potato with wafer-thin slices of beef and, on odd occasions, pickled pig's feet and a cup of coffee. All the while, it appeared, the ship's crew and the infantry officers were being served fresh bread, meat, vegetables and fruit. When he boarded the *Martinez*, Pte. Don Hibbs weighed about 180 pounds. A week or ten days into the Pacific crossing, he was so sick and had eaten so little that he was down to 150 pounds and laid up in his bunk. Then one day, Hibbs awoke to a commotion in the hold.

"Here! Take this!" a friend called as he ran by Hibbs's bunk and shoved two fresh buns and a can of pineapple under the sick man's blankets.

Moments later, a pair of Military Police rushed through the ship's hold demanding to know the whereabouts of the man with the stolen food.

"God, what'll I do?" Hibbs thought. He didn't want to betray his guardian angel, nor lie about the food under his covers. So he just shrugged at the MPs. Hibbs figures that the bread and canned fruit probably kept him alive.

Wayne Mitchell was truly a landlubber. Born and raised on a Manitoba farm, then employed as an Ontario Hydro worker and finally a printer's devil at the Banff Springs Hotel, he'd never been on the water before, let alone packed in "like sardines" on rough seas. He took the advice of a merchant seaman aboard the *Martinez* and spent as much time as he could in the open air near the anchor chains in the bow. He wasn't sick once. However, below where Mitchell was holed up were the heads, the ship's toilets. Actually, they were just toilet seats on long drainpipes. When the *Martinez* was stationary the heads sat at a 30-degree angle, but when the vessel began to pitch in rough seas, Harley Welsh remembered "guys with their arms wrapped around these heads, hanging on for dear life and throwing up with each roll of the ship. If you weren't sick before, when they put one of these poor guys back in his bunk, you sure got sick from the smell . . . It was like that from Puget Sound to Hawaii."

At Honolulu, the PPCLI got its feet back on terra firma briefly. The *Martinez* put in to Pearl Harbor for a few hours to refuel and refill her water tanks. Meanwhile, the Canadians hit the shore and were put through a route march around the US Navy docks with American MPs and jeeps keeping the troops in line. Pte. Welsh remembers the first few yards being the toughest as sea-weary troops learned to walk again without waiting for the deck to come up to each footstep. As he walked the circuit of the route march, PPCLI clerk Mel Canfield recalls the nearby military hospital, where US soldiers already wounded in Korea sat outside in their clean, white slings and bandages. And while they didn't say a word out loud, to Canfield, the Americans seemed to be saying to the Canadians, "You'll be sorry."

It was on board the Liberty ships crossing the Pacific that average Canadian soldiers learned about some basic differences between themselves and their American counterparts. Most of the GIs were draftees, conscripted by US selective service legislation, which required all men between age eighteen and twenty-six to serve twenty-one months in the military, while most of the Canadian servicemen were enlistees. An RCR corporal recalls meeting an American southerner at the rail one morning.

"Hey, boy," greeted the GI. "What y'all? Marine Corps?"

"No," the Canadian answered. "Not a marine. I'm a Canadian."

"Funny-lookin' uniform," continued the American. "When d'you get drafted?"

"I didn't get drafted. I volunteered."

"You volunteered!" said the astonished GI. "You Canadians must go crazy with the cold weather up there."

Finally, on December 14, after nearly twenty days at sea, the pitching and yawing of the vessel ended. So did the retching and vomiting. The ship's cooks no longer inflicted their unidentifiable sea rations on the troops. The final bets in stuke, poker and crown-and-anchor were placed and called. Winners collected their earnings. Losers paid their debts. The *Private Joe P. Martinez* pulled into Tokyo Bay and tied up at the port of Yokohama, and there began Big Jim Stone's first battle of the Korean War.

"There were so many cries from the soldiers about going ashore and sending home presents to their loved ones at Christmas," Stone said. "Much as it was against my better judgement, I relented." To ensure that the men of the 2nd Battalion PPCLI went ashore in an orderly fashion and returned the same way, he assigned each platoon commander to supervise (i.e., chaperone) his unit and have it back on board the transport safe and sound within twenty-four hours.

Debarkation went according to plan; the Patricias marched off the ship and into downtown Yokohama—by the book—with sergeants and lieutenants at the lead. Then the platoon commanders told their men to break off, releasing them to do as they pleased for two-to-three hours. And that's exactly what they did. Some actually did buy Christmas gifts, but most spent their money on beer, Japanese whisky and prostitutes, until they were drunk, dishevelled and broke. When the battalion was finally rounded up, returned to the *Martinez* and assembled on deck, not many were fully uniformed (they'd bartered away army shirts and caps), fewer were able to stand erect, and all received a stern lecture from the battalion's medical officer.

"Men, you know that we're a fighting outfit," began the M.O. "And if one man gets wounded, it takes two to take him away from action. So, you lose three men . . . It's the same with venereal disease. We don't want to have to take you out of the lines because you have V.D." He paused to let that sink in. "So, don't be ashamed," he went on. "Any guy who had sex while ashore in Yokohama better be sure. Be honest, if you had intercourse, step forward and get a penicillin shot."

Both the medical officer and Colonel Stone were horrified when many in the battalion stepped forward. What's more, when the ship pulled out of Yokohama the next day, there was one soldier missing, having presumably deserted. Yet, "somehow he made his way across Japan," Stone said, "got to [the port of] Kobe and joined the ship there. In my own mind I was threatening all of them with the direst of punishments. But when I thought it over, I thought, 'So what? No harm done. We've got more shirts and whatever else they'd traded off,'" and the battalion commander laughed the incident off.

Besides, the colonel had a bigger problem. The Korean War that Stone and his battalion heard about when they departed North America was very different from the Korean War they discovered when they arrived overseas. During the trip from Seattle, the PPCLI had fallen behind on news from the front. The last they'd heard, advance units of the US and Republic of Korea Armies had the Sino-Korean border—the Yalu River—in sight, and their commander-in-chief, Gen. Douglas MacArthur, was promising a quick end to the war. On arrival, Stone was briefed on "the Big Bug-Out" and the UN evacuation of Chinnampo.

At Pier 2 in Pusan harbour on the afternoon of December 18, it was clear that the PPCLI wouldn't be doing "occupation duty." Instead, as he directed the disembarkation of forty-five officers and 873 other ranks, Col. Stone received word that the commander of the Eighth US Army wanted the PPCLI to assist in stopping the advance of Chinese Communist Forces (CCF) into South Korea. As the Patricias marched down the gangplank, the ROK Army and Navy bands gave them an upbeat fanfare and a US Army band played "If I Knew You Were Coming I'd Have Baked a Cake." They climbed aboard trucks and travelled through the city to Mokto, an island on the edge of Pusan overlooking the harbour, There, in an abandoned school playground, the troops of the battalion erected tents and prepared for their first Christmas away from home. Six months before, most of these men couldn't have spelled "Korea," much less described it. Their first contact with the "land of the morning calm" left indelible images.

In 1950, Pusan was the second-largest city in the country. Yet it was little more than what it had been in colonial days of the 1890s—a hamlet consisting of "mud-huts and mat-sheds as far as the eye could see," Jack Henry recalls. He'd grown up in Toronto's east end, where post-war row houses and semi-detached homes were commonplace, but as a PPCLI volunteer he saw that "in Pusan there were no real structures, just endless shacks."

The streets of Pusan were narrow and potholed. The people were poor. Men squatted by the side of the road to hawk apples and American chocolate bars and cigarettes. Half-naked children solicited in the streets for their sisters and mothers, and women in short blouses and ankle-length dresses and slippers carried their wares on their heads in baskets, in pails or tied up in a piece of cloth. Hundreds of people sat in doorways just looking as the Canadians entered. They reminded Don Hibbs of pictures of "life in the Ozark Mountains. No lights. No laughter." By far the most powerful recollection PPCLI soldiers have of their first contact with Pusan was "the smell." According to Mel Canfield, "for five miles out at sea you could smell the stench of this place," because human excrement was everywhere. Al Hill saw people rooting through garbage and thought what most of the Canadian volunteers thought right then: "What in the world am I doing here?"

"Korea is a land of filth and poverty," Col. Stone wrote in a Christmas letter to Brig. Rockingham. "Nothing but hard work will alleviate the boredom that will soon set in . . . Diseases, except venereal ones, probably will not be a problem . . . but as all fertilizing of fields is done with human excreta there is no doubt that there will be a health problem in the spring and summer." His estimation of the perils of both idleness and V.D. were more accurate than he realized, because at the first opportunity, a number of his soldiers found their way into Pusan's red-light district. Despite repeated warnings to avoid such contact with civilians, a steady stream of soldiers passed through the medical officer's tent each night to receive anti-V.D. shots.

There were other problems associated with getting the battalion organized on Korean soil. To start with, there weren't enough tents. Cooking equipment was in short supply. Plugs on platoon wireless sets didn't match receptacles in the batteries, and when boxes marked "Watches" were opened, there was only sawdust and lead inside. Of greatest concern was the order that Col. Stone received when he met with an Eighth US Army operations officer soon after setting up camp outside Pusan.

"Glad you're here," the officer greeted Stone.

The two shook hands.

"I want you to get everything loaded on trucks," the American said, "and I want you to be in Suwon in three days' time."

"But Suwon is in the fighting line," Stone said.

"Yes. You're going to the British 29th Brigade and into action."

"I can't go into action," Stone protested. "We're not fully trained. I came over here to train."

"You came here to fight," the officer corrected him.

"I'm not going," Stone shrugged and then asked, "Do you have an airplane?"

"Yes. What for?"

Col. Stone told the man he was going over his head to Lt.-Gen. W. H. Walker, commander of the Eighth US Army. He boarded a military plane for Seoul, and after being introduced to other commanding officers there, he was presented to Gen. Walker in an office festooned with the flags of all the nations in the UN Command. Again, Col. Stone said he could not comply with American orders to advance to the front.

"Your troops are trained just as well as the reinforcements that come to us," Walker suggested.

"As individuals they might be able to carry their weight," admitted Stone, "but that's not the point." He pulled out his own command instructions from the Canadian government, which stated explicitly, "In the event that operations are in progress when you arrive in Korea, you are not to engage in such operations except in self-defence until you have completed the training of your command and are satisfied that your unit is fit for operations."

Gen. Walker couldn't overrule Stone's orders and said, "We certainly don't want to cause any political trouble." The issue was dropped.

Three days later, Walker was killed in a vehicle accident and his successor, Lt.-Gen. Matthew B. Ridgway, didn't raise it again. Had the Americans forced Stone and the PPCLI into the UN's defensive lines (then located along the Imjin River north of Seoul), ten days later the untrained and untried 2nd Battalion Princess Patricias would have met the communist forces—four Chinese divisions and three North Korean divisions—head-on.

The communist offensive began on New Year's Day. It crossed the Imjin, challenged US positions below the 38th parallel and reached as far south as ROK Army fortifications at Kap'yong. On January 3, 1951, north of Seoul, the British 29th Brigade (the PPCLI's intended battle group) was attacked in strength and suffered heavy casualties. The next day, the capital of South Korea was evacuated by UN forces and fell for the third time in the war. Stone's resolve prevented another Hong Kong for the Canadian army and gave his battalion precious time to prepare for its eventual baptism of fire.

Despite gloomy news from the front, the Patricias celebrated Christmas under canvas. There was actually turkey with all the trimmings brought in. Each man got a bottle of *Asahi*, Japanese beer. There were parcels and letters from home, and some members of the battalion took impromptu gifts to children at a Pusan orphanage. Then, just as quickly as the imported Christmas spirit arrived, the business of preparing for war took its place.

The cone-shaped, rust-coloured hills that nature strung together up and down and across the Korean peninsula were not the least bit conducive to conventional warfare. Steep and spiny, with little natural vegetation except flat dwarf pine trees, the hills chopped up the countryside. In the troughs between these red hills were endless winding tiers of rice paddies notable mostly for the smell of "night soil" (human excrement fertilizer). Beyond every few ridges was a river or creek bed that, depending on the season or the variable weather, could be a bone-dry gully one minute, a raging floodway the next, or frozen solid in winter. This rugged, washboard terrain was devoid of long fields of fire—the view was always broken by the landscape. There was very little space for staging large-scale assaults. The hilltops left even less room from which to defend. Moreover, a general lack of roads hampered rapid and significant movements of tanks, trucks and mobile artillery. Even those Korea volunteers who had experienced fighting in the hills of Italy in 1943–44 had never known anything like this.

The Korean landscape, then, very much dictated the way the war was being fought. It was not being fought by armies, divisions or even battalions, but by small groups of men. Platoons of perhaps thirty soldiers, but more often, sections of about ten men, mostly non-commissioned soldiers, were doing the bulk of the fighting. Each of these small combat units consisted of a Bren-gunner and his No. 2, a half-dozen individual riflemen and a section leader—a corporal or a lance corporal—who had leadership qualities, probably Second World War experience, some understanding of group psychology and a lot of street savvy. The survival of each unit depended on how much each soldier trusted his section leader, how well each man's skills and temperament were used, and how quickly the men could adapt to an inhospitable countryside.

Two days after Christmas, the Patricias moved out of Pusan eighty kilometres north to begin their advanced training. They set up their camp in apple and chestnut orchards at the base of a sheltered, horseshoe-shaped valley along the Miryang River, which had chunks of ice flowing in its current. Absent for the moment were the malodorous rice paddies, but there were still plenty of those characteristic hills and gullies where valuable lessons had to be learned. The men's training emphasized mobility in the hills and establishing defensive "islands" on high ground at night. To regain physical fitness in the battalion, Col. Stone drove his men hard with extensive hill-climbing, cross-country manoeuvres and battle exercises incorporating their own firearms—.303 Lee-Enfield bolt-action rifles and Bren guns—plus their support weaponry—American-made 81-mm mortars and British-built Vickers medium machine guns. This time, no one was using blanks.

The use of live ammunition presented an unexpected opportunity for the men of the PPCLI. Before too long, some of the Patricias spotted wild fowl in the Miryang, including Chinese ring-necked pheasants, which apparently made "really good eating." When the battalion authorities made it known that venison would also be a nice addition to the soldiers' diets, riflemen kept an eye out for wayward deer. "C" Company clerk Mel Canfield recalled a morning when a rifle platoon, dug in for a twenty-four-hour front-line exercise, spotted four deer about 200 yards downhill from the platoon's position.

"In no time, the platoon's commander gave the order to fire," Canfield wrote. "There was an explosive roar as the men who were on guard were joined by those who had been sleeping . . . But the four deer managed to move across in front of the platoon's position and then disappeared into the woods. There was a moment of stunned silence as each member of the platoon looked at his neighbour . . . unable to believe their eyes. Almost forty men had fired and not one had hit a single deer."

In mid-January the PPCLI suddenly found itself in the war zone. One of its platoon commanders, Lt. Harold Ross was wounded by a sniper's bullet. Communist guerrillas, known to be active in the Miryang area, had also recently killed two New Zealand artillery trainees. So the Patricias' "B" Company was assigned to clear the guerrillas from a 2,700-foot hill feature called T'ogok-san. Within five days, three PPCLI platoons had killed two guerrillas, wounded numerous others, uncovered caches of ammunition and food and rescued several US engineers who had come under fire. The action prompted one PPCLI officer to write: "I consider hunting guerrillas the best company exercise . . . Men learnt to live, keep warm and alive in the open."

If the trek up T'ogok-san didn't make fighting men of his soldiers, Stone's discipline made up the difference. While at Miryang, the colonel built his own battalion prison—a large tent with sixteen strands of barbed wire around it—which the commander called "the toughest field punishment camp since Admiral Nelson." Any man caught stealing, drunk, absent-without-leave or in dereliction of duty had his hair shaved off and a yellow mark painted on the back of his fatigues. Each day, he had to run obstacle courses—up and down hills, under barbed wire and through pits of filthy water—all with a full pack on his back. He ate while running on the spot and wasn't even allowed time to relieve himself. When several soldiers stole a day's beer ration, Stone paraded them in front of the entire battalion, chewed them out verbally and then sentenced them. The four men were forced to dig their own detention cell in a riverbank, install a plank floor and a door with bars, and then serve their fourteen-day term in "Stone's stockade."

This was also a time when the colonel weeded out what he described as "non-battle casualties." During the Miryang exercises, Stone shipped home sixty men suffering from such afflictions as atrophied leg muscles, cardiac palpitations, broken eardrums, flat feet, arthritis of the spine, chronic bronchitis, hernia and hypertension. They were the so-called "scruff" described in the early days of the Special Force recruiting. Indeed, back home in Canada, in February, the government reported that more than a thousand—or one in ten—had been discharged from the Special Force as men "unlikely to become efficient." Fortunately for the battalion, this so-called elimination of "wastage" missed the fact that Sgt. Tommy Prince had varicose veins in his legs. The twice-decorated Second World War Native Canadian would complete two tours with the Patricias despite having to limp across the Korean countryside on a wooden cane.

Besides shipping home some of its Special Force recruits, when it finished training exercises at Miryang near the end of January, the 2nd Battalion of the PPCLI left behind its first casualty. One of the regimental sergeants major, Jimmy Wood, was killed in an explosion during the demonstration of a Chinese anti-personnel mine. A party of Patricias transported his body to Pusan, where a huge empty field had been designated as the United Nations Cemetery. On the day the burial detail brought Wood's body to Pusan, Don Hibbs remembers there were only three Canadian graves in the cemetery—one of a soldier already buried, a second for Wood and a third as yet unoccupied; 378 Canadians would eventually be buried there.

For Pte. Hibbs, burying Wood made that January day in Pusan among the bleakest. However, February 19 proved to be worse. By this time, the Patricias were on the move. The PPCLI had joined British, Australian and New Zealand units of the 27th British Commonwealth Infantry Brigade in a general advance against Chinese and North Korean forces fighting rearguard actions south of the 38th parallel. At about 11 o'clock in the morning the Canadians left the village of Chuam-ni and moved northward up a valley toward their first objective—Hill 404 (each hill was identified by its height in metres). En route they discovered an entire company of American soldiers that had been ambushed during the night.

"The first thing I saw was a jeep with a guy lying across it," remembers Hibbs. "He was draped over a machine-gun on the jeep. Empty cartridges were piled up over his ankles in the bottom of the jeep. He was a black man, a sergeant. I saw his stripes and the name on his hat, 'Lewis.'"

Sometime during the previous day's action, sixty-five members of the US 1st Cavalry Division, using jeeps with mounted guns, had chased Chinese soldiers up the valley. The Americans had returned to the mouth of the valley to set up an overnight camp. Most found hollows or dug slit trenches for their sleeping bags and crawled in for the night, but the Chinese crept back down the valley and killed the entire company while it slept.

"They were just slaughtered in their underwear," recounted another Canadian, "More than half of the bodies were still in sleeping bags, bayoneted to death."

Harley Welsh was horrified by what he saw: "I came across a couple of them in a trench. It was February and cold. And we used to do this too. They had put straw in their trench to keep warm. The trench had been set on fire and the two guys were burned right up."

Another Canadian picked up an American helmet that lay off to the side, and kept it for the remainder of his stay in Korea, partly because it made a better washbasin than his Canadian-issue helmet, but mostly as a reminder never to use a sleeping bag at night. In fact, as the Patricias stopped to take stock and to eat a meal of American C-Rations that midday, Col. Stone ordered that there would be no sleeping bags when troops were in the line; in addition, at night soldiers were forbidden to pull parka hoods over their heads to hamper their hearing. The horrible juxtaposition of eating lunch while an entire company of American soldiers lay strewn over the valley floor was too much for Don Hibbs.

"I put my stuff down," Hibbs recalled, "took out my writing pad and began to write a farewell letter to my mother: 'I'm sitting here amongst dead people eating lunch. I saw dead people up in the hills at Miryang, the guerrillas. But these are our own. This is war. It's the biggest shock of my life . . .' And I finished by saying, 'I don't know if I'm going to make it. Look at these guys! What chance have we got?'"

The world was not supposed to know about the American massacre, but Canadians read about it two days after it happened. The headline read: "Pats Learn Grim Lesson From Sight of Slain GI's." The story indicated permissible details of the Patricias' advance. It described the American attack and the Chinese counterattack "mowing down the troops mercilessly." The two-column article quoted PPCLI battle adjutant Maj. Gordon Henderson of Calgary: "It's a tragedy. But it's a terrific lesson for our fellows." The story was datelined "With the Canadians in Korea, Feb. 22." and the byline credited reporter Bill Boss.

"When I reported [the massacre] all hell broke loose," explained Boss, who saw his story first deleted and then "passed by the censors. But the Pentagon queried Tokyo and Tokyo queried the Eighth US Army headquarters and so it came down the line. This battalion had lost an entire company and there had been no mention of it in army briefings."

Sporting a black beret, green scarf and red goatee, Bill Boss hardly looked the part of a front-line war correspondent. Nor did his affinity for symphonic music and his fluency in six languages necessarily help him fit in among average front-line soldiers. However, his other habits—sometimes chain-smoking and drinking scotch with the best of them—helped Boss break the ice among both officers and enlisted men. At thirty-two, Bill Boss was a seasoned and shrewd reporter. As a war correspondent, he had followed the Canadian army from North Africa to Sicily to Italy during the Second World War; in fact, he'd reported on Col. Stone's career commanding the Loyal Edmonton Regiment in Italy. It is not surprising, therefore, that when war broke out in Korea, he easily won top job for Canadian Press covering the PPCLI's mission to Korea. He came over with the Patricias aboard the *Martinez*, and no sooner had he landed at Pusan, when he'd horse-traded a case of scotch for a jeep, a trailer, a tent and a generator to establish a war correspondent's office. "Telling Canadians at home the score about Canadian soldiers overseas" became his self-chosen assignment; even the chief censor in Korea recognized that Boss was doing "the most intimate job of troop activities coverage."

However, they didn't expect Boss to be their primary source of classified information. So, posthaste, Boss was summoned to a meeting behind the front lines. A helicopter arrived and disgorged none other than Lt.-Gen. Matthew B. Ridgway, commander of the Eighth US Army, in search of correspondent Boss. When they met, the general began dressing Boss down, saying, "I'm here about your story on the first engagements of the Patricias . . . a very good piece of reporting . . . but divisive of the United Nations war effort."

"With respect, I don't think so, sir," Boss countered, then stood silent, looking at the two grenades fastened to the front of the general's battle dress (the source of his famous nickname, "Old Iron Tits"). Given the general's renowned assertiveness and outspoken nature, the reporter feared he'd soon be on a slow boat home to Canada.

"Are you a fisherman?" Ridgway asked suddenly.

"Oh yes, I am," said Boss, a little surprised at the change of subject.

"Ever fish in the Ste. Croix River in New Brunswick?"

As quickly as the official critique had been delivered, Boss realized the general's expressed sentiments were not his own; Ridgway was just going through the motions for his superiors.

"Between you and me," the general confided, "I hope you keep on doing the job you're doing."

Consequently, Bill Boss went right on doing what he was doing. He kept a room in Seoul in the press billet, where he could return once in a while to clean out his kit, have a bath, send out longer background pieces and catch up with the rest of the war. Otherwise, he lived with the Canadians, near the front lines with the Patricias, moving with the soldiers, "pitching my tent outside the brigadier's sentry post. It was the only way to cover the war. My job was to be with the Canadians and report on them and that's what I bloody well did!"

The Patricias thought of Boss as a booster. Indeed, it appeared that way to both brass and infantrymen. While he dutifully quoted PPCLI officers' appraisals of a battle, correspondent Boss devoted most of his energy searching out the sections and platoons that had fought it. For example, during the assault on Hill 419 on the road north of Yoju, he gave the company commander credit for organizing the attack, but he reserved most space and best prose for rank and file, such as the stretcher-bearer from Mount Dennis, Ontario: "Pte. John Miles, who earned the company's acclaim by ignoring hazards to attend the wounded . . . According to Princess Patricias who saw him in action, 'Miles ran into direct line of fire with no regard for his own life whatever and carried back four or five wounded. He should have got the Military Medal.'"

A thorough reporter, Boss also went looking for problems, and he found them. In spite of his extensive experience covering warfare, even Boss was sometimes horrified by the actions of these "first wave" soldiers. Among the Patricias, whom Boss sometimes described as "buccaneers," there were those who treated Korean civilians with absolute disdain (even the war diaries describe Koreans as "gooks.") Some brutalized, a few murdered and at least one was court-martialled for the rape and murder of civilian women. Such incidents repulsed the seasoned reporter who said "in some situations, I was ashamed to be a Canadian."

Correspondent Boss reported on activity both at and behind the front. On March 17, 1951, the Princess Patricias came out of the line for a rest near Chipyong-ni. Seoul had been liberated again. The Chinese Communist Forces appeared to be pulling back across the 38th parallel. The battalion had suffered losses—fifty-seven casualties in its first three weeks, fourteen fatal—but morale was high.

Coincidentally, it was the birthday of the regiment's namesake, Lady Patricia Ramsay, so the battalion staged a parade to celebrate. There was a sports meet in the afternoon. In the evening, the Argyll and Sutherland Highlanders, a sister regiment in the brigade, presented a pipe-band concert. And this was followed by a bonfire and beer issue. But for some, the *Asahi* was not enough and several soldiers scrounged more alcohol. That night they mixed canned fruit juice with canned heat (Sterno), shoe polish and alcohol from the tank of a flame-thrower. Two Patricias died. Two went blind. Several more went to a field hospital to have their stomachs pumped.

True to form, Colonel Stone made an example of the tragedy. The following morning, he formed up his troops, described what had happened and paraded every man in the battalion by the corpses of their fellow Patricias for full impact. Adding to the regiment's black eye, the same night a group of Canadian and British soldiers attempted to rape a Korean woman; beaten off, they killed three Koreans with a grenade and wounded four others. Though he was not on hand to witness either event, within ten days, correspondent Boss had pieced together the two stories including both Stone's displaying the dead soldiers and the Canadians' promise to apprehend the culprits in the killing of the Koreans. He filed the material in the normal way, but it never reached Canadian Press for publication. (It was finally printed in *Time* magazine in September.) Not only was his report censored, Boss himself was subjected to "a campaign of vilification from United Nations public affairs officers" and called "subversive." For a while he was persona non grata around the Patricias, and there was an abortive attempt to oust Boss from the Korean theatre.

That same spring of 1951, in the skies over the Pacific Ocean, Larry Motiuk was getting into the rhythm of the Korean Airlift. Originally a bomb-aimer aboard Lancasters in the latter stages of the Second World War, Motiuk had retrained as a navigator, rejoined the RCAF and been assigned to No. 426 Transport Squadron and Operation Hawk. One of Canada's earliest commitments to UN Command in

Korea, the airlift was a vital supply link between North America and the main distribution centre at Haneda Airport in Tokyo.

The airlift route was a circuit from McChord Air Force Base, near Tacoma, Washington; to Anchorage, Alaska; to the island of Shemya, at the western tip of the Aleutian Islands; to Tokyo; then back to Tacoma via Hawaii and San Francisco. Flying Officer Motiuk recalls those runs. Navigating the four-engine, 77,000-pound North Star and her crew and cargo along the first leg from McChord to Alaska was a piece of cake, "but the weather in the Aleutians was bloody awful."

Due to its size and location in the northern Pacific, Shemya was almost never visible from the air. The Americans had transformed most of the island into a runway, 10,000 feet long and 600 feet wide, three times the width of a normal runway. The edge lights were a standard 200 feet apart, but the extra pavement on either side of the lights allowed pilots to stray up to 200 feet either side of centre in the strong winds that whipped over the island up to 80 knots. Landing there was a unique experience.

On his first approach to Shemya, navigator Motiuk was invited up to the cockpit by seasoned RCAF pilot Dean Broadfoot. The flying officer did that for a number of his first-timers to Shemya.

"Ceiling is low," Broadfoot said.

Motiuk peered into the cloud and fog outside the windshield. Sometimes the soup hung less than 200 feet from the surface of the island.

"When you see the lights," Broadfoot continued.

"What do you mean?" Motiuk said. He couldn't see a thing.

"As soon as you see a string of lights," the pilot said.

Motiuk was aware that the first runway lights on Shemya were only 150 feet in from the seashore. Then supposedly there was lots of runway on which to bring the transport down. Just beyond the other end of the runway, however, it was ocean again.

"You just aim for the lights," said Broadfoot, bringing the North Star down quickly out of the soup. "Then you straddle them. And you're on the runway!"

Navigator Motiuk admitted it wasn't the kind of landing he'd like to experience on a daily basis. But with Broadfoot at the controls, he felt reasonably secure.

Trained between the wars, Dean Broadfoot had intentions of becoming a fighter pilot on Vampires, but instead was posted to No. 426 Transport Squadron in the fall of 1948. He helped break in the new North Star transports and then found himself virtually living on them during the Korean Airlift. The crews initially referred to Operation Hawk, under the command of the US Military Air Transport Service (US MATS) as "Pacific Panic." Broadfoot remembered the commanding officer, Wing Commander C. H. Mussells, gathering all the flying crews in a movie theatre at McChord for a briefing as the operation began.

"MATS headquarters says we've got to do a trip per day per squadron," Mussells told his pilots. "The Americans have twenty-four airplanes and fifty-two crews per squadron. No. 426 Squadron has six airplanes and nine crews. Bennet [the commander of the US transport wing] said they'd have to make some accommodations for 426. . . . But no, if the commitment is a trip a day per squadron, that's what 426 will do."

The C.O. then looked at his crewmen and said, "I have no goddamned idea how you guys are going to do that. Just do it!"

Eventually the squadron grew to ten aircraft and then to sixteen, but the routine remained the same. Each day of the airlift, RCAF aircrews and ground crews loaded North Stars at McChord, flew them across the North Pacific route to Japan, then unloaded and reloaded them in Tokyo and flew them back across the Pacific via Wake Island, Hawaii and San Francisco. The 11,000-mile round trip took 80 to 85 hours to complete. At any time of day or night, as much as half the squadron could be in the air somewhere along the circuit.

The pace was gruelling. The demands of instrument flying (flying nearly blind) never stopped, and sometimes RCAF pilots bent both US Air Force and RCAF flying regulations in order to get their cargoes through, because, as airlift pilot Cy Torontow pointed out, "A few times at Shemya, we landed in zero-ceiling and zero-visibility. Thank God for those GCA operators."

On a tour of the Aleutians, Bob Hope translated GCA as "Greetings—Congratulations—Alive!" In fact, it stood for Ground Control Approach, the radar system and operators employed to guide transport aircraft along corridors between West Germany and West Berlin during the Berlin Airlift in 1948. As far as Cy Torontow was concerned, "The Shemya GCA guys were absolutely fantastic . . . They could tell you, when you were about to touch down, 'Okay, start lowering your nose wheel.' They were that good."

"They had a guy on a headset outside the GCA shack," added Dean Broadfoot. "He looked at the weather and gave you weather calls, the wind, the visibility and the ceiling. My favourite ceiling call was, 'A low crouch and three yards.' That's low ceiling."

Most RCAF aircrews agreed that the Pacific run presented some of the worst flying conditions in the world: there was plenty of radio interference; comparatively low flight altitudes often meant that cloud cover hampered astro-navigation; and the unpredictability of winds made dead reckoning and lining up a landing approach difficult. The US Air Force B-17 that sat nosed-over at the end of the Shemya airstrip provided a constant reminder of the power of Pacific winds. The Flying Fortress had been blown off the edge of a runway in a severe crosswind. It was a write-off.

During one run between Anchorage and Shemya, RCAF navigator Eric Glustien had a trainee out from Dorval airfield, near Montreal. After making sure the young navigator was on track for the eight-hour run to Shemya, Glustien decided to grab a well-deserved nap. The North Star then encountered a low-pressure system with particularly strong winds. Several hours later, Glustien was wakened by a tap on the shoulder.

"Can you come up and take a look at something?" asked the trainee.

"What do you mean?" asked Glustien.

"I don't know where I am," the navigator admitted.

The new navigator had guided his pilot, Dean Broadfoot, around the extremities of the bad weather system. The outer edges of the system were accompanied by strong winds, winds that would not have affected them had they flown through the system. Instead, the winds had drifted the North Star so that it was now flying into the middle of the Pacific. When Glustien took a fix to establish their position, he found the plane was off course and called for a 90-degree course alternation.

"What the heck are you doing?" Broadfoot called back.

"You'd better do it or we're in deep trouble," said Glustien. When he listened for the Shemya beacon, all he could hear was a weak signal. "We have to come back from 180 miles off track!"

For the next few hours, the North Star crew fought the wind that had blown them off course. All the while, Glustien made calculations to see how long their fuel would hold out and listened as the Shemya beacon finally grew louder and guided them to the island runway.

"I certainly learned my lesson," Glustien said. "Never let a new navigator whip around without being checked closer. And never underestimate the weather."

Operation Hawk freight varied, "from bullets to broomsticks." When the ROK Army and American forces were in danger of being pushed into the sea at Pusan in the summer of 1950 and again in the winter of 1951 when the Communist Chinese Forces threatened Seoul, the RCAF North Stars carried troop reinforcements, mostly American draftees. During the earliest flights to Korea, each RCAF pilot was issued a .45-calibre revolver.

"What the hell is this for?" Dean Broadfoot asked.

"Many of these guys don't want to go," explained an American army sergeant. "They've got their rifles, but no ammo."

Beginning in January 1951, on many of the return trips through Honolulu and San Francisco, the North Stars were rigged with bunks to carry out as many as thirty-five wounded soldiers each. While the North Star was durable and reliable, it was neither soundproof nor pressurized, which would expose the evacuees to twenty hours of pain-threshold engine noise and the stink of fuel fumes. However, on many return flights, an inhospitable cabin area didn't matter. The RCAF crews were bringing home coffins containing American war dead.

"I can remember them stacked up back there," Dean Broadfoot said. "We didn't like that much. I don't know why, but we used to lock the cockpit door. It just made us very uneasy."

BLOODING OF
THE BRIGADE

―――――――――

"**A** SOLDIER'S SPIRIT is keenest in the morning. By noonday it has begun to flag. And in the evening, his mind is bent only on returning to camp. A clever commander, therefore, avoids an enemy army when its spirit is keen, but attacks it when it is sluggish . . ." This philosophy, dating to 500 BC and the Chinese military commander Sun Tzu's *The Art of War*, shaped the strategies of Communist Chinese Forces in Korea. That tactical doctrine, combined with a natural north-south invasion route in the valley of the Kap'yong River, prompted the communist spring offensive back into South Korea in late April 1951.

At the time, the Princess Patricias had just completed operations into a range of hills code-named Kansas. After two weeks of chasing Chinese troops northward, not allowing them to break contact or regain strength, the PPCLI had crossed the 38th parallel for the first time. The Canadians had then turned over the job to the 6th South Korean (ROK) Division and had moved south to a rest area near the village of Kap'yong.

Among other things, while the battalion was in reserve, several members of "B" Company pulled together a poker game. Accustomed to living in the close quarters of slit trenches and small tents, in the rest area the floating poker game found a larger circular tent with enough room for five or six poker players and a handful of spectators.

"No money on the table," somebody warned as the players sat down around the table. If anybody of authority came in, there should be no evidence.

"So who'll be banker?" another player asked.

"I will," Pte. Don Hibbs piped up. He tore up strips of different-coloured magazine paper, one colour worth a dollar, another worth five dollars, a third worth ten. The players bought the slips of paper from Hibbs and would cash them in at the end of the game.

One of the poker players, Pte. Wayne Mitchell, produced a bottle of rum, liberated from somewhere, to take the edge off the cool spring night and to inspire those who were dealt poor poker hands. The game and the rum lasted until nearly 3 in the morning, when a sergeant happened by.

"He storms into the tent," Hibbs recalled, "throws over the table, grabs the booze and screams at everybody to get out." It wasn't until some time later that Hibbs reached into his pocket and realized he still had more than $100 of the poker players' money. Likewise, when Mitchell reached into his pocket, he found $38 in uncashed coloured paper, his poker earnings for the night. He never did get to claim his winnings.

It was Easter Sunday, in the view of communist military leaders an opportune time to attack. Meanwhile, UN Command had learned that troops from the 2nd and 3rd Chinese Communist Field Armies were on the move southward from the North Korean capital, P'yongyang. Even Chinese and North Korean prisoners predicted an assault from the north. It was clear, UN forces would have to prepare to meet a renewed communist offensive.

As George Cook recalled, "We knew something was up." A corporal in a pioneer platoon of explosive specialists in the PPCLI's support company, Cook, like the rest of the battalion, was enjoying the rest behind the lines near Kap'yong. "The battalion padres were preparing for Easter Sunday church parades, when we were suddenly given orders to get our gear and move." The Princess Patricias were headed back into the fighting.

Just before midnight on Sunday, April 22, more than 200,000 Chinese and North Korean soldiers began a massive assault on the western and west-central regions of the United Nations line, about twenty kilometres north of the PPCLI's reserve area. The apparent objective was to recapture Seoul. In the west-central area—the Kap'yong valley—the offensive first concentrated attacks on troops of the US I and IX Corps. The Americans fell back south, leaving two regiments of the 6th South Korean (ROK) Division to hold the UN line. The shock of the attack sent thousands of ROK soldiers, South Korean civilians and Chinese communist infiltrators streaming down the valley. The front protecting the way to Seoul was collapsing.

To the south, where the Kap'yong River valley narrowed like a funnel from 3,000 metres in width to several hundred and passed through three natural elevations, was the spot where the men of the 27th British Commonwealth Brigade were ordered to halt the oncoming Chinese offensive. The Middlesex Regiment with three companies and the New Zealand 16th Field Regiment were sent to Hill 794 in the north to assist the ROK Army withdrawal. The 3rd Battalion of the Royal Australian Regiment (RAR), with support from the US 72nd Heavy Tank Battalion, was assigned the eastern side of the valley on Hill 504 to cover a ford in the river and block enemy action along the road from the northeast. Meanwhile, the Princess Patricias went to the western side of the valley to defend the two kilometres of steep, scrub-covered ground around Hill 677.

By 8 o'clock Monday evening, the Australians had set up their roadblock. Two hours later, the last of the retreating ROK Army troops came down the road with troops from the 3rd Chinese Field Army in hot pursuit. To add to the confusion, the Middlesex and New Zealand gunners were falling back with the ROKs, and the Australians found themselves facing Chinese forces on three sides. The Chinese probed Australian trenches and machine-gun positions all night. The RAR held its position. However, by Tuesday afternoon, the forward Australian rifle companies had been battling waves of Chinese soldiers for sixteen hours; they were now low on ammunition, and they were up to four kilometres behind the communists'

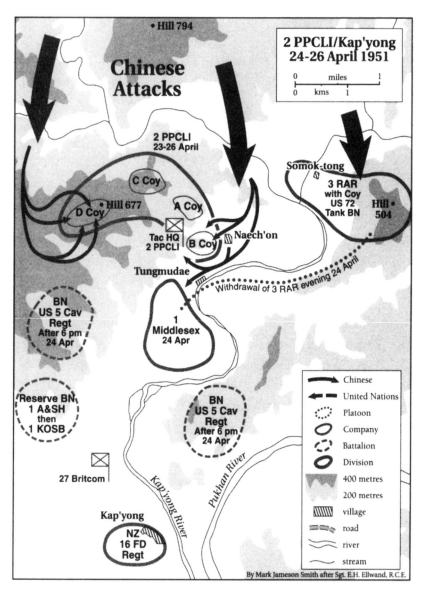

deepest advance. They were ordered to withdraw. Under cover of smoke laid down by the New Zealand artillery, and with American tanks ferrying out the wounded, the Australians—with nearly a hundred casualties—came off Hill 504 fighting their way south to reach the Middlesex Regiment's new position to the rear of the Princess Patricias.

That left the Canadians alone on Hill 677 to stop the Chinese.

The PPCLI was deployed across the north face of the hill: "D" Company positioned to the left; "C" Company in the centre; "A" Company to the right; and "B" Company occupying a salient trench-line in front of "D" Company. Colonel Stone's specific orders were: "Be steady, kill and don't give way!" The Patricias had some sense of the overwhelming numbers of Chinese soldiers they faced, but didn't know they were outnumbered eight-to-one.

Wayne Mitchell recognized the odds early. It was during the day-light hours of April 24. From his position in "B" Company on the west side of Hill 677, he could see "there must have been hundreds of thousands of people, mostly refugees" racing south through the valley toward their position. "Orders were to stop them, because the enemy was in there among them. I felt horrible, but I set up . . . and fired low."

The eighteen-year-old Pte. Mitchell hadn't fired more than a few bursts from his Bren gun, when three American fighter aircraft swooped down over his position and began strafing and bombing the people in the valley. Mitchell didn't have time to think about what was happening in the valley. His platoon commander, Sgt. Roy Yalmer, told Mitchell they were moving to the eastern side of Hill 677 to protect the "back door" to the battalion area. Mitchell trusted Yalmer implicitly. The sergeant was experienced; he'd fought the Germans in Italy during the Second World War.

"Just before dark [April 24] we saw them coming out of the hills to the north," Yalmer said. It was about 10 o'clock when Chinese mortar bombs began falling on the Patricias' positions. "B" Company com-mander Maj. C. V. Lilley estimated there were 400 Chinese on the flat ground in front of his position, but as Yalmer remembered, "They were well on top of us (with those rubber shoes of theirs) before we knew it."

On a hump of land at the forward corner of "B" Company's posi-tion, Cpl. G. R. Evans and his section were among the first to hear piercing whistles and bugle blasts only metres in front of their slit trenches. This was the Chinese call to attack. They tossed grenades into the Patricias' position. Then the first wave of Chinese infantry stormed out of the darkness. In minutes Evans was wounded in the leg and chest. Only the continuous firing of Bren-gunner Ken Marsh saved the section from being wiped out in the first attack. However, Lt. Harold Ross, the platoon commander, ordered a pull-back from the position. Though they got Evans out, he later died of his wounds.

Noiselessly and almost invisibly, the next "human wave" of Chinese soldiers moved into position. One wave came close to knocking out the battalion's tactical headquarters in "a well organized and well executed attack in strength . . . between one and two companies, which 'B' Company was powerless to stop as it came through our back door."

"The Chinese fought extremely well at night," Col. Stone noted. "They lived in the dark. We lived in the light . . . Luckily we had these half-tracks with a .50 calibre and a .30 calibre machine-gun. When they fired it was four balls and then a tracer [to light the direction of gunfire]. Suddenly these grey shapes came out of the dark. And all these machine-guns opened up," and eventually the Canadians drove off the attack.

It was only midnight. The waves of Chinese Communist Forces kept coming. One assembly of Chinese troops gathered at the Kap'yong River across from the Canadian position and began fording the current. This time, however, the Patricias were aided by weather conditions. Bright moonlight silhouetted the Chinese and "they made wonderful targets," said Pte. Carl Deschamps, who watched as machine guns mounted on half-track vehicles opened up. The respite was temporary. Very early on the morning of Wednesday, April 25—the beginning of the second day in defence of Hill 677—every weapon in "B" Company was firing at advancing Chinese troops.

"We just fired at everybody," recalled Don Hibbs from "B" Company. On the way into the hills, Pte. Hibbs imagined being shot at, so when he walked, he got into the habit of stepping then bobbing his whole body one direction and then the other, like a boxer. In his slit trench he kept moving too, firing, ducking into the trench, reloading and firing again. "There was so much confusion, so much firing and the smell of weapons . . . the dust, the dirt and the fear. You're sweating. Your mouth is dry . . . You're terrified."

In Wayne Mitchell's No. 6 Platoon area, there were few able-bodied soldiers left. A clerk, who'd been brought up to replace Mitchell's No. 2 on the Bren gun, had been hit in the face with shrapnel. During a lull, Mitchell removed him and another wounded rifleman from the line and returned to his slit trench.

"I'm all alone out there," recalled Mitchell, who by now had shrapnel wounds in his back, his chest and on his face. He could only see through his left eye. "And suddenly they were in on top of me. I remember being hit in the back with a shovel or something. But I had the Bren gun in my hands. And as I fell I landed on my back firing. The bodies were falling on top of me. It was fight, or be buried there."

Fortunately, his section leader, Roy Yalmer, was nearby, heard his shouts for help and joined Mitchell in the trench. By this time, neither Mitchell nor his sergeant had much ammunition left. Still, the Chinese infantrymen kept charging up the hillside until "I yelled at Roy to look to his left. He wheeled around and just pitched his rifle, bayonet first like a spear. Then he grabbed Hayes [another wounded rifleman] and dragged him out and we came back down the hill." Unfortunately, their friend Pte. C. A. Hayes was dead by the time they reached tactical headquarters. Mitchell, too, could hardly stand for loss of blood.

As savage as the fighting had been on the eastern side of the ridge, it was only a diversion for a larger assault that was coming. For most of the preceding day, "D" Company, at the west end of the north face of Hill 677, had been spectators to the battle. That changed for No. 10 and No. 12 Platoons of "D" Company just after 1 o'clock in the morning, April 25, when suddenly the hillside exploded with light. Flares, triggered by tripwires laid the previous day by George Cook's pioneer platoon, lit up the sky. Again "there was the [Chinese] bugle call, then the sound of the beating of sticks," said Jim Waniandy, a lance corporal in "D" Company. "That was followed by the blowing of shrill whistles. They came in with a shout like a screaming jabber."

Hundreds of Chinese troops were now silhouetted as they climbed the hillside toward the Patricias' positions. The flare light gave Sgt. Tommy Prince and his Vickers machine-gun partner, Pte. McGillivray, early advantage against the Chinese offensive. Some distance away, at a second Vickers position, gunners Maurice Carr and Bruce Mac-Donald were aided by two Korean houseboys armed with US army carbines. However, it was clear by the persistence of the attack that the defenders were heavily outnumbered. The Chinese focused the assault on that Vickers position and soon overran it, killing both Carr and MacDonald. The western reaches of the battalion position were now falling into Chinese hands and there was a distinct danger the invading troops would turn the Vickers machine gun on the Patricias' vulnerable left flank.

"At 0300 hours, 10 Platoon was cut off and 12 Platoon was completely overrun," Mel Canfield wrote in the regimental war diary. "Lt. Mike Levy [10 Platoon commander] asked for close in mortar and artillery support," that is, for friendly fire to be brought down on "D" Company's position while the defenders hunkered down in their trenches. The company commander, Capt. Wally Mills, endorsed the plan and ordered the New Zealand artillery to commence firing on "D" Company's sector. "The stratagem was successful in driving off the attacking Chinese, although the Chinese continued to engage 'D' Company until 0700 hours."

Equally important to the successful outcome in "D" Company's sector was the action of Pte. Kenneth Barwise, a tall sawmill worker from Vancouver. Immediately following the bombardment that drove the Chinese from the area, the twenty-two-year-old Barwise dashed over from "C" Company sector and single-handedly recaptured the Vickers machine-gun position lost at the beginning of the assault. In the course of the assault, the six-foot four-inch Barwise killed six Chinese soldiers before picking up the Vickers barrel, lock and tripod (about 200 pounds), and packing it back up the hill to his platoon headquarters. Barwise's only comment to war correspondent Bill Boss after the battle was: "There sure were a lot of strangers in hell that morning."

When dawn finally broke on April 25, the sky was clear and bright. The sounds of the night—the continuous booming of the New Zealand 25-pounder guns from behind Hill 677, the thumping of exploding grenades, the chatter of Bren guns, the bursts of the Chinese burp-guns and even the whistle and bugle calls—all died down. The Patricias' situation, however, was no less precarious. Even though the waves of Chinese infantry had stopped swarming the hilltops, the communist forces had nearly encircled the Patricias. Their supply route was cut off. Col. Stone called for a re-supply of the battalion by air.

As they waited, PPCLI patrols began moving through trenches in search of Chinese and Canadian wounded. At about 7 o'clock, a reconnaissance (or recce) patrol from "C" Company blundered into some booby-trap grenades (a defensive line laid by a Patricias' pioneer platoon). Cpl. Smiley Douglas and Cpl. George Cook ran to the top of the ridge to help. Moments later, Douglas found an unexploded grenade. He shouted a warning. Cook hit the dirt to protect one of the wounded patrol members, and Douglas tried to throw the grenade away from the patrol. It went off in his hand.

The battalion was in desperate need of re-supply and relief.

At 11 o'clock that morning, Cpl. Cook saw the four US Army Air Force C-119s coming in low over the battlefield. "The four Flying Boxcars roared overhead at about 200 feet altitude. Then they made a second pass and we could see the crews pushing the boxes of ammunition, rations and water out of the hatches. They must have dropped a hundred packages of supplies to us," and only four landed outside the battalion-held position.

"The supply pallets under the parachutes came down really fast," Harley Welsh recalled. Originally working at "B" Company tactical headquarters behind Hill 677, Welsh and an intelligence section officer, Lt. Peter Mackenzie, had been reassigned to defensive position manning American .30-calibre machine guns. For nearly two days the two had sat back-to-back looking at the hillside through gunsights. On this morning, however, Mackenzie was keeping watch while Welsh caught up on lost sleep, when the air drop occurred. (In fact, it was Mackenzie who had suggested the air-drop idea to Col. Stone.) "One pallet bounced three feet from me," Welsh said. "God, if it had hit me I'd have been a pancake."

By Wednesday afternoon, April 25, American air strikes and patrols from the Middlesex Regiment had cleared Chinese snipers along the road from the town of Kap'yong north to Hill 677. The US 5th Cavalry had arrived from Seoul to reinforce. Meanwhile, with their forward momentum halted, the Chinese Communist Forces withdrew north.

UN Command began to take stock. Sixty kilometres to the west, in a similar defensive action against the Chinese spring offensive, the Royal Gloucester Regiment had nearly been wiped out; of 1,000 men in the regiment, only 100 survived the battle. New Zealand gunners had fired 14,500 artillery shells during the battle at Kap'yong. Coincidentally, April 25 was ANZAC Day, the thirty-sixth anniversary of the disastrous assault New Zealand and Australian troops had made at Gallipoli, Turkey, during the First World War; at Kap'yong, they'd sustained 31 killed, 59 wounded and 3 captured. Together, the Canadians and Australians—about 700 men—had held off two Chinese regiments, more than 6,000 troops. The Princess Patricias had suffered 10 killed and 23 wounded, testament to the skilful way they had defended Hill 677.

For his actions, Pte. Kenneth Barwise was awarded the Military Medal. For calling down fire on his own position, Capt. Wally Mills won the Military Cross (although diary records show that Mike Levy made the original call, but no honours were awarded to the lieutenant). L/Cpl. Smiley Douglas had to be flown out by evacuation helicopter (he'd lost his hand and a lot of blood), but was later awarded the Military Medal for his selfless act of bravery. Pte. Wayne Mitchell, also severely wounded and evacuated, was awarded the Distinguished Conduct Medal.

Two weeks after Kap'yong, the entire 2nd Battalion of the PPCLI was assembled in a field behind the front lines. A VIP helicopter arrived and American general James Van Fleet emerged. The new commander of the Eighth US Army inspected the battalion and read out the United States Presidential Distinguished Unit Citation. In the opinion of the senior commander in field, the PPCLI deserved public recognition in the name of the President of the United States, the only Canadian unit ever to be so honoured. Gen. Van Fleet was not aware that awards to Commonwealth troops had to be approved first by the British monarch. The breach of protocol didn't seem to matter to either British or Australian authorities, but it would take almost five years before the Canadian government formally permitted the 2nd Battalion PPCLI—whom some media and politicians back home had labelled "soldiers of fortune" and whose colonel had once described as "scruff"—to wear its Kap'yong citation ribbon.

Pte. Ron Trider, of the 2nd Battalion RCR, and his seagoing companions found out about Kap'yong in the middle of the Pacific Ocean. The RCR troops, as well as other units of the 25th Canadian Infantry Brigade, had finally set sail from Seattle aboard the troopship *General Edwin P. Patrick* and its sister Liberty ships, the *Marine Adder* and the *President Jackson*, on April 19, 20 and 21, 1951. While at sea, their only link with the outside world was a daily news sheet called the *Patrick Press*. Amid news of the day—including the successful opening of *The King and I* on Broadway and the results of a new Canadian census reporting a population of just over 14 million—the Canadian soldiers "greeted reports of the Patricias' epic stand at Kap'yong . . . with a mixture of quiet pride and resentment. With half of an eighteen-month contract expired, the other members of the Special Force were bitterly disappointed because they were not sent with the Patricias earlier to fight as a brigade." The truth was, there was plenty of fighting ahead, enough for every eager volunteer.

Among the other bits of news that the Royal Canadian Regiment, the Royal 22e Régiment, the Royal Canadian Engineers, the Royal Canadian Dragoons and the Royal Canadian Horse Artillery learned en route to Korea was that President Truman had fired the UN commander-in-chief, Douglas MacArthur.

Having witnessed the failure of two separate phases of UN action in Korea—the "war for containment" and the "war for rollback"—

Truman and most members of the UN Command now desired "stabilization," or re-establishing the 38th parallel as the front or stalemate line in hopes that UN peace negotiations might then end the conflict. Gen. MacArthur still openly advocated extending the war to China, on the ground and in the air, in a second bid for complete victory. In fact, he had concocted a plan to use Nationalist Chinese troops in an all-out land invasion of China and to drop between thirty and fifty atomic bombs across the neck of Manchuria, effectively rendering China's border lands with Korea a radioactive no-man's-land for sixty years. On April 11, Truman recalled MacArthur and stated in a radio broadcast: "By fighting a limited war in Korea, we have prevented aggression from succeeding and bringing on a general war . . . We are trying to prevent a world war, not start one."

With that announcement, MacArthur lost all his command titles, but not his public voice. Despite criticism, even from fellow generals Omar Bradley and George Marshall, MacArthur continued to speak out against US policy in Korea, and on April 9 he addressed a joint session of Congress. He reiterated his tough approach to "neutralizing" Chinese influence in the Far East and concluded with his famous "I now close my military career and just fade away, an old soldier who tried to do his duty as God gave him the light to see that duty. Good-bye."

As abhorrent as MacArthur's speech was to the Truman administration, it began to shift public opinion against the war. Casualties were mounting. Winning the war was now questionable. And while a Gallup poll showed a majority of Americans supported MacArthur's policy in Korea, only 30 percent favoured all-out war with China.

The MacArthur firing left many Canadian Special Force troops bewildered. In 1950, Larry Moore had jumped on his motorcycle and raced to Chorley Park in Toronto to join up when he heard the call. He felt that joining the UN action in Korea was important, but "I was disillusioned [by the firing]. I thought I was part of the United Nations force. And here was the President of the United States firing my boss, General MacArthur. It made me wonder."

The Liberty ships carrying the rest of the 25th Canadian Infantry Brigade arrived at their Far East destinations during the first week of May. The administrative, signals, movement control, postal and dental units were offloaded at Kure, Japan; the fighting troops at Pusan, where they were immediately transported to an empty prisoner-of-war camp outside the city.

"I didn't know if the compound was to protect us or to protect the people from us," admitted Ken McOrmond. An advance party had transformed the prison into a staging area, where the soldiers drew stores and "de-preserved" 1,500 vehicles and about 2,000 tons of stores and equipment, because "anything metal had been covered in this thick petroleum jelly preservative, to keep it from corroding from salt water during the Pacific crossing," recalled Don Flieger, who was part of the Service Corps advance party. "To remove it we had to wash everything in hot water. Or sometimes we cheated and used gasoline, but that was pretty dangerous."

There were other dangers the newly arrived RCR and Vandoos troops were warned about, including which bars and "hooches" were out-of-bounds and which laundry establishments (or "washy-washy" women) could be trusted. The advance party even suggested that the RCR assign an armed escort to its canine mascot Major in case he was innocently "coaxed home for dinner." At any rate, Major and the rest of Canada's Special Force survived their stay at Pusan, and on May 11 began a training exercise—Charley Horse—to harden the troops, acquaint them with battle tactics in hilly country and get them used to some additional American weapons. After four days of climbing the hills around Pusan's airport, the brigade followed the 2nd Royal Canadian Horse Artillery group north toward the front.

As a "tech able," Sgt. Bob Somers served at a command post with the 2nd RCHA; he worked at a battery plotting board, converting map locations and distances to gunnery instructions. The trouble was, his unit barely stood still long enough for him to do the conversions. No sooner had Somers set up on the back of a half-track vehicle, when it would be time to move. Artillery gunners were nicknamed "the seven-mile snipers" because they were generally located well behind the lines, but "once we got going, between the Han River and the 38th parallel, we moved our guns thirty-one times in thirty days."

If nothing else, the early experience of Canadian infantrymen in Korea had taught those who followed that the land was master of everything. In particular, the Patricias had learned that only a thin layer of topsoil covered the hills, ridges and spurs of the landscape. In the wartime circumstances of 1951, that meant precious little from which to build protection against small arms, mortar or artillery fire. And so, Canadian soldiers became inveterate diggers in Korea. Whenever he and his RCR platoon moved toward the front, Ron Trider knew that meant the renewed digging of every manner of army hole: "There were trenches, slit; trenches, communications; posts, command; posts, observation; pits, ammunition; pits, garbage; pits, weapons; bunkers, living in, for the purpose of; latrines, hygienic; [and] graves, enemy."

The one night 2nd Battalion RCR soldiers didn't have to dig in was the night before their first brush with Chinese Communist Forces. It was May 24, 1951. When the last troops arrived at the battalion concentration area near the village of Kumyangjang-ni, they were told their overnight campsite was a graveyard, so there would definitely be no digging-in on this occasion. By now, the communists' spring offensive had collapsed and the Chinese had mostly withdrawn north of the 38th parallel, attacking only when their strength was replenished. The UN operation—its third advance to the 38th parallel and just beyond—consisted of "a movement forward of regimental groups in line abreast against opposition."

No. 9 Platoon was part of the 2nd Battalion RCR's "C" Company advance toward Hill 407 on May 25. During a short stop en route, platoon commander Dave Renwick had his men rest and change their socks. The lieutenant knew that his men would soon be climbing a series of ridges to engage the Chinese, so dry, unblistered feet would be a must. It was a distraction too; broken field guns and bullet-riddled, burned-out vehicles along a pockmarked road gave graphic evidence that the territory they were passing through had been fought over before. Next, Renwick had his men fix bayonets. This was no longer an exercise. It was their first charge into action, except that "when we got to the crest of the first hill," Pte. Ken McOrmond said, "there was another hill just beyond it, and another."

At the top of the first hill, Renwick positioned McOrmond on his .303 rifle and Pte. Gerry Beaudry on a Bren gun to cover the platoon's next advance. Beaudry and McOrmond were friends from Sudbury, Ontario. They'd both joined the Special Force the previous August.

As "C" Company climbed a second ridge on Hill 407, the Chinese began tossing down grenades and firing at the RCR attackers. McOrmond and Beaudry answered by raking the top of the ridge with gunfire to force the Chinese defenders below the crest. Miraculously, Renwick led his No. 9 Platoon to the top of the second ridge and took it without losing any of his party. When they returned to the first ridge, however, they found that Beaudry had been killed by a single sniper's shot through the head. Eventually, the RCR troops came down off Hill 407 with the body of their fallen Bren-gunner. That night, Pte. McOrmond took out a 1,000-won Korean banknote he'd kept since Pusan. On it were the signatures of every man in his section, including that of his friend, Gerry Beaudry, the first RCR casualty in Korea.

For Pte. David Graham, "losing Gerry didn't hit me until later in the day, but we'd been friends in Sudbury, and it hurt." And that's all the emotion Graham allowed himself to feel. There was neither time nor room in this war to grieve, only distractions to help make it through. Because he had left a job as fireman on CPR locomotives, Graham fantasized about trains a lot. Once, out on patrol, "we came across this old steam engine in a little Korean railroad yard. I thought, 'Boy, if I could get this thing going, I'd take her all the way to North Korea.'"

Pte. Pat O'Connor was a little older than the others. He was a company stretcher-bearer. At age twenty-seven, he had a wife and two young children at home in Sarnia, Ontario, where he'd left his job delivering bread from a horse-drawn wagon. "Paddy" O'Connor carried a notepad with him, and in quiet moments wrote poems and rebus stories (stories with drawings) to his three-year-old daughter, Terri, and his infant son, Michael. Sometimes the rebus showed stick men or trees or the sun, but every note or story signed off "Love and kisses. Pat."

Pencil and paper also helped Lt. Don Stickland cope. In Korea as a platoon commander, Stickland began documenting on his sketch pad what he called "a most important time in my life." Sometimes he captured the smallest details of landscape—a graveyard or truck tracks on a dirt road—but more often he depicted army life in single-frame cartoons. The characters were quickly drawn and one-dimensional, but they covered every aspect of army life—recruitment, training, needle parade, R & R leave and life in the line. Sometimes these drawings afforded him a much-needed release from the stresses of battle.

"On May 30, the major [Harry Boates] told us we were moving north toward this huge Gibraltar-of-a-hill," remembered Stickland. "And he says, 'You'll be covered first of all by artillery and then by aircraft. Nothing to it, just go to the top of the hill and occupy it.'"

Easier said than done. The "Gibraltar-of-a-hill" was actually a topographic feature called Kakhul-bong, or Hill 467. Its peak offered a clear view northward some thirty kilometres up the Hantan River valley to the strategically vital staging area of the Ch'orwon Plain and communist stronghold known as the Iron Triangle. To the south one could see all the way to the 38th parallel, and though the Royal Canadian Regiment and Royal 22e Régiment didn't know it, Chinese troops on top of Hill 467 had been doing exactly that. They had been observing the Canadians' advance and had dug in for the impending attack.

On their fifth day in the line, the move up Kakhul-bong and into the adjacent village of Chail-li was to be the RCR's first full-scale battalion action of the war. "A" Company had orders to push quickly up the road to the west of Hill 467 and capture Chail-li. "B" Company would protect the left flank by occupying positions on Hill 162. "C" Company was to skirt the base of Hill 467 and take the lower Hill

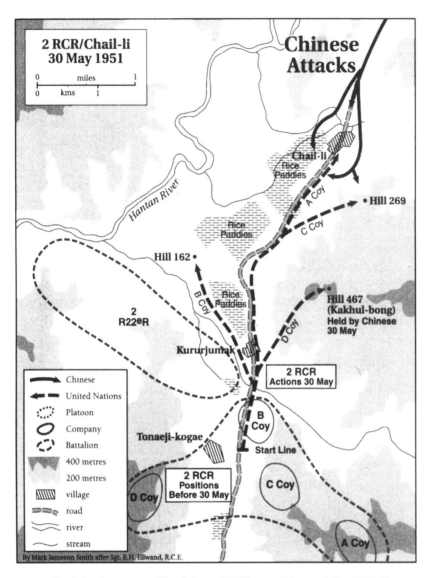

2 RCR/Chail-li
30 May 1951
0   miles   1
0   kms   1

Chinese
Attacks

Chail-li
Rice
Paddies

A Coy

• Hill 269

Rice
Paddies

C Coy

Hantan River

Hill 162 •

Rice
Paddies

B Coy

Hill 467
(Kakhul-bong)
Held by Chinese
30 May

2
R22eR

D Coy

Kururjuntak

2 RCR
Actions 30 May

Chinese
United Nations
Platoon
Company
Battalion
400 metres
200 metres
village
road
river
stream

B
Coy

Tonaeji-kogae

Start Line

2 RCR
Positions
Before 30 May

D Coy

C Coy

A Coy

By Mark Jameson Smith after Sgt. E.H. Ellwand, R.C.E.

269, which lay between Chail-li and Hill 467. Meanwhile, "D" Company would tackle the twin peaks of Kakhul-bong. That's the way Brigadier Rockingham and his senior officers saw the day's operation going. What the men at the front experienced, however, was vastly different.

The morning dawned grey, misty and drizzly. With small packs and web-belt pouches loaded with rations and ammunition, RCR soldiers moved through the Vandoos, who had been holding slit trenches at the start line of the day's action. By 0600 hours, as "B" Company headed northwest toward Hill 162, the weather had changed to driving rain. Skin quickly numbed with the damp cold and boots had no traction in the sloppy mud. As Pte. Reg McIlvenna slogged toward the objective, he thought he heard . . . music. He did. "It was unbelievable, but heart-warming. Everyone recognized it as the rollicking air of our regimental march. Then through the rain we saw the man whose melody was inspiring us. Sitting on the side of his anti-tank platoon half-track was Stan Lopez, puffing on his harmonica in the rain. In our minds we were all singing 'The RCR have gone to war . . .'"

Meanwhile, "A" Company dashed up the road on armoured half-tracks and reached its objective—the village of Chail-li—well ahead of schedule. However, as company sergeant major George Fuller recorded, "The Chinese were welcoming us to Chail-li with ever increasing machine-gun and mortar fire." Soon No. 1 Platoon reported Chinese approaching from the north in company strength; No. 2 Platoon found enemy infiltrating through rice paddies on the left flank, and by 1 o'clock the right flank was under fire. "A" Company suddenly found itself nearly surrounded and cut off from the rest of the battalion.

Just as quickly as the others, "C" Company reached its objective—the low sprawling rise of Hill 269—and established its position to defend "A" Company's right flank and "D" Company's left. Before long, through the fog and rain, Ken McOrmond recalled seeing soldiers dressed in ponchos moving around the eastern edge of Chail-li. Who were they? There were Puerto Rican soldiers nearby and they wore American-style ponchos. Canadian soldiers wore them. It wasn't clear until somebody peering through field glasses realized that under their ponchos these soldiers wore tight-fitting pants and puttee leggings. They were Chinese! Somebody fired a single shot, and in an instant, the Chinese had taken cover and had "C" Company pinned down with return gunfire. The RCR's two forward actions—to Chail-li and Hill 269—were in position, but were pinned down.

The scene up Kakhul-bong was worse still.

As a young lieutenant, Don Stickland had just been put in charge of No. 12 Platoon in "D" Company, and it was a real cross-section of men—from air force vets to a barber to a baker to some ex-convicts. "Our guys were pretty gung-ho when we started. I had one platoon ahead of me and a couple more behind . . . And there was no problem. Half way up the hill, approaching a small plateau, there was a sudden burst of firing."

Stickland first heard moaning ahead of him. Then another machine-gun burst. More shouts. A bunch of reactions he'd learned in training rushed through his head—"smeacs"—situation, mission, execution, administration, command and signals. None of those textbook responses seemed appropriate. One man had been hit in the stomach, another nicked in the head. A third was hysterical and screaming, "I'm hit! I'm hit! Save me!" To his left, Stickland's corporal, R. A. Edmonds, was crumpled over with his Sten gun slung awkwardly around his neck.

"Where are you hit?" Stickland asked Edmonds.

"I can't move," whispered the corporal. Bullets through his spine had paralyzed him. "Take the Sten gun off."

Stickland reached to remove the gun and it came off just as Edmonds died in the lieutenant's arms.

Meanwhile, the same light machine-gun fire from the Chinese had pinned down the two platoons that were following Lt. Stickland up the slope. They too had sustained wounded, and stretcher-bearer Paddy O'Connor had successfully removed several of the fallen. Stickland knew the machine gun had to be silenced. He called to his sergeant and two section leaders to lay down covering fire and he began a flanking move to the right. When gunfire from the Chinese position stopped momentarily, Stickland turned to see his stretcher-bearer, O'Connor, dashing up toward him to assist in removing the wounded. There was another burst from the machine gun. It caught O'Connor in the body. He stumbled over his stretcher and rolled over dead.

It was about this time that Stickland also realized that none of the air strikes nor any of the artillery cover promised by Maj. Boates had ever materialized. To add to the discomfort and confusion, the farther up the western peak Stickland's platoon moved, the heavier the rain and the muddier the ground became. All the while, Stickland's radio operator, Pte. Mancuso, kept sending messages and information over his 88 set to the rear, where company headquarters was located. In spite of Mancuso's excited tone, the only response heard was the calm voice of the company commander, Maj. Boates, saying, "Move on. Move on. They're not firing now!"

Again Stickland moved forward with three of his remaining platoon privates—Digger O'Dell, Red Trott and Vern Roy. On its right flank, the western peak of Kakhul-bong was steep and muddy. Still, the four soldiers slopped as best they could toward the top. Stickland took a grenade, pulled the pin, shouted and heaved it up the hill toward the Chinese machine-gun position, angling his throw so that the grenade didn't roll back down the hill and explode on his men. After a few minutes, he crawled to the top of the ridge, peered over the edge and saw his own mortar officer, Lt. John Barrett, and some other members of his platoon right where the enemy was supposed to be. He called "Hold your fire!" Barrett and a sergeant were standing over a narrow trench that contained the bodies of two Chinese machine-gunners. The skirmish for the western peak had been won, but not the battle.

Fighting for the eastern peak of Kakhul-bong continued into the afternoon. Repeated attempts to take out the Chinese positions there failed. In fact, returning Chinese mortar fire had scored a direct hit on RCR company headquarters at the base of the hill, where Maj. Boates had been commanding "D" Company's operations. At the nearby regimental-aid post, the padre attached to the RCR, Rev. George Bickley, saw the hit. A sergeant was dispatched in an armoured ambulance to retrieve Boates.

"Padre, will you help me with Major Boates's body?" the sergeant asked Bickley when he returned.

"Of course," answered the padre, and the two took hold of the stretcher and slowly pulled it from the ambulance.

Maj. Boates lay still and white as a sheet. He'd been hit by shrapnel, had lost a lot of blood and looked dead, but then he slowly raised himself up in front of Bickley and said, "Hello, Padre . . ."

At brigade headquarters, Brig. Rockingham found the entire day's operation stalling badly. "D" Company was stuck on the western peak of Kakhul-bong. "A" Company was nearly surrounded in Chail-li. Meanwhile, "B" and "C" Companies were becoming increasingly isolated from the two main battle areas. Rockingham ordered all companies of the 2nd Battalion to begin a fighting withdrawal. By 1900 hours, with the 2nd RCHA artillery laying down a screen of fire, the last company had pulled clear of the hills. The twin peaks of Kakhul-bong would be wrested from the Chinese on another day. For now, the Royal Canadian Regiment had endured its first test in battle. Military Medals were awarded to RCHA gunner K. W. Wishart and RCR Bren-gunner J. A. Sargent for service in the battle, but the cost at Hill 467 was high. The brigade had sustained 6 killed and 54 wounded.

A week after the battle for Chail-li and Kakhul-bong, when he was behind the lines, Don Stickland drew a cartoon of RCR soldiers crawling up Hill 467. Bullets from the Chinese machine guns are ricocheting everywhere, including off the radio set from which the major's words were still ringing: "Move on. Move on. They're not firing now!"

Then Stickland faced the tough task of writing to Pat O'Connor's widow, Vera, in Sarnia, Ontario. Stickland tried to console the woman and her family by explaining that the stretcher-bearer "came running up the hill, ignoring the danger to himself in his desire to get to the wounded. A burst of fire hit Pat . . . He lived only long enough to reach for his missal . . . He died as he had lived, trying to aid others with unselfishness." A short time later, O'Connor's personal effects arrived at the family home in Sarnia, including that prayer book, a wallet, a bracelet, a comb, some snapshots, a tobacco pouch and a writing pad. Vera hid them from her children because they were splotched with his blood. In December, a letter arrived from the parents of Howard Root, a wounded soldier O'Connor had brought away from the battle for Hill 467. Enclosed was a slip of paper and a poem that the stretcher-bearer had written and given to Pte. Root before the day's action.

There is blood on the hills of Korea.
'Tis blood of the brave and true
Where the 25th Brigade battled together
Under the banner of the Red, White and Blue

As they marched over the fields of Korea
To the hills where the enemy lay
They remembered the Brigadier's order
These hills must be taken today

Forward they marched into battle
With faces unsmiling and stern
They knew as they charged the hillside
There were some who would never return

Some thought of their wives and their mothers
Some thought of their sweethearts so fair
And some as they plodded and stumbled
Were reverently whispering a prayer

There is blood on the hills of Korea
It's the gift of freedom they love
May their names live in glory forever
And their souls rest in Heaven above.

In the weeks that followed May 30, 1951, Don Stickland's No. 12 Platoon in "D" Company of the 2nd Battalion RCR and the rest of the brigade continued to advance. The 25th Canadian Infantry Brigade now consisted of the RCR, the Royal 22e Régiment and the Princess Patricias all fighting together for the first time in the war. North of the Canadians lay territory that, according to the UN

Command, had to be cleared of Chinese occupation because it left the capital, Seoul, vulnerable to attack. Ahead lay the Ch'orwon Plain and the Imjin River valley. Through the month of June, UN forces would move the front line in North Korea (just above the 38th parallel) almost to the position it would occupy for the rest of the war.

Tactics changed during this period. Perhaps because of the experiences at Kap'yong and Kakhul-bong, large frontal engagements, either offensive or defensive, were avoided. The advance consisted of establishing patrol bases that could be defended, then sending deep patrols ahead to reconnoitre, probe and seek out new defensive bases. Each new defensive position was dug in deeper, protected with more barbed wire and defended by more entrenched artillery and wider minefields than the last.

Each day groups of soldiers, usually platoon-strength, would go forward as a "deep patrol." The patrol would proceed a distance down the road by truck, dismount and then walk through its appointed patrol area searching for Chinese patrols doing much the same thing. One of the Vandoos platoon commanders, Phil Plouffe, preferred to call these missions "scout and sniper patrols," consisting of men he had trained specially to protect the left and right flanks of any larger company-size advances by penetrating deep into the "no-man's-land" of the Ch'orwon plain. Fellow Vandoos section commander Leo Gallant remembers these operations as mopping up actions, although, in his case, he came within one step of disaster. One day, he was leading about ten men along a path through a rice paddy, where a Korean child jumped out of the brush and began waving frantically at him. The lance corporal stopped in his tracks as the girl pointed to a trip-wire directly in front of him. The wire was scarcely above the ground and attached to an American pineapple grenade on a stick a few metres away. Had Gallant tripped the booby trap, the grenade would have killed or maimed his entire section.

Regardless of the setting, no soldier could forget that he was in hostile territory. L/Cpl. John Dalrymple of the PPCLI made a habit of documenting his Korea experiences on paper. He recorded the tale of one Ch'orwon village, where "bearded farmers stood ankle deep in the paddies, poking patiently with wooden sticks to cultivate the crops . . . [where] women carried bundles of washing down to the clear flowing stream," and where a Princess Patricias patrol had been ambushed. In response, the Canadians brought down artillery fire on the paddies and village, followed by an even larger infantry patrol, which retrieved the bodies of dead comrades and hustled the civilian population down the road away from the village.

"As we withdrew," Dalrymple continued, "a pair of Wasp flame-thrower carriers clattered from hut to hut. They would pause in front of each dwelling, swing in to face the primitive mud and wood structure, then spit with vengeful snarl a savage hundred-foot blast of flame. The little mountain rimmed valley was filled and overflowing with thick white smoke from the burning straw roofs. Not a home was left standing, not a cattle shelter, nor a chicken coop.

"As for the quiet, noble peasant who had lived out his strange idyll of peace in the midst of war, waste no useless tears. For as that thick gray smoke floated upward, it was streaked with flashes of red that should not have been there . . . Beneath the thatched roofs shelter-ing these gentle people, under the protecting straw, each hut was jammed to the eaves with thousands of rounds of enemy ammuni-tion, mortar bombs and hand grenades."

During the United Nations advance along the Imjin River, count-less roads were built and rebuilt in order to ensure plentiful supplies for front-line soldiers. Day in and day out that spring, hundreds of UN vehicles churned up the dirt along the roadway that led to the 25th Canadian Infantry Brigade command post north of Seoul. Unknowingly, they also passed over unexploded landmines.

Rev. George Bickley was doing his rounds near the Canadian com-mand post one morning, when there was an explosion over a nearby hill. He looked up in time to see dust and pieces of paper cascading to earth.

"Must be one of those propaganda shells," suggested one observer.

"I'm not so sure," Bickley said.

Moments later, the call came up the road for stretcher-bearers. A jeep containing Reuters-Australian Associated Press correspondent

Derek Pearcy, Canadian Army public relations officer Joe Levison and their British driver had set off a landmine. Both Levison and Pearcy were killed; the driver was seriously wounded. Levison had come to Korea with the Princess Patricias; he was the first Canadian P.R. officer killed in Korea. Pearcy was celebrating his twenty-fifth birthday that day; he was the fourteenth war correspondent to die in the war.

"Picking up their body parts," Chaplain Bickley said, "was the most horrific experience."

Anti-personnel landmines, booby traps, sniper attacks, deep penetration patrols and skirmishes in no-man's-land—these were the new tactics that evolved in mid-1951. As combat looked less and less like its predecessors in the two world wars, the idea of the same type of decisive outcome for Korea also began to fade.

Diplomacy also entered the picture. July 5 marked the first time since the North Korean army crossed the 38th parallel on June 26 the previous year that the Chinese communist government in Peking responded to American invitations to discuss cessation of hostilities and an armistice. It agreed to "the dispatching of three liaison officers by each side to hold a preparatory conference in the Kaesong area." The so-called peace talks began at the 38th parallel three days later. They would consume more than two years.

GOD KEEP ME
FROM HEROES

L ATE IN JUNE 1951, several Dakota transport aircraft landed at k-16, the airport serving Seoul, South Korea. They contained a priority cargo for Canadian troops. When the freight doors were opened, an airport group known as Movement Control went into action. On a regular day, this Royal Canadian Army Service Corps (RCASC) crew could unload and process the paperwork for up to twenty dc-3s delivering military supplies to the front. This freight, however, simply identified as "welfare supplies," was considered a rush shipment. It was nearly July 1, and members of the 25th Canadian Infantry Brigade were to receive the contents of this shipment—3,440 cases of Canadian beer—in time for Dominion Day celebrations.

The beer was a gift from John Labatt Brewery in London, Ontario. And no sooner were the skids of twelve-ounce beer tins off the Dakotas, than Movement Control loaded them into trucks for the trip north toward Ch'orwon and the Imjin River. When they arrived at "A" Echelon, a service terminus a few kilometres behind the front lines, the more than 40,000 quarts of Labatt 50 beer were distributed to all troops in the brigade on the basis of two tins per man. It happened to be hot that summer in central Korea, and correspondent

Bill Boss noted that "cooled in a mountain freshet, the liquid was as ambrosia in the 80-degree sun."

"That's the first beer you can say is beer we've had since leaving Canada," announced Pte. Bob Anthony of the PPCLI.

"Number One," added Pte. Goldie Howard.

However, when Pte. Bob Lusty exclaimed, "With two beers a day like this, I'd gladly stay here six months longer," his 2nd Battalion buddies, looking forward to the end of their eighteen-month enlistment in the Special Force, playfully booed down his overzealousness.

Like the safe conveyance of so many essentials—food, water, fuel and ammunition—the prompt delivery of that imported beer went virtually unrecognized and mostly unacknowledged by the front line troops. The rule was, "It takes seven people behind the lines to keep one man on the battlefield." Whether it was the American C-Rations that fed Canadian soldiers or the boxes of shells that fed their weapons, everything came from offshore and came via Service Corps people.

Almost without stopping, RCASC troops battled the elements, red tape and the clock to get the necessary supplies through. Sometimes the freight was as inappropriate as greatcoats in the middle of summer. Some shipments were as quirky as shotgun shells for a skeet-shooting club the officers occasionally operated behind the lines. Other times the freight was as vital as boxes marked "Welfare Stores" consisting of books, magazines, cigarettes, mail and beer, or crates embossed with the red maple leaf or the Red Cross signifying urgent medical supplies. Whether freight was urgent or seemingly superfluous, however, the guiding principle of the Service Corps Movement Control was: "Delays are not permitted." The work often seemed invisible and was rarely rewarded.

"That's okay," commented one RCASC member. "We managed to get a case or two of that [Dominion Day] beer . . . It was simply reported as 'breakage,' I think."

Don Flieger was a Service Corps corporal. He'd begun his Korea service weeding out the medically unfit and AWLs at Petawawa when the Special Force was first announced. As advance party in Pusan, he'd supervised the depreserving of military equipment off the boats before the RCR and R22eR moved inland. At Kimpo Airfield it was back to the paperchase, living under canvas at the airport and joining the tarmac crews unloading freight for the front lines. Flieger, and hundreds of RCASC troops like him, did his tour keeping the army supply lines open and moving. While he was never "within the sound of battle, we constantly saw the wounded and the American coffins going out on Lodestar transports . . . sometimes up to a hundred coffins at a time. The Americans lost a hell of a lot of men."

Other members of the Service Corps were closer to the fighting. During the time of the Ch'orwon patrols and the probing missions toward the Imjin River, the front line sometimes became remarkably fuzzy. It changed every day. As a result, in the spring of 1951, when everyone seemed to be on the move, even the service locations, known as "A" and "B" Echelon, found themselves in the middle of the action.

On the afternoon of May 28, as Canadian infantrymen advanced north of Uijongbu toward the 38th parallel, the brigade's Mobile Laundry and Bath Unit (MLBU) was in hot pursuit. This elaborate assembly line of showers, washtubs and clothes dryers allowed a continuous stream of men to enter showers at one end and emerge from the other with a clean change of clothes in under thirty minutes. The MLBU could process hundreds of men each day and was euphemistically referred to as the "Chinese Hussars." However, during this particular day's action, the Canadian advance inadvertently bypassed some communist Chinese positions. Consequently, when the MLBU caught up to the fighting troops and set up facilities at a stream along the brigade's centre line, it found itself outnumbering a small Chinese patrol and took two prisoners. They were the first POWs taken by the brigade in Korea.

The MLBUs and the Royal Canadian Army Medical Corps' (RCAMC) doctors and medics moved in close proximity behind the front lines. For field doctors, like Frank Cullen, the laundry and bath units were at least a temporary stopgap to infection and disease. In the summer of 1950, Cullen had been interning at Toronto Western Hospital, working eighteen-hour days and making $60 a month. Since

Cullen also was in the RCAMC reserve, he suddenly became a prime candidate for Korea. By the spring of 1951, he was the medical officer in charge of No. 1 Section of the 25th Field Ambulance, dealing with Canadian wounded in the dust and heat near the 38th parallel.

"Nothing was ever really sterile there," Cullen recalled. "Rats ate your soap, chewed your toothbrush and the only way to discourage them was not to organize your medical equipment on open tables, the way you're supposed to." Instead, Cullen insisted on keeping surgical tools and dressings in metal panniers only to be opened by his staff when actually administering first aid. What made matters worse, the battle lines were constantly changing, which meant that medical units were forever setting up camp and then breaking camp. "I remember at Ch'orwon . . . we set up this big bloody tent, got ready for the wounded . . . then nothing happened. Then we're told we're moving again. I think we set up and moved five times in one day."

Cullen served at a Regimental Aid Post (RAP), the first point behind the front lines to which wounded were brought by stretcher-bearers for immediate first aid. Often working at night, Cullen packed wounds or tried to stop the bleeding by the light of a Coleman lantern or by directing a light he wore on a headband at his working area. From Cullen's RAP, a litter jeep carried wounded to the Casualty Clearing Station (CCS), where another medical officer could remove dressings, perform minor surgery, administer splints and stabilize the men. Beyond the CCS, wounded went farther back in four-stretcher box ambulances to the bigger Advanced Dressing Station (ADS), where they could be attended until they were stable enough to move by helicopter to a sixty- to seventy-bed Mobile Army Surgical Hospital (MASH) or flown to a hospital in Japan.

One of Frank Cullen's friends in Canada, Keith Besley, left his internship at St. Michael's Hospital in Toronto and came to Korea to establish the Casualty Clearing Station behind the Vandoos' front lines. Like Cullen, Besley had to grapple with the mobility of the war. On one occasion, Capt. Besley found a dry riverbed where he and his crew set up their CCS for the night. They had just settled down to catch some sleep in anticipation of the night's work, when a British mortar platoon moved in beside them and began firing at nearby Chinese positions. Before long, the communist artillery had zeroed in on the riverbed location and began returning fire. To stay in one piece, Besley's medical station was forced to make a hasty retreat.

Sometimes, however, encounters with enemy soldiers couldn't be avoided. At 6 o'clock one morning, Capt. Besley was up doing his daily ablutions. He'd placed a mirror on a tree to shave, when he sensed he was being watched. He turned and found himself facing a Chinese soldier armed with a rifle. The man began chattering at him, suddenly dropped his gun and threw his hands in the air. Interrogators soon arrived to take away "the first prisoner-of-war captured by the RCAMC!" On another occasion, Besley's unit wasn't so fortunate; Chinese snipers ambushed an ambulance and killed the driver before guards in the area were able to return fire.

The mortality rate during the Korean War was thirty-four per 1,000 wounded (it had been sixty-six per 1,000 in the Second World War.) A wounded soldier in Korea benefitted from greater accessibility to air-evacuation transportation, the advent of better drugs and antibiotics and quick access to surgical and medical treatment. No doubt the presence of a physician aboard HMCS *Cayuga* saved the life of at least one South Korean soldier. During her second tour in September, 1951, *Cayuga* supported units of the South Korean marines who were conducting raids along the west coast of North Korea. One such raid left about a dozen South Koreans wounded, including one with a bullet in his lung.

On the after-canopy deck aboard *Cayuga*, RCN Surgeon Lt. J. C. Cyr did a triage of the South Korean wounded and requested an operating area be readied for the soldier with the punctured lung. Capt. J. Plomer offered his cabin for the operation. With a gunnery officer acting as his assistant and an ordnance officer as his anesthetist, Dr. Cyr "opened up the marine's chest, took out a bullet, held it up and said it had been a quarter of an inch away from his heart. He sewed the man up and proceeded to deal with all the other wounded on deck.

"Later, we all joked about Fred Little being the surgical assistant and Frank Boyle the anesthetist," recalled the ship's supply officer, Bill Davis. "It felt like just another event on board ship . . . Anyway, our public relations officer wrote up a piece for publication about Joe Cyr, that he had taken a bullet from next to this guy's heart, that he had attended all the wounded and on another occasion had even removed the captain's abscessed tooth."

The newspaper in Joe Cyr's hometown—Grand Falls, New Brunswick—printed the story. And among those who read it was the real Dr. Joseph Cyr. When he informed the RCMP of the coincidence, the extraordinary tale of Ferdinand Waldo Demara came to light. Born in Massachusetts in 1921, Fred ran away from home at sixteen and entered a monastery. As well as participation in a number of religious orders, Demara moved on to secular study of law and zoology; he became dean of philosophy at a college in Pennsylvania and even served as an assistant warden at a Texas prison, but he never became a doctor. Along the way, as a monk named Brother John, Demara met Dr. Cyr and disappeared with the physician's credentials. In March of 1951, Demara presented himself to the RCN in Saint John, New Brunswick as Dr. Joseph Cyr, and was assigned to ship duty, arriving aboard *Cayuga* in time for her second tour to Korea.

On October 24, 1951, a month after the lung surgery, *Cayuga* received a message informing the captain he had an impostor aboard. When Capt. Plomer confronted his ship's doctor with the information, Demara produced Joe Cyr's notarized birth certificate and his physician's sheepskin and then retreated to his cabin. Unmasked and accused of impersonating a doctor, Fred Demara took an overdose of barbiturates and slashed his wrists. He was given first aid at sea, transferred ashore, shipped home to Canada and discharged from the Navy. The real Dr. Cyr did not press charges because Demara hadn't harmed anyone and another shipmate, Gil Hutton, claimed some RCN officers offered Demara funds to pay for a real medical education. Ultimately Fred Demara was deported to the United

States, where he became a hospital chaplain and where, in 1960, Hollywood released its version of his story as *The Great Imposter*.

Even in the relative quiet and security behind "A" Echelon, away from the sharp end of the fighting on the front lines, the horror of the war could not be avoided. RCAMC medic Les Pike never forgot the sight of nine dead RCR soldiers lined up on stretchers outside his Regimental Aid Post following the battle of Chail-li and Kakhul-bong on May 30, 1951. Yet, in terms of raising his awareness of the realities of war, "the scariest time I remember was helping an ambulance get to the aid post . . . It was nighttime. We knew there were snipers, so the driver couldn't use any lights . . . and couldn't see where he was going. So I walked out in front of the vehicle about ten or fifteen feet ahead. He saw my outline in the darkness and followed me back."

As valuable as Pike's shepherding the ambulance through the darkness was to the Service Corps driver that night, the service of medics behind the lines was greatest to those wounded in the fighting. In fact, Pte. Don Leier, who served at an ADS, remembers that most soldiers didn't think much of medics, "but as you got closer to the front lines, the fighting men suddenly got friendlier," sensing their lives might depend on the concern and skill of a medic in an emergency.

On his very first day behind "A" Echelon, medic Cosmo Kapitaniuk was assigned to a motor ambulance convoy transporting wounded PPCLI soldiers from the Advanced Dressing Station to the American 8055th MASH unit. Despite being twenty-eight and a Second World War veteran, Kapitaniuk remembers he was so nervous he lay down fully clothed in his blankets to wait for his first orders.

"The wounded are already in the ambulance," a corporal told Kapitaniuk as he woke him. "Just watch for bleeding. And make sure the IVs don't stop along the way."

Kapitaniuk was shaking as he climbed into the back of the box ambulance. In fact, the Canadian private, a very religious man, prayed too.

The ambulance had hardly set out when a wounded soldier started moaning, "My eye is bleeding."

Kapitaniuk thought, "What will I do?" He approached the wounded man and saw that both his eyes were bandaged. From the documentation, Kapitaniuk found that the soldier had already lost one eye and the other was injured. "Which eye is bleeding?" he asked.

The wounded soldier anxiously pointed to his good eye.

The medic looked and realized that perspiration was running down the soldier's cheek in the heat of the ambulance. Kapitaniuk gently touched the drop of sweat beneath the soldier's good eye and said, "Look, it's sweat, not blood. It's all right."

The wounded man exhaled a deep sigh of relief and in seconds fell asleep. Pte. Kapitaniuk relaxed too. He had administered aid to his first patient in Korea and all it took were words of reassurance. Unlike many in the war, Kapitaniuk was there on a mission. Not just to provide medical assistance. Not just to assist South Korea, although his deep hatred of communism went back to his family's mistreatment at the hands of the Bolsheviks in Ukraine after the Russian Revolution. In addition, Kapitaniuk felt instructed by God to join up and save souls. He volunteered for the medical corps again as he had done in the Second World War, and headed for the battle-fields of Korea to be a nurse, a chaplain and a missionary, or as he described himself, a "bible puncher."

Not long after he arrived in Korea, Kapitaniuk sent home for gospel tracts that he could hand out in his spare time. Within a few weeks, bundles containing 3,000 tracts arrived and Kapitaniuk wondered what he was going to do with them all. En route back to the front lines, his ambulance cab jam-packed with pamphlets, he stopped at a Norwegian MASH unit just as a South Korean Army unit was passing through. To Kapitaniuk this was a sign and he leapt out of the ambulance and began distributing the pamphlets to the ROK soldiers. Before long, Pte. Kapitaniuk caught the eye of a South Korean officer.

"Who's handing out these tracts?" shouted the major.

"I am," said Kapitaniuk, fearing a severe tongue-lashing from the senior officer.

The heavy-set South Korean soldier approached Kapitaniuk, grabbed the tracts from him, identified himself and said, "I'm a Christian doctor in the 1st ROK Division. I want these tracts."

Kapitaniuk gladly gave the ROK officer almost 2,000 of them. He later learned that this same ROK unit had been mauled in a fierce battle with the Chinese. Hundreds of the South Koreans were killed. Kapitaniuk found some solace in the possibility that his pamphlets had brought "the gospel to many of those men for the first and last time before they died."

Bible punchers aside, whenever a soldier felt he needed a sympathetic ear, he was generally told, "Tell your troubles to the padre." Indeed, in Korea the army chaplain was officially responsible to the commander for the moral and spiritual welfare of the troops. Throughout the war, Protestant and Roman Catholic clergymen, six at a time, were assigned to Canadian military units. The chaplain's (or padre's) job was to take services with the men—to preach, conduct sermons, instruct and console—and to do so for every denomination in the force. The chaplain had a licence to go anywhere. He worked in uniform. Whatever the number of pips on his shoulder, however, tradition dictated that the chaplain was always the equivalent rank of the man to whom he was speaking. In a sense, the padre was the conscience of the entire unit. He helped men deal with fear and confusion, death and grieving. He listened to their problems and passed on their concerns, recognizing that it was his role to help hold civilized men together in an uncivilized situation.

"There are no atheists in foxholes," said Rev. Bill Buxton, echoing the Second World War adage. An Anglican chaplain from Tisdale, Saskatchewan, Buxton, thirty-two, was university-educated, had been parish curate in Edmonton and Fort Saskatchewan and formerly the chaplain of the Loyal Edmonton Regiment reserve. In Korea, he was attached to a Casualty Clearing Station with the 38th Field Ambulance, located below the Imjin River, where "you're dealing with the insanity of the whole thing. You're constantly saying that these things which seem to be signs that God does not care, are not God made. They are human made. And you're telling the soldier he's under-appreciated . . . that he's there to meet the enemy, to defeat him and to bring peace."

In 186 days in Korea, Rev. Buxton conducted 183 services. He was constantly on the move, travelling just behind the front lines in a jeep that sported a brass crucifix his military parishioners had welded to the hood. He towed a small trailer that contained his books, robes, holy communion and even a small field organ "that unfolded and you had to pump like crazy during hymn singing." Some soldiers appreci-ated the distraction of a service and the singing of "Onward Christian Soldiers" or "Abide With Me," others the tobacco or note paper Bux-ton dispensed from his trailer. He claimed the trust he earned from men in the field came from "a little pastor psychology and just plain horse sense."

In Korea, among the experiences a soldier dreaded most was receiv-ing a Dear John letter from home. To some at home the Korean War seemed "pointless" and had "no glamour." For whatever reason, this war had no less destructive impact on family ties than any other, but without batteries of military psychologists or counsellors, such per-sonal problems fell to the army chaplain to resolve. This was entirely appropriate; when he encountered a soldier upset over a lost sweet-heart or potential marriage break-up, Rev. Buxton had greater power to intercede than even the generals.

"I relied on 'the purple net' in these kinds of situations," Buxton said, purple being the colour associated with clergy and part of their shoulder flashes. "A soldier from London, Ontario, gets a Dear John letter from his wife. I have a chaplain in London I can communicate with immediately. I can have that chaplain go see that man's wife, child or parents. And it doesn't have to go through the commanding officer, the adjutant, the signals office . . . I can probably have word back to me and advise the soldier the next day . . . The purple net was the chaplains' communication network."

Church services were celebrated wherever and whenever conditions allowed—outside a Regimental Aid Post after a battle, in a slit trench during a lull in enemy shelling, or on board the RCN destroyers at sea. On one occasion, says Father Walter Mann, "I celebrated mass one afternoon in the bottom of a mortar pit." Though it was generally frowned upon, the thirty-five-year-old Roman Catholic priest kept a diary of his year as a chaplain with Canadian army units in Korea. A typical entry reads:

"Set out early this morning for forward positions. Vehicles cannot enter this Company area after first light . . . because of enemy observation. But now have been camouflaged by the engineers. Hats off to these boys.

"Visited the boys at the sharp end, on the front lines . . . Said mass in one of the mortar pits. Three shells landed not 100 yards back of me. And the shrapnel went whizzing over my head and about me. Debated about calling the mass off since the communion time had passed, but trusted to Divine Providence.

"We had just barely finished and two more shells came in. Came out of the bunker and learned that one of the boys was hit . . . two legs and an arm blown off."

As conspicuous as medics and chaplains, carrying Canadian wounded off the battlefield, were the thousands of Korean civilians recruited (and in some cases simply rounded up) and put to work as porters. These were the latter-day "Gunga Dins" of the UN Command in Korea. With no pay, no uniforms and certainly no acknowledgement (save the generosity of their military employers), these Korean men, women and children were seen everywhere behind the lines acting as stretcher-bearers. They also hauled supplies of every shape and weight—food, water, ammunition and occasionally cases of *Asahi* beer—from the jeep-head (where roads ended behind the front) to the trenches. Korean porters, or "rice-burners" as they were euphemistically called by UN troops, routinely carried twenty-five kilograms of supplies on their backs, held there on an A-frame (three poles lashed together in a triangle with shoulder straps of woven straw). In return, the porters survived on whatever the troops behind the lines could offer them in leftover food, clothing and shelter.

What began as an ad hoc arrangement, by 1951 was established as the Korean Service Corps (KSC), with most units serving with the Republic of Korea Army, but with the 120th KSC Regiment assigned to the Commonwealth Division. Absolute loyalty was demanded from all KSC bearers. Discipline was strict and summary. One Canadian recalled that a razor was stolen from a soldier's kit bag. An ROK officer soon appeared with the apparent guilty party, a Korean porter, and after giving the man a tongue-lashing, the officer pulled out a pistol and executed the porter on the spot. Others remember some mornings when a bridge over the Han River would have corpses hanging from its girders—porters and other civilians allegedly found guilty of spying or theft.

Despite the realities of the war zone, the KSC grew in strength to more than 100,000 people. In addition to providing a lifeline of supplies, many adult Koreans worked as interpreters or translators during interrogation of Chinese prisoners. Women, or mama-sans, served in rear echelon areas as laundresses. And then there were the Korean boys, ranging in age from mid-teens to mid-twenties, who served as houseboys for officers in intelligence sections or at the headquarters of the mortar, pioneer or machine-gun platoons. In return for subsistence, these boys polished boots, washed clothes, brewed coffee or tea, and cleaned officers' tents or bunker living areas. Among the best-remembered houseboys, fourteen-year-old Cho Nam-Soum became attached to the Princess Patricias' battalion headquarters and he "so endeared himself by his industry and willingness," wrote correspondent Bill Boss, that the battalion "decided to make a little Canadian of him . . . with a suit of blue denim overalls, a scarlet neckerchief [and] Canadian running shoes."

In August 1951, when the 2nd Battalion of the Royal Canadian Regiment was patrolling north of the Imjin River, platoon commander Don Stickland recalled "a little boy of eight or ten, who had strayed away, perhaps from a family massacre . . . was found, wandering in what had recently been a rural village. Whatever the precise day and place, that's when the small boy acquired a family, a name and a future. For almost two years he had no home other than the echelon camps behind the battle lines of the Royals."

The 2nd Battalion RCR adopted the boy and named him Willie Royal. They dressed him in cut-down bush pants, a well-shrunk khaki-issue sweater and a pint-sized pair of combat boots. In return, the boy devoted himself to the soldiers, particularly those in the anti-tank platoon and the mechanics and drivers at the transport compound near "A" Echelon.

"Willie was the pet of the regiment," recalled Lt. Scotty Martin. When the lieutenant and the 1st Battalion RCR arrived in Korea to take over for the 2nd Battalion, Martin and his fellow officers also took over responsibility for Willie. By now, RCR troops had instilled such pride in Willie that he too polished his combat boots and buffed up the RCR hat badge he wore on his issue field service cap. However, his soldier-fathers had also passed along a unique vocabulary, which Willie readily parroted back to whomever would listen. That's when the C.O. and the chaplain made more formal arrangements to care for the boy. A trust fund of soldiers' contributions—more than $1,000—helped place the boy in the charge of the bishop of Seoul.

Not so passive among the young Korean civilian recruits were Yong Sang-Rock, a twenty-four-year-old houseboy who was nicknamed Pete, and seventeen-year-old Moon Pyong-Hee, referred to as Joe. In addition to carrying out daily cleaning and maintenance responsibilities for the Princess Patricias, the two boys refused to be left behind. They equipped and armed themselves and regularly joined the battalion when it went into the line. During the battle at Kap'yong, Pete and Joe helped defend a "D" Company machine-gun position during some of the toughest fighting on Hill 677.

Behind the lines, duty above and beyond came in all shapes and from all units. During the frigid winter of 1952, at the British Commonwealth medical unit in Seoul, nurses, under Canadian matron Capt. B. Pense, managed to equip each hospital cubicle with its own heating stove while some of the medical staff went without. Wherever there were wounded soldiers—at forward stations in Korea or at the British Commonwealth Hospital in Kyoto—members of the Canadian Red Cross Welfare Team helped out; Muriel White recalls writing letters home, providing handicrafts as therapy and "sometimes just offering a female voice in a man's world."

Another unsung unit in Korea was the road-building crew of the 57th Independent Field Squadron of the Royal Canadian Engineers (RCE). In the summer of 1951, when the 25th Canadian Infantry Brigade was operating in the Ch'orwon Valley, Maj. Don Rochester's sappers were suddenly ordered to build an airstrip just behind the front lines for Brig. John Rockingham's observer aircraft. The Canadian engineers quickly chose a barley field, bulldozed and graded it flat, then cleared the surface of stones by hand. It took "the Rochester General Construction Company," as they became known, only four hours to complete a single airstrip 1,350 feet long and 60-feet wide.

One week later, on July 6, the Supreme Commander of the Far East, Gen. Matthew B. Ridgway, suddenly chose that day and Rockingham's airstrip for a hasty fact-finding rendezvous with UN commanders in the Ch'orwon area. Rochester's crew was told that the airfield would have to be expanded to accommodate not one aircraft, but a dozen, and not in four hours, but in one. Called into extraordinary action were Spr. Ed Rollheiser operating a bulldozer, Spr. Hec Gravel manning a grader, L/Cpl. Glyn Nott driving a truck as a roller and Sprs. F. A. W. Jones and Bill Milson hauling water trailers to tamp down the new airstrip surface. Total construction time: forty-seven minutes.

Less than an hour later, Gen. Ridgway's personal aircraft, complete with its four-star insignia, landed on the strip, as well as that of Lt.-Gen. James Van Fleet, commander of the Eighth US Army, and ten other taxi aircraft belonging to corps, divisional and regimental brass of the United Nations Command. Each of the dozen planes was guided onto the strip by a seventy-foot-tall mast complete with brand-new airport windsock. Of course, little or no fuss was made over the impromptu runway and tarmac area, let alone the Canadian sapper crew that had built it in record time. Besides, "the Rochester

General Construction Company" was probably already off building another new road or rebuilding one that the weather or Chinese artillery had destroyed—all before most people behind the lines even noticed.

Nobody in UN Command travelled behind the front lines in Korea very quickly. The closest that politicians, diplomats and generals got to rapid transit was in a single-engine airplane—the Beaver. Built in 1947 by Canadian manufacturer de Havilland, the Beaver was designed for use in the bush. In 1950, the aircraft caught the eye of those equipping the US Army, who were "looking for a tough short-take-off-and-landing, utility aircraft capable of carrying six people for a radius of 200 miles and able to land anywhere." In other words, they needed "a flying jeep." Instead of such competing American aircraft as the Beechcraft Bonanza, Aero Commander, Republic Seabee amphibian or Cessna 185 and 195, officials of the US Army Test Center at Fort Bragg, North Carolina, chose the Beaver. They bought more than 200 Beavers, 50 of which were packed and sent to Korea under the supervision of de Havilland field representative Bruce Best.

"They gave me officer status in the American army," Capt. Best recalled. A civilian aircraft mechanic during the Second World War and later chief engineer with the Toronto Flying Club, Best also had his commercial pilot's licence. He joined de Havilland to assist in the US Army testing of the Beaver and in 1952 was shipped to "a base called Ascom City, between Seoul and Inch'on . . . about sixteen miles from the front . . . I was my own boss . . . I got hold of my Beavers and maintained them there for a year."

Best's Beavers fanned out across the front. Most were equipped with underwing bomb shackles, not used for bombing but for dropping food and ammunition in tight spots, or for running communication wires from one position to another. When a Beaver was rigged with litter straps, it could carry twice as many wounded soldiers, in greater comfort, than the Bell Sioux evacuation helicopters. Other Beavers earned the moniker "the general's jeep" by flying military VIPs (including Dwight Eisenhower) on their appointed rounds in

Korea. One even had its doors removed so that a piano could be transported to an officers' mess behind the lines.

"This might seem crazy," Best explained, "but in Korea booze was cheaper than water. Mix was expensive as hell. So I'd fly over and give the Brits some soda water to mix with their booze. And they'd give me gallon jugs of Pusser rum to bring back to Ascom City."

The Korean War turned out to be a perfect testing ground for the Beaver and for its first wartime field representative. Pilots flew the aircraft roughly, and Capt. Best regularly had to deal with broken undercarriage legs, missing rear wheels, buckled fuselages and burned-out engines. He eventually requested and got twenty-one modifications to the Beaver's design. Based on his experience at the Ascom City repair and maintenance depot, Best recommended they double the plane's skin, strengthen its wings and change the location of its air intakes to reduce the damage from airborne dust.

"I was a bit of a doctor," Best said. "I was there for the airplane and it did a superb job . . . When other tech reps got back to the States, they were given a diploma for making history . . . for being part of the first battalion under combat conditions to do this type of work in the US Army. But I left in a hurry and never got mine . . . I was hired for one job and did it."

Best wasn't alone. Technical expertise in Korea generally went unnoticed.

In spring of 1951, Bill Tigges, an instrument technician in the RCAF No. 426 Transport Squadron, was reassigned from McChord Air Force Base at Tacoma, Washington, overseas to the Tokyo instrument section at Haneda Airport in Japan. Almost from the very day Canada joined the UN mission to Korea, in July 1950, Tigges had found himself crawling in and out of North Star transport aircraft maintaining cockpit gauges and meters and patching oxygen lines and joints, "because the vibration of the aircraft kept breaking them all the time. And the repair could take hours and hours of straight bull work."

Near the end of one eighteen-hour stint repairing an oxygen system aboard a North Star, Leading Aircraftman Tigges refused to let

the aircraft go until it was fixed. When the LAC emerged in his overalls, covered in grease and mud, he suddenly found himself facing his
spick-and-span commanding officer, Wing Commander C. H. Mussells (whose nickname, ironically, was "Muss"). The C.O. chewed
out Tigges for his appearance and "conduct unbecoming." However,
when Muss found out why Tigges was so dishevelled, he returned
and commended him for the effort and held up the bus to the barracks until Tigges had finished the job.

In the early days of the war, when three Canadian destroyers
maintained a blockade in seas off the coast of Korea, the vessels regularly encountered floating mines. UN sailors safely detonated 1,535
Russian-made "contact" mines during the war. On one occasion,
when it was too dangerous to take HMCS *Athabaskan* close enough
to fire on the inshore mines, one of the ship's dinghies was rowed into
the minefield. There the ship's gunnery officer, David Hurl, a petty
officer and two able seamen, including sonar operator Ed Dalton, set
to work. The group rowed close enough to the mines to allow Dalton
to hold each one steady and Hurl to attach charges. The party blew
up four mines this way, and while Hurl received a Mention In Dispatches honour for displaying iron nerves, Dalton was rewarded with
a welcome but ephemeral "extra tot of rum."

Equally dirty work was carried out by teams of the Royal Canadian Electrical and Mechanical Engineers. Among their missions
was the recovery of vehicles overturned on steep embankments,
bogged down in mud or shot up by the enemy. Their recoveries were
often conducted at night, with repaired equipment back in operation
by morning. Ironically, these units served in Korea longer than any
other. During twenty-three months of duty these troops piled up an
incredible record of 21,983 field repairs on everything from radio
equipment to armoured vehicles. The record of Sgt. T. "Trapper"
Allen, a recovery specialist attached to the Lord Strathcona's Horse
armoured regiment, was typical.

In the spring of 1952, when the tank regiment got bogged down
in the Korean countryside just behind the front lines, Allen, the driver
of an Armoured Recovery Vehicle (ARV), was dispatched forward to

recover a dozer tank that had broken down while attempting to build a road for the PPCLI across a rice paddy dike. The location was in plain view of North Korean gunners and it wasn't long before they found the range. First mortar, then 120-mm artillery shells began falling closer and exploding all around the recovery scene.

Canadian engineering officer F. W. Chapman watched Allen continue the recovery operation in spite of the shelling. "Disaster was imminent, I thought . . . [but] Sgt. Allen, standing in the open and using hand signals, was oblivious to the enemy shells as he directed the ARV and crew into relative safety . . . No one was injured nor was equipment damaged . . . There's no doubt in my mind that Sgt. Allen, through his personal efforts, dedication to the job and knowledge of recovery, had made the operation a complete success." Ten days later, Sgt. Allen's heroism was recognized when he was awarded a Military Medal.

During a tour of duty in Korea, Canadian fighting troops left the front lines in only one of three ways: as a medical evacuee, as a fatal casualty, or on rest and recreation. Soldiers were regularly rotated out of forward positions for R & R at "B" Echelon locations, where they could sit down to a hot meal and take advantage of the Mobile Laundry and Bath Unit. Better still was an R & R leave, which meant five days and five nights in Tokyo, plus several days travelling to and from Japan. There were few more welcome words from the sergeant or platoon commander than, "Get cleaned up! You're going on R & R!"

"You'd get down on your hands and knees and crawl out of a trench," said one Korea veteran, "just to get R & R in Tokyo!"

As inviting as the sound of that was, a vacation from the war required a substantial readjustment. Ron Trider, a private in the Royal Canadian Regiment, aptly assessed the anticipation and anxiety in his own diary of a soldier's R & R experience: "For many months there had been no privacy. He was never alone. It had been a long time since he had slept in a bed or sat on a chair for a meal served on a table. Far too long had it been since he had opened a door, switched on a light, or had even seen sheets, or a building lit up at night. Too many months had passed since he had made choices as to when and what and where he would eat and drink, since he had strolled down a street, and since he had looked in shop windows, or enjoyed the privacy of an indoor toilet . . .”

Between his Spartan existence at the front and the Utopian one he expected in Japan lay a number of hurdles. The first was inspection. Somehow, his badly scuffed and worn boots, his threadbare trousers and tunic *sans* elbows, all of which smelled of stove smoke, stale sweat and his visits to the latrine, would have to pass. His packs and pouches containing a hand towel, socks, underwear and extra shirt, a sewing kit of needle and thread, a small flannel patch he used to clean his weapon, part of a C-Ration chocolate bar or cigarettes would be surveyed. Meanwhile, the soldier attempted superficial repairs: 9-mm ammunition rounds to weight his pant legs at the cuff to give the impression of being pressed, cleaning solvent to spruce up webbing and Kiwi polish to shine boots.

At “B” Echelon, some distance back of the lines, kit bags in storage were reclaimed, parade-square boots retrieved and new bush uniforms issued. Then it was on to Seoul for the night at the British holding barracks. Next morning, there was time for breakfast, another inspection and then on to the parade square, where “the soldier rather naively assumed he would board an aircraft in Korea and somehow, through an absurd leap in logic, land on the Ginza with a beautiful Geisha on each arm and a bottle of *Asahi* beer in each hand.”

Not so. At the other end of the DC-7 flight to the Japanese island of Honshu was Ebisu Camp, the Tokyo Commonwealth leave centre. Again, despite anticipating early freedom, the soldier on leave had to endure more of the army's routines, rules and regulations. At Ebisu, all troops received their third shower in two days, an inspection (from a medic with a flashlight and a magnifying glass), another issue of bush uniform, socks and underwear, another trip to a mess hall, assignment to another barracks and yet another parade, this time for pay—some British pounds sterling, some US dollars and the rest in Japanese yen. The penultimate stop was the mandatory speech from a supervising officer, who “droned on, tantalizing his captive audience with references to lust, drunkenness, over-indulgence and fleshpots." Finally, the men were marched to the front gate area. Here was a room with a little blue light on the outside, where all Commonwealth troops passing out the gates of Ebisu Camp had to draw stores. This place ensured that all the men delivered forth onto the streets of Tokyo were protected against the perils that might ambush the careless soldier. "Only then," wrote Pte. Trider, "could the frantic troops explode through the gates for five days and nights of FREEDOM!"

The Tokyo that Canadians on R & R found outside the Ebisu camp in 1951 was a strange blend of cultures. It looked and felt like a collision between East and West. It was a picture of pop-North Americana superimposed on a scroll painting. Canadian soldiers were entering a world of Buddhist temples and beer halls, of mama-sans and military police, of speeding taxicabs, bicycles and rickshaw carriages. Affluence and poverty resided side by side. All the energy and excitement of the city circulated around the famous shopping and entertainment centre of Tokyo, the Ginza.

Ernie Banks and an RCR buddy on leave emerged from Ebisu Camp with a personal card, provided by a previous draft of R & R troops; the card offered directions to and assessments of various bars, hotels and bathhouses. Ultimately, however, the two neophyte visitors left their fates to the "ex-Kamikaze pilot-type" taxicab drivers lined up outside Ebisu. In downtown Tokyo, the Canadians encountered women almost immediately. Some were geishas. Others described themselves as either "tenderly hostesses" or "heavenly hostesses," hired by some hotels to engage and direct newcomers to "proper cultural exchanges." The soldiers also saw corpses in the street, apparently victims of a sleeping-sickness epidemic that struck the city that year.

Eventually, a cab deposited the two at a hotel, where a hostess passed out paper slippers, motioned them to remove their boots and led them through tiny hallways to select "their [female] cultural guides." When arrangements were made, kimonos were issued and uniforms shed; the tunics and pants would eventually reappear completely cleaned and pressed and with pockets still containing cash and personal belongings. The soldiers' "guides" then "introduced the men to the Japanese ritual of the bath . . . If the military authorities were shower-parade crazy, the tenderly hostesses proved absolutely mad . . . the baths were hot enough to boil the bloody hide off a rhino . . . Following each cultural exchange between soldier and hostess, it was back to the tub!"

"We called them pompom houses," remembered RCN Leading Seaman Glenn Wilberforce, who did two tours aboard the HMCS *Huron*. The navy also enjoyed R & R in Japan. "They weren't normal brothels. They were clean and respectable."

"You'd pick out a woman you liked," agreed *Huron* stoker John Rigo. "And once you came to a deal with the mama-san, you paid her and then you had that girl for the night . . . You'd go into her room, take off all your clothes and put on a kimono. You'd dance. And if you felt a little amorous, you'd go into the room and then come out and dance some more. It was all night for 500 yen . . . about two dollars."

How far a draft of R & R soldiers or seamen explored the nightlife along the Ginza varied, often depending on the personality of the vacationing serviceman, or more likely how much alcohol was consumed. One night, Pte. Don Hibbs and a fellow Princess Patricia, Pte. White from P.E.I., managed to crash an American Officers' Club in Tokyo. The two indulged a while at the club bar. Before long, Whitey had disappeared, only to re-emerge playing a violin he'd "borrowed" from a Japanese chamber orchestra on the premises. His enthusiastic performance à la Don Messer, complete with hoots and hollers, wild fiddle-scratching and loud foot-stomping, wasn't what the club patrons expected and the two Canadians were soon shown the door.

Elsewhere, a group of Australians on leave teamed up with some Canadians on a Tokyo hotel balcony one morning. The senior-ranking soldier in the group—an Aussie corporal—ordered the combined unit to strip to the buff and, with their backs to the street, to perform a series of calisthenics to astonished Japanese passersby on the street below. On another occasion, a R22eR soldier, on R & R leave over Christmas in 1951, was particularly attracted to a huge

Christmas tree erected by the proprietor of a beer hall on the Ginza. Deciding the tree was too tall (and inspired by liquid courage), the Vandoos soldier scaled the evergreen like a lumberjack and quickly sawed off the top. The toppling limb sparked a riot for no other reason than it seemed like a good idea at the time. It took American MPs and two buses most of the night to clear the hall of hundreds of brawling troops.

R & R changed most who ventured to Japan. The soldiers who returned to Ebisu Camp following leave were not nearly as parade-square sharp as the ones who had left there five days before. Indeed, few even looked like uniformed soldiers. Roll call at the Commonwealth leave centre revealed many of them wearing smoking jackets or kimonos instead of tunics, paper sandals not boots, and all manner of headgear, including US Navy caps, forage caps, wedgies, Irish tam-o'-shanters or Australian Stetsons, not to mention the various non-military accoutrements, such as pool cues, fishing rods and ceremonial swords.

The greater impact on servicemen such as Banks, Hibbs, White, Wilberforce, Rigo and the thousands who went on leave to Tokyo before and after, was re-entry, the return to the business of warfare. As Ron Trider put it, "their leave expired, they returned flat broke, dead tired and emotionally drained. In camp they stood meekly in line for whatever food was tossed on their plates. They moved to the left, or shifted to the right on command, while resigning themselves again to the grand order of things and events that belong to the military. They again parked their imaginations and individuality on hold, and glumly boarded the aircraft for Korea to re-enter the world of reality."

Parading naked on a hotel balcony, chopping down Christmas trees in beer halls or engaging in "cultural exchanges" with heavenly hostesses seemed permissible on R & R leave in Tokyo. In Korea, however, there was very little tolerance for such things as theft, drunkenness, desertion, rape or black marketeering. Such actions generally led to court martial, but often meant imprisonment at the military prison in Seoul.

A number of Nissen huts surrounded by barbed wire and guarded by provosts comprised the Commonwealth detention barracks, or DB. Depending on the crime, a soldier sent to the DB in Seoul got seven, fourteen or twenty-eight days' detention. Upon entry, the soldier serving a sentence had every badge, button and military insignia ripped from his uniform by the prison C.O. From that moment on, the prisoner was ordered to do everything on-the-double. No matter what activity—eating, shaving or urinating—he had to keep his eyes skyward and his feet pounding out the rhythm of a quick march. Additional punishment included no rations but bread and water, or "piss and pump," for three days, solitary confinement in "the box" or, finally, running a ninety-pound pack up and down a hill within the compound night and day.

"You didn't ever want to go to the DB in Seoul. It was like a dog kennel," recalls Cpl. Bob Douglas. During the Second World War he'd served in Farnham, Quebec, guarding Luftwaffe aircrew brought to Canada as POWs. When the Korean War broke out, he was transferred to the Canadian Provost Corps, whose members were stationed behind the front lines to handle security matters. He relished every aspect of his service job, "except escorting prisoners down to the DB in Seoul . . . Once while a bunch of performers were visiting behind the lines, this one corporal tried to take one of the young ladies off into the woods. But he got caught and was given twenty-eight days' detention . . . Being a provost himself, this corporal knew what was coming, so he put his leg across a foxhole and dropped a hundred-pound bag on himself. Broke his leg, so that he'd get shipped back to Canada instead. But he did ninety days when he got back to Borden."

Not unlike the Service Corps, members of the Provost Corps slogged through the muck, dust and military red tape behind "A" Echelon, unnoticed by the generals, the fighting troops and the war correspondents. After the front-line soldiers captured a Chinese prisoner (and generally enjoyed congratulations from commanding officers and a photo opportunity), it was up to the provost to escort the POW away. Once artillerymen or infantrymen installed a new hill position and camouflaged it, the job of guarding the installation during the heat of the day and the loneliness of the night fell to a couple of provosts in bunkers. Or when a convoy of vehicles planned to use a bridge, it was up to the provosts to secure it before, during and after its use.

"It was damn hard and dirty work," Gerry Emon remembered. After enlisting with an armoured corps and finding himself sidelined at Petawawa instructing, Cpl. Emon transferred to the Canadian Provost Corps hoping he'd get to Korea sooner. Once there, "I did a lot of guard duty . . . stuck in a bunker at the bottom of a hill by yourself for nine hours . . . And every once in a while [the Chinese] would try to hit the hill, so you'd grab your ass and duck until the bombardment let up."

Whenever troops and equipment moved en masse behind the lines, it was under provost supervision. One night, in a buffer zone along the Imjin River, the Princess Patricias were moving out of a front-line position as Royal Australian Regiment troops moved in. Five provosts, Cpl. Bob Douglas among them, were ordered to provide security for the move along a single-lane road. Throughout the night, Douglas and the rest of his platoon directed traffic both ways. In the middle of it all, a convoy of two-and-a-half-ton trucks full of American troops suddenly appeared on the road. Douglas radioed to his superior, who responded without sympathy.

"I'm sorry," Douglas reported to the American lieutenant, "but your six trucks are in the middle of our move."

"So, what am I supposed to do?" asked the US officer.

"I've got orders, sir. They'll have to go into the ditch."

"You can't do that!" protested the lieutenant. "I'll get killed when I get back!"

"You should never have got lost," said Douglas. And he supervised the lieutenant's men as they disembarked and pushed all six trucks into the ditch. It was not work the military recognized with medals or even Mention In Dispatches, but if the rest of the night's troop movement went smoothly, there was at least satisfaction in a job well done (and perhaps a little pleasure at an officer's expense).

Even without the threat of direct bombardment or hand-to-hand combat, work behind the front lines could still be deadly. On a chilly December day, provost Gerry Emon joined his buddy, Pte. Benny Larson, for a trip in Larson's carry-all truck. The private from Edmonton always took great pride in maintaining his three-quarter-ton, army-issue truck, but especially for the few days' leave he and Emon had been allotted in Seoul, Larson seemed to have the vehicle in tip-top shape. In good spirits, as usual, the two friends sped along the dirt supply road south from Uijongbu away from the battle lines. It wasn't long until Christmas, and Emon carried in his pocket a sterling-silver cigarette case that he planned to have engraved for his girlfriend back in Wainwright.

Not far into the trip, Larson slowed the carry-all as he steered it onto a short wooden bridge. As the truck bounced onto the flat of the bridge, Emon was suddenly engulfed in a blinding light and catapulted from the passenger seat through the truck door and down toward the creek below the bridge. An explosion inside the carry-all forced it off the bridge. It came down on its front end in the creek bed and nosed over, crushing Benny Larson beneath it. Even though Emon was thrown clear, the explosion lacerated his face, hands and stomach, and the impact of being driven through the door and smashed into the creek bed shattered his shoulders and nearly severed his legs at the knees. Luckily, a jeep ambulance was travelling in the opposite direction along the same road and raced to the scene. The attendants found Emon with his leg stumps driven into the mud.

"I tried to get up," remembers Emon. "But I couldn't find my feet because they were back behind me. What saved me, I guess, was that it was the first of December. The water was ice-cold, so it slowed down the bleeding."

When he came to, on a six-foot folding table at an Advanced Dressing Station, the next morning, Emon was told that Chinese or North Korean infiltrators had probably set a mine—booby-trapped to explode when the truck hit a bump in transit—in the glove compartment of the carry-all. The four tires were all that was left of the truck. Nearly all of Emon's clothes and his boots had been blown or burned off. The only belonging that survived the bombing was the twisted and singed sterling-silver cigarette case, which he eventually presented to his girlfriend in Canada.

Quick work behind the lines at the ADS saved Emon's life in Korea; two years of orthopaedic and plastic surgery at Sunnybrook Hospital in Toronto eventually put him back on his feet.

"God keep me from heroes," Gerry Emon had often said. "They draw fire." As a Korea volunteer, he had never expressed a need to be at the sharp end of the fighting to feel he was contributing. Nor did he regret not being there. Still, it hadn't been fire from fighting on the front lines that killed his friend Benny Larson and maimed him so severely. It had been wartime duty behind the lines, away from heroes.

THE IRREMOVABLE
DIGIT

W HEN Charlie Company of the Royal Canadian Regiment reached and secured the banks of the Imjin River from the Chinese Communist Forces in mid-1951, many of the troops did what any red-blooded Canadian would do on a blistering summer day. At the first opportunity, the soldiers stripped down and jumped into the blue-green waters of the current to cool off. Until then, despite all the water the men of "C" Company had encountered—the rain and snow at Fort Lewis, the pitch and yaw of the Pacific Ocean crossing and the mud of the trenches and rice paddies in Korea—this was the first opportunity to enjoy the water. The troops, even the chaplains, swam and splashed around like children.

"We had troops down there by the truckload," one RCR soldier recalled. "Everybody wanted to have a great, long swim in that fresh, cold water . . . Till somebody saw a body floating in the river. That's when medical authorities checked the river and figured out the water was polluted . . . Then, the only way you'd swim in the river was if you stuffed medicated cotton balls in your ears, your nostrils, your anus—every orifice."

The Imjin River was more than a refuge from the heat and, as it turned out, an exhaust for much of the country's natural and man-made effluent. That summer it became a vital part of the United Nations' strategy against the Chinese and North Korean armies in the field and their negotiators at the peace talks in Kaesong.

In the western part of the Korean peninsula, the Imjin ran east and west, roughly along the 38th parallel and along a military front the UN Command named the Kansas Line. About halfway across the peninsula, the Imjin Valley turned north well into North Korean territory. That summer, UN Command decided to send patrols deep into the Chinese-held territory beyond the Imjin River to establish a new "western" front in North Korea, designated the Jamestown Line. The strategic aim of these operations was to keep unrelenting pressure on the communist armies and force their diplomats to a speedy ceasefire. The tactical aim was to push the UN front line forward about ten kilometres northwest in order to keep Chinese artillery away from the Seoul-Ch'orwon-Kumhwa railway, the primary UN supply line to that sector of the front. As part of the newly formed 1st Commonwealth Division, the 25th Canadian Infantry Brigade joined the new military initiative.

The probes across the Imjin River began that summer of 1951. There were Operations Slam and Dirk in early August. Operation Claymore involved the 2nd Battalions of the Princess Patricia's Canadian Light Infantry and the Royal 22e Régiment late in August. Then in early September, the United Nations Command conducted Operation Minden and in early October Operation Commando, to establish a permanent bridgehead on the enemy side of the Imjin. As symbols of the UN's determination to stay, engineers built the Teal and Pintail Bridges, which would be strong enough to carry tank traffic and fend off the extremes of river flooding and icing.

During nearly a week of continuous fighting in early October, units of the Commonwealth Division battled forward to reach their objective—the Jamestown Line. The Royal Australian Regiment captured Hills 199 and 317. The Canadians took Hill 187 and Hill 159. The 1st Royal Northumberland Fusiliers gained Hill 217. The King's Shropshire Light Infantry secured Hills 210 and 227. And the King's Own Scottish Borderers eventually captured Hill 355. At 355 metres above sea level, this final feature towered over all the rest like a fortress. The Koreans knew the mountain as Kowang-san. When the Americans were assigned to it, they nicknamed it "Little Gibraltar." But when Canadians moved onto its heights they simply referred to it as "Three-five-five."

Operation Commando alone had cost 58 killed (4 of them Canadians) and 262 wounded (28 Canadians). In return for those casualties, by October 8, the Commonwealth Division occupied a front that extended 21,000 yards—from the western bank of the Imjin River at one end, to the eastern bank of the Sami-ch'on River at the other. In the front line—the Jamestown Line—seven Commonwealth battalions now began to dig in, with one battalion in a back-stop position and another in reserve, approximately 20,000 men.

The war now entered yet another phase. The first phase—the "war for containment"—had attempted to stem the southward advance of the North Korean armies in the summer of 1950. The second—the "war for rollback"—had been Gen. Douglas MacArthur's attempt to push the communists right out of Korea in the fall and winter of 1950–51. That had drawn the Chinese Communist Forces into the war and they had pushed the UN armies all the way back down the peninsula below the 38th parallel in the spring of 1951. In the third phase— "stabilization"—UN Command had re-established the 38th parallel as a stalemate line in mid-1951 in order to precipitate peace talks.

During all three phases, troops and supply lines had ebbed and flowed with the victories and setbacks at the front. There had been few major battles, that is, engagements designed to decisively defeat the enemy. Instead, campaigns had consisted of running offensives or raids with hasty retreats and even hastier defensive stands. With the summer and fall actions—Operations Dirk, Claymore, Minden and now Commando—the warfare was becoming positional and more static. To the soldier on the front lines this transition in the war was subtle at first, but became more obvious as the fall of 1951 wore on.

Robert Clark's corporal stripes were freshly sewn on his sleeve when he arrived in Korea as a reinforcement for the 2nd Battalion of the RCR in September. The day he and fourteen other reinforcements reached the reverse slope of their "B" Company front-line position, they were greeted by a sudden Chinese mortar bomb barrage. During his first days across the Imjin, Clark watched Princess Patricias on the RCR's right flank winching a 17-pounder anti-tank cannon onto the crest of a hill. No sooner did the cannon fire its first shell, pinpointing its position with a flash of muzzle fire and a cloud of dust, when Chinese guns replied, "and soon we were all getting plastered by shell fire.

"The war had now taken a new turn," Clark wrote. "The line wasn't moving anymore. And the Chinese increased their use of mortars and artillery. The dash and élan of infantry advancing had all ended. Instead of advancing on a broad front and taking hills now, we would move up onto them and stand fast in static positions while the enemy lobbed shells at us."

The first night of his Korean War experience, Art Johnson was led up to the RCR's "C" Company trenches on Hill 187, where he joined No. 9 Platoon. There in a slit trench, reinforcement Johnson met fellow rifleman Ken Gorman enjoying the day's ration of a tot of rum. Word was buzzing around the company position that one of their own—Pte. G. G. Rowden—was to be awarded the Military Medal for his bravery during Operation Dirk in August. The men decided unanimously to pool the next day's rum ration to celebrate his award.

Otherwise, Johnson noted that things remained relatively quiet, except that "various patrols from 'D' Company came forward and began rigging aprons of barbed wire and entanglements between our own position and the 'A' Company position. The pioneers laid many mines, too, and it was suddenly tricky picking your way through the concealed minefield gap in the wire."

Soon after, Johnson remembers a lieutenant from the R22eR visiting his own platoon commander. The Vandoos officer was there to reconnoitre the layout of wire and mines in front of the RCR position before taking a R22eR night patrol out into the valley in front of Hill 187. That night, not long after the Vandoos patrol was escorted through the barricade of wire, Johnson's platoon heard an explosion out in front of its position. Everybody was ordered to stand-to anticipating a Chinese attack. Then they heard familiar voices calling for help and realized that the Vandoos patrol had become disoriented in the dark and had wandered into the defensive minefield. The rest of the night, Johnson and his platoon gingerly wove their way through the barbed wire and mines to bring in the wounded, including "the body of the Vandoos lieutenant. It was a shame. He was fresh out from Canada. It may well have been his first patrol."

New faces at the front lines signalled another change in the war. The same week Commonwealth Division troops had fought their way to the heights north of the Imjin River, two companies of Canadian 1st Battalion troops arrived at Pusan harbour in South Korea. They were heralded ashore by the same band that had welcomed all inbound soldiers. They were serenaded by the same song, "If I Knew You Were Coming I'd Have Baked a Cake," and the men received the same meagre, tasteless, dockside breakfast that all new UN soldiers received upon arrival. These were the first Canadian troops sent to replace the original Canadian volunteers—the 2nd Battalion soldiers of the PPCLI Special Force—who had nearly completed their eighteen-month tour of duty. These 1st Battalion PPCLI soldiers would soon be rotated into the front lines.

At the Tokchong railhead north of Seoul, where the 1st Battalion PPCLI troops transferred from rickety train cars to British Army Service Corps trucks, the incoming officer commanding "A" Company, Maj. Jeffery Williams, was met by Lt.-Col. Jim Stone and Lt.-Col. Norman Wilson-Smith (battalion commanders of the PPCLI) and Brig. John Rockingham (commander of the Canadian brigade). Rocky and Williams were old friends from Second World War days.

"You've got a good-looking lot of men," Rocky said.

Williams nodded in agreement.

"Nothing quite like well-trained regulars," Rocky added proudly.

"It wasn't the time to tell him," thought Williams, "that we had had no tactical training and that I hadn't a clue what my officers and NCOs were like in the field."

Unlike the 2nd Battalion troops who were volunteers in for an eighteen-month hitch, their 1st Battalion replacements were mostly career soldiers. As permanent force troops, Williams's soldiers had joined the army in a desire to serve their country in an honourable profession. They most certainly had wanted a taste of the adventurous life, in secure and interesting jobs, in some cases to uphold a family's military tradition and, of course, out of a sense of patriotism. Soldiering was their life's choice and "Korea was just another exercise, but with live ammunition."

Nevertheless, like their brother unit before them, the 1st Battalion Princess Patricias needed some orientation. Their officers went forward to reconnoitre the sharp end, while, behind the lines, the rank and file immediately began special courses in American weaponry and marches to offset the effects of the Pacific Ocean crossing. The training culminated in a two-day march, in mid-October, during which some troops collapsed in the heat or from drinking too much water to compensate. Others, who weren't used to climbing so many hills, injured their legs and feet. A final initiation awaited the newcomers when they were rotated into the line to the right of Hill 187 on October 14, 1951.

"When we got to the top of the hill," Bill Jackson remembered, "I could smell this terrible smell of death. It was in the wind from up the hill." Just beyond the crest of the new PPCLI position, Pte. Jackson and his platoon found the bodies of scores of Chinese soldiers, killed weeks earlier. He had seen dead people before, when some of the 16,000 German POWs he was guarding at Medicine Hat, Alberta, during the Second World War killed others in the camp, but "seeing a body that's been dead in the hot sun for six weeks was revolting." Before the platoon could bed down for the night, each man had to bury one of the dead Chinese soldiers. If that weren't initiation enough for Jackson, during his first nights on the hills of the Jamestown Line, he was constantly awakened by shelling duels between UN and Chinese gunners.

Pte. Jackson and the rest of "A" Company of the 1st Battalion PPCLI had only been in the front lines nine days when they were called upon to join a battalion-size raid across an open valley 2,000 metres wide in front of the Jamestown Line. Their objective was to capture the Chinese-held Hill 156, while a company of the 2nd Battalion RCR and one of R22eR were to probe the Chinese-held Hill 166. The raid was code-named Operation Pepperpot. It was designed to test the strength of the Chinese, destroy their defensive bunkers and direct artillery fire onto Chinese positions behind the objective.

At 3:30 in the morning, Maj. Williams and his "A" Company were up, and by 6 o'clock on their way through wire and mines laid by the 2nd Battalion. It was still dark when No. 3 Platoon, with Pte. Jackson as company runner, entered the valley. He was with his sergeant major, Paddy Lynch, when the sky suddenly lit up with what Jackson thought were fireflies.

"What's that?" Jackson called out.

Lynch turned to look.

"What're those goddamn lights coming?" Jackson asked.

"Tracer bullets, you asshole," shouted Lynch. "Get down!"

Minutes later, the New Zealand Field Regiment answered from the UN side of the valley with an artillery barrage to distract the Chinese machine-gunners from the company advance. With shells bursting on their objectives across the valley in front of them, the Canadian companies dashed through a wide-open no-man's-land. Within an hour, the RCR and R22eR were on the lower edges of Hill 166. By 8:30 the PPCLI were partway up Hill 156, but pinned down by Chinese machine-gun and mortar fire.

"We were running when the machine-guns came on us," Bill Jackson recalled. "That's when Jack Currie got hit. He got up and started running again, but fell and stayed there. He was shot through the heart."

When his No. 3 Platoon reached a knoll, Jackson stuck with Capt. J. E. W. Red Berthiaume, a Forward Observation Officer (FOO) who had been assigned to the PPCLI to direct Canadian artillery strikes during the operation. After a few minutes in the shelter of one position, Berthiaume said, "That's long enough, here," and he moved to a different spot. Jackson followed.

"Sure enough," Jackson said, "we'd no sooner get to the new hole and they'd drop a mortar right where we were." In the midst of the shelling, one of Jackson's friends from Saskatchewan, Pte. E. F. Bradshaw, was wounded and placed on a stretcher. He was bleeding badly from internal wounds, The next incoming mortar bomb exploded right on top of him.

From his command position, Maj. Williams couldn't see the Chinese machine-gun or mortar positions and called to his forward platoon commander, Capt. Gordon Gunton, "Give me an Oboe Tare," that is, an Observer to the Target reading, to guide tank fire from the rear using compass bearings.

"That's difficult," replied Gunton.

Williams realized that Gunton couldn't raise his head long enough to spot the Chinese gun position without being shot, so instead he guessed at a target location near the enemy bunkers and radioed it back to the Strathcona tanks behind the Canadian lines, hundreds of metres away. Seconds later the shell crashed into Hill 156.

"Damn good!" called Gunton over his wireless. "Go left one yard."

The Strathconas gunner received the correction via Williams on the radio and was told to "adjust his sight by breathing on it." The second shell was a direct hit on the Chinese bunker, so the tanks opened up with continuous fire as the two PPCLI platoons charged up the slope of Hill 156 to seize the position. Through the middle of the day, the sappers accompanying Maj. Williams set about clearing and destroying the Chinese defensive bunkers.

By early afternoon, with nearly all the objectives reached and dismantled, except the very top of Hill 166, the Canadians began to withdraw. Initially, the pull-back was unnoticed by the Chinese, but then UN gunners began shelling Hill 156 to set up a smokescreen to cover the Canadian withdrawal. This action drew the attention of remaining Chinese units in the area. Suddenly, the combined friendly and enemy fire was raining down all around the withdrawing Canadian troops.

"We heard these goddamn shells coming in on us," Jackson said. "We were hiding from our own shells. We didn't know what to do."

"I instructed my very gallant FOO, Berthiaume, to get that unprintable stuff off our necks," recalled Maj. Williams. "He sat down in the midst of the mixture of Chinese and Commonwealth artillery fire and lifted the concentration off us by wireless," and eventually, the Canadian infantrymen made it back through the valley to the Jamestown Line positions.

The Canadian advance across no-man's-land and successful demolition of Chinese forward positions during Operation Pepperpot that day had cost 5 RCR, 7 R22eR and 4 PPCLI casualties. The withdrawal, however, added 10 more casualties, including several soldiers who, racing back through UN defensive fortifications, stumbled into their own minefield. Nevertheless, the operation earned Maj. Jeffery Williams the American Bronze Star, and artillery observer Capt. Red Berthiaume the Military Cross. The action was also observed throughout the day by commanders of the 1st US Corps, the Commonwealth Division and the Canadian Infantry Brigade, and in Williams's words "had in effect been a sort of grandstand performance."

For Pte. Bill Jackson it was his first action in Korea. Immediately afterward, he felt light-headed and cocky about having survived. Weathering live fire and several brushes with death had given his system a shot of adrenaline. He felt invincible for at least the first few hours back at "A" Echelon behind the lines. However, the experience hadn't made him any the wiser, because after the battle, when he saw a soldier with a gaping neck wound lying on a stretcher, he wondered aloud, "How come he's not bleeding?"

"You dumb bastard," said a medic, "he's been dead four hours."

However dashing their advance to the top of Hill 156 and partway up Hill 166 had seemed to the UN commanders that day, no Canadian soldier ever again penetrated this far into North Korean or Chinese-held territory—except as a prisoner of war. The operation was also the last large-scale Canadian army raid against North Korean or Chinese forces. From this point on, Canadians took part in a holding action along the front. Even so, the defence of the Jamestown Line would prove even more costly than Kap'yong, Chail-li, Kakhul-bong and all the operations in Ch'orwon and north of the Imjin River during the summer and fall of 1951 put together.

"Everything that occurred in Korea after the fall of 1951," wrote one veteran, "was a waste of time and lives."

Two days after Operation Pepperpot, on October 25, 1951, negotiators from both the UN and Chinese sides renewed discussions for an armistice. The talks, begun on July 10, had broken off August 23 due to distrust among the negotiators and manoeuvring on the battlefield.

Meanwhile, the release of new and shocking casualty figures as a result of United Nations offensives north of the Imjin River reached North America. American army statistics indicated that while the August, September and October 1951 operations had inflicted severe punishment on the communists (more than 200,000 casualties), they had also come at a cost to UN Command (60,000 casualties). In the United States, the so-called "yo-yo" war—the back-and-forth fighting for seemingly inconsequential ridges—had finally and conclusively turned most Americans against a desire to win the Korean War. American casualties since 1950 were approaching 100,000 killed or wounded. A poll taken in October showed that only 33 percent of Americans disagreed that Korea "was an utterly useless war." Interestingly, magazine and newspaper reports often included such phrases as "let's get the boys back home" and "war-weary troops."

Whether a coincidence or a reaction to news of the war, in Canada the flow of volunteers to the armed forces had slowed to a trickle. Unlike the weeks and months immediately following Canada's recruitment of the Special Force in August 1950, by the end of 1951 the 25th Canadian Infantry Brigade was understrength nearly 400 soldiers. The military reported a disappointingly low number of infantry being enrolled. For example, French-speaking recruits were not coming forward in sufficient numbers to enable the Royal 22e Régiment to keep up to strength.

When both sides in Korea agreed to reconvene peace talks, October 25, it was not at Kaesong. Instead, the talks would move ten kilometres east to the shattered village of Panmunjom. Amid what was left of civilian mud shacks, military tents, with flooring, heating and lighting, were set up for conferees, their staffs and correspondents.

Nearby, a mess, communications, security and engineer facilities were hastily erected. Finally, negotiators set up a massive searchlight to demarcate and protect the location from hostilities. Its vertical and stationary beam could be seen all along the front.

Nam Il, the chief of staff of the Korean People's Army, and C. Turner Joy, commander of US Navy forces in the Far East, and their delegations began to talk again about the conclusion of an armistice and determination of a military demarcation line between the UN and communist forces. The ceasefire line or a demilitarized zone between opposing armies remained to be determined. No one, least of all the soldiers in the front lines, knew where that might be, nor when a diplomatic breakthrough might come.

The commander of a mortar platoon in the 2nd Battalion of the Royal 22e Régiment summed up the fears of most front-line troops: "I cannot avoid a tightening of the heart," Capt. Charly Forbes wrote, "at the thought that this night I could be killed and that tomorrow the war would end with a sudden armistice." The thirty-year-old officer, who had fought with Le Régiment de Maisonneuve in the 2nd Canadian Infantry Division during the Second World War, rejoined the army for Korea, but now thought of his wife and son "Pierre, who might grow up never knowing his father. How do we reconcile duty and sacrifice, family and country, life and death at a time like this?"

Beginning on Wednesday, November 21, there was little time for Forbes or any other member of the 2nd Battalion R22eR to consider such questions. Not even the sumptuous Thanksgiving feast the cooks at "A" Echelon served could be savoured. At a briefing with his commanding officer, Lt.-Col. J. A. Dextraze, Capt. Forbes learned that his mortar platoon's new position would be a vulnerable one. He was told to pack all his reserve ammunition and to dig in just back of the crest of Hill 210. There his platoon was to defend all four companies of his R22eR against an expected Chinese attack on the western slope of Hill 355, "Little Gibraltar," currently occupied by the 2nd Battalion of the US 7th Infantry Regiment.

Lt.-Col. Dextraze positioned the four companies of the R22eR like a fist and pointing finger, Companies "B" and "C" making up the fist across Hill 210, "A" Company just ahead in reserve position, and "D" Company at the tip of the finger pointing out into no-man's-land, with the Americans to the right and the Chinese to the left and straight ahead. "Jadex," as he was known, delivered simple and direct orders for the coming engagement: "No withdrawal. No platoons overrun. No panic."

At 0400 hours, in the darkness of Thursday morning, November 22, the rifle platoons of "D" Company moved forward to a saddle, or ridge, of land between the Americans on Hill 355 (to the right) and the Chinese on Hill 227 (to the left). Rhéal Liboiron, the commander of Dog Company, found that the saddle of land was smaller than anticipated. "D" Company's three forward platoons—No. 11, 12 and 10—dug in left to right across the front of the saddle, each platoon in a space that would normally house a section of men. There was no time to dig deep positions in the mud, so the R22eR gun positions took shape as sandbag castles or "hotdog stands," making them vulnerable to the Chinese artillery.

At the same time, Capt. Forbes's platoon was digging six mortar positions on Hill 210 at the rear of the battalion position. In the darkness, each crew of five men excavated a pit seven feet in diameter and one foot deep. Aiming posts and base plates were installed, while empty ammunition boxes were filled with earth and built into a parapet around each mortar position. Then more holes were dug to house the mortar bombs and to protect each of the mortar teams.

The weather was foggy and damp, and the ground was freezing. The air remained calm until mid-afternoon when Chinese rockets and artillery shells began slamming into American positions on Hill 355. Gradually, the sustained shellfire crept down Little Gibraltar toward the R22eR positions. Few noticed, but afternoon rain turned to snow overnight and by mid-morning of November 23, most positions were slushy quagmires.

The Chinese bombardment was intermittent that morning, but by early afternoon the shellfire intensified. The first Chinese assault came at 1500 hours, when Capt. Forbes and his mortar platoon were

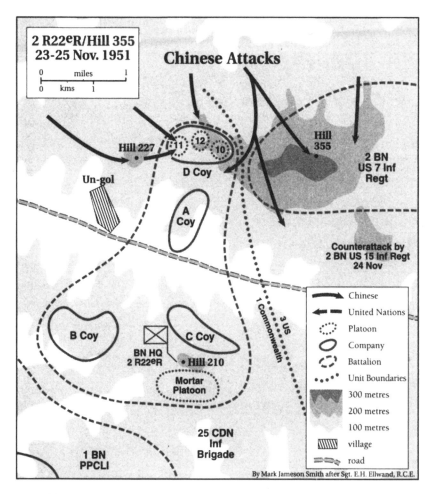

jolted by a sudden, deafening barrage of Chinese shells exploding to their right up Hill 355. The ground shook. The sky filled with the black spots of shell bursts that began falling on "D" Company up in front. Forbes pulled his headset to his ears.

"Target! Target! Target!" shouted Sgt. Walter Zaluski, the forward mortar controller with No. 12 Platoon of "D" Company at the front line. "Grid reference 190 375. Scale Twenty. Fire!"

Forbes computed the order. Twenty mortar bombs a minute from each mortar position. He asked Zaluski for verification.

"Three Chinese columns, coming in our direction from the hills in front of our position," roared Zaluski. "Fire!"

Forbes passed coordinates and the order to fire to his crews. In seconds, they began launching mortar bombs.

"Hello, Niner Niner Delta," Forbes called back to Zaluski. "Bombs away." He waited the sixty seconds it took for the first mortars to explode in front of "D" Company's position.

"Good show," called Zaluski on the phones. "On target. Right in the middle. Repeat."

The order was given. Then Capt. Forbes began calculating. At this rate—six teams firing twenty bombs a minute—his 4,000 mortar bombs would quickly disappear. Fortunately, Jadex had anticipated the problem and troops were already moving the entire ammunition reserve forward to the mortar platoon position.

The Chinese force of approximately two companies' strength was merely probing the Canadian lines. Its real objective was the American position to the east of the R22eR lines up the heights of Hill 355. First reports from the top of Little Gibraltar indicated that the Chinese were attacking in battalion strength. Within an hour, two companies of the US 7th Infantry Regiment were forced to contract their defences while a third had been overrun.

At 1730 hours an unidentified voice was heard on the wireless at the R22eR battalion headquarters: "Collapse! This is collapse. Over."

In the fading light of the late afternoon, Maj. J.A.A.G. Vallée from the Vandoos' "A" Company position reported American soldiers approaching his sector below Hill 355.

"Collapse," repeated the voice. "This is collapse. Over."

"Collapse, sit down, stand up. Do what you want," shouted Dextraze into his microphone, "but for God's sake, get off my battalion net!" His fury hid his real fear. The US 7th Infantry Regiment was bugging out. "You realize what this means," he said to his mortar platoon commander, Capt. Forbes, on the radio.

"I do."

The Chinese had retaken the highest ground in the sector, Hill 355. Its permanent loss meant loss of control of roads running through the American sector. Its vantage point—commanding the highest ground for kilometres in every direction—could make the PPCLI and R22eR positions untenable. Already, with Hill 227 to the west, and now Hill 355 to the east, in enemy hands, the Vandoos' position on the saddle was open to encirclement. Lt.-Col. Dextraze had two choices: Retreat to safety as the Americans were doing, but jeopardize all the gains made north of the Imjin River in the previous three months. Or hold firm.

Dextraze addressed the entire Royal 22e battalion on wireless radio. "We're being attacked by a major Chinese force. We will hold our positions. We will fight to the end."

Dog Company's three forward platoons—No. 11, 12 and 10—took the brunt of a Chinese bombardment. Shells from tanks, self-propelled guns, artillery pieces and mortars began falling on the "D" Company positions at a rate of 300 every two minutes, 9,000 an hour, "the worst," recalls Maj. Rhéal Liboiron, "since the Hochwald Forest," where German artillery fired relentlessly on Canadian soldiers during the Second World War.

For a twenty-six-year-old sergeant from Quebec, Denis LaPierre of No. 10 Platoon, it was "the first time ever going through anything like this. . . You get afraid, but you talk it off. You talk, you joke if you can and you say your prayers."

In the short lulls between rounds from Chinese guns, the three forward platoons of "D" Company awaited the first Chinese infantry attack. Out in the darkness in front of No. 12 Platoon, Cpl. Guariepy heard strange rustling noises; he realized it was the rubbing of trouser legs of Chinese soldiers just beyond the defensive barbed wire. Moments later, the first wave of Chinese infantry crept through the wire and attacked with grenades and burp-guns. The second wave, carrying bayonet-ended sticks, used carpets like stiles to cross the barbed wire. The third wave, armed with the weapons of those who had fallen ahead of them, charged headlong toward the Canadian trenches.

Sgt. LaPierre told his section of riflemen to hold their fire to conceal their positions in the dark. So, instead of gunfire, the R22eR platoon answered each wave of Chinese with a shower of grenades. Just below the parapet, Pte. J. L. Bougie and Cheh Sang Sup, a Korean Service Corps worker, primed each grenade by pulling the safety pins.

The sergeant cupped his hands and rhythmically took each grenade, tossing it like an egg over the parapet at the advancing Chinese. Along the trench the rest of the platoon did the same.

In the course of the battle, No. 10 Platoon threw forty cases of grenades to repulse the waves of attacking infantry. Word of the rate of fire got back to "D" Company headquarters. Lt. Wally Nash's No. 10 Platoon needed a re-supply. Without hesitation, Pte. Ernest Asselin volunteered to bring forward fresh Bren magazines, oil, rifle flannel, water and two cases of grenades. He carried double the normal load—175 pounds—saying, "I might not make it a second time." It took him four hours, through shellfire and mud, to reach No. 10. He stayed the night, manned a Bren gun and in the morning carried down the body of a fallen Vandoos soldier.

Throughout the night, the riflemen of Lt. Ray MacDuff's No. 11 Platoon on the western side of the "D" Company position faced probing attacks from Chinese infantry. Mortar flares in the dark sky revealed that a larger communist force was assembling off to the west atop Hill 227, apparently to mount an assault on the R22eR's forward positions. Before long, the Vandoos were facing Chinese infantry from the west, the north and the east. Intelligence officer Tom Webb looked at the battalion's status on the operations map back at battalion headquarters and referred to the Vandoos' position sticking out into no-man's-land as "the irremovable digit."

By dawn on Saturday morning, November 24, the battle zone had fallen silent. That morning, a cavalcade of jeeps arrived at Lt.-Col. Dextraze's observation post on Hill 210: the pennant on one of the jeeps was that of Maj.-Gen. A. J. H. Cassels, commander of the Commonwealth Division; another identified Brig. Rockingham; and finally, with his American entourage in tow, came corps commander Lt.-Gen. J. W. "Iron Mike" O'Daniel. There was very little chit-chat. The meeting lasted just fifteen minutes, but at its climax O'Daniel spoke to his infantry commander in the field:

"Bill, where were your men yesterday?"

"On top of the Hill [355], sir," answered the American officer.

"Well, by 1400 hours this afternoon," the general said, "you're going to roll back up there with a punch!"

In the worst of weather—rain, low cloud and freezing temperatures—American artillery, eight-inch guns nicknamed "the Persuaders," began shelling Little Gibraltar in preparation for a counterattack against the Chinese by the US 7th Infantry Regiment. The Vandoos knew very few details of the battle for Hill 355, but for Forbes, "judging by the number of helicopters coming and going, the losses must have been frightening. I was told there were more than a thousand dead and wounded."

The fierce battle atop Hill 355 spread to the saddle of land occupied by the three forward platoons of the R22eR. Chinese artillery again concentrated their fire on "D" Company positions, pulverizing even the most secure of the Vandoos' defensive dugouts. No. 11 Platoon, commanded by Lt. Ray MacDuff, on the western edge of the company position, took the worst pounding from the shelling. At No. 10 Platoon, on the right flank, a direct hit on Cpl. Earl Istead's Bren-gun firing pit buried him in mud temporarily, but he emerged with himself and the Bren intact and took a new position. In the same area, Cpl. Joe Harvey realized that the shellfire could bring down all the defensive structures and smother his platoon mates, so he scaled several old parapets with a pick and hacked them down.

By six o'clock in the evening, a Chinese infantry attack had begun. First came the charge call of Chinese buglers. From his position in a trench with "A" Company, L/Cpl. Leo Gallant heard "those goddamned bugles . . . and with every note, the hair on my arm stands on end." The Chinese troops were so close to the "D" Company area that MacDuff said, "We can look right down their throats." Some 300 Chinese troops swept up toward the Vandoos' trenches in their characteristic three waves—"like buffaloes over a bridge, there is no stopping them." Despite the returning fire of Commonwealth tanks and mortars, the attack surrounded No. 11 Platoon so quickly that the Chinese broke through the wire and overran the position. Transmissions suddenly ceased from MacDuff's platoon.

At the "D" Company command post where Maj. Liboiron awaited word from his No. 11 Platoon, a private burst into his tent.

"We're finished! Our platoon is overrun."

Liboiron grabbed the private and shook him: "Tell me one thing. Have they come through the barbed wire?"

"Like animals," wept the soldier.

Realizing that MacDuff's No. 11 Platoon had abandoned its forward trenches, Liboiron picked up his radio microphone and called the tank commander. "Fire everything you've got on MacDuff's position."

Ninety seconds later, the first tank shell was airborne. As the rest of the troop joined in, the barrage from the Lord Strathconas proved devastating. It broke the Chinese attack momentarily, allowing MacDuff enough time to join Lt. Mario Côté and No. 12 Platoon at the centre of the Vandoos' forward area. Together they consolidated the position. The intensity of the shelling at MacDuff's position surprised the Chinese troops. Perhaps fearing a larger counterattack or encirclement, the Chinese field commander pulled back.

By midnight, a scout and sniper platoon, led by Cpl. Léo Major, had come forward with orders to retake MacDuff's trenches on the left flank of the Vandoos' position. With Major's unit of fifteen Korean troops advancing just behind a curtain of bombs laid down by Capt. Forbes's mortar platoon, the position was regained by 1 a.m. and Cpl. Major called back to Jadex with the code word "Buick," to indicate mission accomplished.

Minutes later, Major reported to Jadex. "We're being attacked by infantry."

"Come back with your men," radioed Jadex.

"I'm not pulling out. Engage with mortars."

"I'll have artillery brought down in a few minutes," promised the colonel.

Cpl. Major directed Capt. Forbes's mortars, and together they repulsed four new Chinese attacks. The mortar bombs were falling so continuously and so close to Major's position that Forbes could hear them exploding when Major came on the radio phone. Some

3,000 rounds of 81-mm mortar ammunition were fired that night, until a mortar platoon sergeant told Forbes that the mortar barrels were glowing red hot. In fact, the barrels had become transparent; Forbes could see each mortar bomb as it was dropped into the barrel. Fearing a bomb might explode in a barrel before launch, he ordered a ceasefire. His mortars were done.

By 2:30 Sunday morning, November 25, the worst was over. The Vandoos remained on the saddle position between Hill 355 and Hill 227. Their positions had been reduced to rubble—not a single bunker at No. 11 Platoon's position was intact—but the three original platoons of "D" Company held firm. In four days and four nights of fighting, the R22eR suffered 54 casualties—16 killed, 36 wounded and 2 taken prisoner. But their resolve to hold the position turned the tide atop Hill 355. The Americans had recaptured Little Gibraltar.

On Monday, November 26, at daybreak, the Jamestown Line was quiet. The Chinese, as in previous battles, had retrieved their dead and wounded, so the battlefield appeared clean, except for the telltale splotches of blood on the snow (although estimates put the number of Chinese dead at 1,500). What remained of "D" Company handed over its positions to incoming "B" Company. The Vandoos survivors were muddy, bearded and exhausted. They'd gone without food, water and sleep for the duration of the battle.

"We were there to fight," Sgt. Denis LaPierre reported to Bill Boss of Canadian Press, "and if need be to die. And we did."

What LaPierre and the rest of the Royal 22e Régiment had experienced at the base of Hill 355 was the sharpest of the sharp end.

The same morning, November 26, an officer from the American ordnance corps brought up new equipment for Charly Forbes's mortar platoon. According to the rules, however, he was supposed to take out the old mortars.

"Can I keep the original mortar base plates?" asked Forbes, handing the American soldier a cup of rum.

The ordnance man scratched his head as he surveyed the scene of burned-out mortar barrels and mountains of empty ammunition boxes.

"We fired more than 15,000 bombs in four days," Forbes said, to emphasize his attachment to the base plates.

"You can keep them all," the American marvelled. "You guys are fantastic. In my entire career, I've never heard of anyone burning out 81-mm mortars."

Fantastic? Yes, according to the veteran mortar platoon commander. But more than that, Capt. Charly Forbes insisted that the Royal 22e Régiment—like the Princess Patricias at Kap'yong—deserved a Presidential Citation for standing firm against the Chinese. They had fulfilled their colonel's orders of "No withdrawal. No platoons overrun. No panic." They had also kept a toehold on Hill 355 until the Americans could regain the heights. The regimental recognition never came. Nevertheless, a Military Medal was awarded Pte. Ernest Asselin for re-supplying No. 10 Platoon. For his initiative with No. 10 Platoon, Cpl. Joe Harvey was decorated with a Distinguished Conduct Medal. Cpl. Léo Major earned a bar to his Distinguished Conduct Medal for regaining and holding the No. 11 Platoon position. For the overall action, a Distinguished Service Order went to Maj. Rhéal Liboiron.

Two days after the Vandoos' heroic defence of Hill 355 along the Jamestown Line, delegates to the peace talks gathered at Panmunjom, in communist-held territory. René Lévesque, later premier of Quebec but then serving as a CBC radio correspondent, recalled the "deathly silence" that greeted the press in the fortified area, surrounded by barbed wire and stone-faced Chinese troops.

However, on November 27, 1951, Wilfred Burchett, a former journalist and communist, installed in Peking as the "white voice" of the Mao regime, emerged to inform the media that the two sides had agreed on the line of contact, or a demarcation line that would become a potential truce line. Should the negotiators fail to settle the other terms of an armistice, the agreement on the demarcation line would expire on December 27. And so, with the final line in the Korean War more or less decided, senior delegates turned to the next two major items on the agenda: provisions for enforcing the armistice and the exchange of POWs.

AN UNHOLY MESS

W HILE NEGOTIATORS at Panmunjom waged a war of words through November and December 1951—scoring and yielding propaganda points at the peace talks—the troops at the front adapted to a war of entrenchment and information gathering. Besides digging deeper bunkers, putting up strands on strands of barbed wire and laying more powerful mines, UN Command began sending out regular patrols to capture prisoners in order to find out what the other side was up to.

On a night early in January 1952, a Royal Canadian Regiment patrol headed out into the valley of the Sami-ch'on. Only 2,000 metres wide, this narrow valley was currently the no-man's-land between Chinese Communist Forces to the west and UN positions to the east. It was also the territory where Maj. Bill Hill and his snatch patrols conducted a bizarre form of bingo.

This night, Sgt. C. H. Cole had split his patrol. He had taken half the platoon forward with him and left the other half behind to establish a firm base, or back-up position, under Cpl. Sam Harbinson. The patrol had just begun, when Cole spotted a couple of thatched houses ahead and decided to investigate. In the dimly lit interior of one, Cole spied six men; there were five in the other. He dispatched Pte. T. W. Stack to retrieve Harbinson's half of the platoon to assist in a search of the huts.

Stack had barely turned for the firm base when a Chinese soldier jumped up in front of him, blocking his path. Cole immediately fired a shot. It felled the Chinese soldier and temporarily confused what Cole realized was a Chinese ambush. He radioed his commander, Maj. Hill, and called for artillery fire down on the thatched huts. Within seconds, shells were landing on their targets, scattering the Chinese.

"We're still playing bingo, right?" Hill asked over the radio.

"Right," Sgt. Cole said. And that was the last communication for some minutes as the platoon commander regrouped his men and organized an assault on the huts. As he approached one of the burning huts, Cole heard moaning. Inside was a Chinese soldier, wounded but conscious.

"Bingo!" radioed Cole to his commander.

"Fine," Maj. Hill said. "Bring the card back and we'll check it."

Sgt. Cole was soon winding his way back through RCR defences at the "D" Company position. His platoon was unscathed. His Chinese prisoner received first-aid dressings for his wounds. He would live. The winning "card" had been delivered and checked. Sgt. Cole's platoon had won that night's POW bingo match.

As primitive and macabre as this game seems, it was one way Canadian intelligence units gathered information about Chinese troop movements and attacks. As with any intelligence there was plenty of chaff among the kernels of truth in the information that Chinese POWs provided. One report told of Chinese soldiers attacking while under the influence of opium. Another claimed that unarmed women regularly joined attacks as an inspiration to rank-and-file soldiers. One story, gleaned from a prisoner interrogation, indicated that the Chinese army included a "monkey division," a special unit of animal handlers that trained apes to fire pistols and throw hand grenades. Few of these reports could be substantiated. All had to be recorded in intelligence summaries.

Though patrols were plentiful during this new phase of the war, successful captures were not. Only seven prisoners were taken by Commonwealth troops between the time of the agreement of the demarcation line, on November 27, 1951, and mid-February 1952.

This situation was likely due to the changing nature of the war, but it may also have been due to a general fear among Chinese troops that, if captured, a soldier was cruelly treated by his United Nations captors.

That fear was vividly recorded by then-*Maclean's Magazine* war correspondent Pierre Berton. Sent to Korea aboard an RCAF North Star aircraft from No. 426 Transport Squadron, in the spring of 1951, Berton shot photographs, drew sketches and prepared numerous background pieces on Canadian servicemen and the war itself. Among his story objectives was to put a face to the enemy Canadian soldiers were fighting. By the summer of 1951, Berton had written a piece chronicling the lives of three Chinese soldiers—a former Nationalist soldier, a former communist officer and a young recruit. That last, a communal farmer named Wu who was conscripted into the Chinese army, eventually found himself in a trench covered with logs and earth. He was ordered to defend his position to the death, because, he was told, "if Chinese were captured . . . their fingers and noses, ears and feet would be hacked off." In Berton's magazine story, Wu was not captured, but killed in an American counterattack near Suwon.

Had Wu been captured, he would not have lost his appendages, but would most certainly have been transported to the island of Koje, a rocky outcropping in the sea a few kilometres off the south coast of Korea near Pusan. Here, under American army supervision, prisoners-of-war had constructed four barbed-wire enclosures, each subdivided into eight compounds. Each compound was designed to hold 1,200 men, but by the spring of 1951 each was jammed with five times that many. By the end of the year, Koje-do ("do" meaning "island") housed over 130,000 Koreans and 20,000 Chinese POWs. Congestion at the island camp might have gone unnoticed except that early in 1952, while negotiations at Panmunjom addressed the repatriation of prisoners, Koje-do suddenly stepped into the limelight for all the wrong reasons.

At the peace talks, UN delegates first proposed an early, "fair and equitable" exchange of POWs, the sick and wounded to be swapped first. Communist delegates cited Article 118 of the Geneva Convention and demanded an all-for-all swap without delay. Then the UN

side asked for an exchange of POW lists. When they were produced, both sides cried foul, claiming that names had been withheld.
Finally, when the UN team introduced its real position—voluntary
repatriation—a screening of UN POWs began at Koje-do. Partway through the polling process, in April 1952, the UN was pro-
jecting that of the 150,000 POWs it held, only 70,000 would elect
to return to China or North Korea. The information appeared to
be a propaganda coup for the UN. It looked as if the communists
had lost face. Ultimately, on April 28, they walked out of the talks at
Panmunjom.

Meanwhile, the communist side had set in motion a propaganda
campaign of its own. Early in the year, communist agents allowed
themselves to be captured as POWs. The agents were sent to Koje-
do, where they were "instructed to organize the hard-core communist
POWs to foment riots and other disturbances inside the UN POW
compounds . . . for the purpose of incurring UN punitive counter-
measures which the communists could then exploit." According to
plan, riots occurred on February 18 and March 13, 1952, during which
American guards fired into the ranks of the POWs, killing 89 and
wounding 166. The communists then denounced the actions world-
wide as "barbarous massacres" and "atrocities."

Matters worsened. Even though American authorities had screened
out some 38,000 prisoners as South Koreans and released them as civilians, the riots at Koje-do intensified. The prison leaders demanded
more humane treatment and better food and clothing. Word filtered
out of the compounds that communist organizers inside were running kangaroo courts to punish prisoners who tried to take advantage
of the screening to get out.

"Pro and anti-communist factions are killing each other," recounted one member of the former Student Volunteers Army from
North Korea. An anti-communist, Young Sik Kim worked as an
interpreter at Koje-do and kept a diary of the atrocities on both sides.
"American GI's cuss, kick and mistreat the POWs," he wrote. "It is
painful to watch fellow Koreans treated like animals. But we are
treated no better than the POWs.

"[When] agents are inserted into POW compounds . . . some 6,000 POWs die in the camps. Many die in the most cruel ways imaginable—sharp stakes [through the body,] beaten to death, suffocated to death, hanged. Bodies are buried under the tents."

Mindful that an armistice might be in the offing, the commander of the Koje-do camp, U.S. Army Brig.-Gen. Francis Dodd, tried to appease the leaders inside the compounds. Locks were removed from outer compound gates. Only guards carried guns and security personnel were instructed never to shoot except in an emergency or self-defence. Dodd often met with POW spokesmen and entered the main enclosure—Compound 76—unarmed. When he did so on the afternoon of May 7, the inmates surrounded and grabbed the general, rushed him to a tent that had been prepared for him and informed Dodd he was to be tried.

The kidnapping lasted three and a half days, during which the camp commander was forced to endorse a list of demands and sign a statement agreeing to cease immediately the "barbarous behaviour, insults, torture . . . [and] mass murdering" of POWs by UN guns, germs, poison gas and atomic weapons, and to halt the screening of POWs for the purpose of complying with the UN's "illegal and unreasonable" voluntary repatriation program. Even the new I Corps chief of staff, Brig.-Gen. Charles Colson, sent to Koje-do to free Dodd, decided against using force and signed a document conceding "that there have been instances of bloodshed where many PW have been killed and wounded by UN forces." The statement went on to "assure in the future that PW can expect human treatment according to the principles of International Law." Dodd was released. And the prisoners rejoiced at their stunning victory.

Three days later, US general Mark Clark assumed Far East Command from Lt.-Gen. Ridgway and appointed Brig.-Gen. Haydon "Bull" Boatner to quell the uprising at Koje-do, break the conspiracy inside the compounds and clean up "what any reasonable soldier would call an unholy mess." But the propaganda damage was done. Throughout the communist world, headlines proclaimed Dodd's confession. Pictures of the rioting, death and the signs of protest the

POWs had posted outside Compound 76 appeared in *Stars and Stripes*, the American army newspaper. They were followed in the same paper by a two-page spread of pictures supplied by the communists showing smiling UN Command prisoners playing games and relaxing, thus proving to the world how humanely the communists were treating *their* prisoners.

During the third week of May 1952, an officer in the 1st Battalion of the Royal Canadian Regiment was just getting his feet wet as a platoon commander in Korea when things changed dramatically. Capt. Herb Cloutier should have expected it; it seemed to be the story of his military career. When he tried to get overseas to Europe during the Second World War, they made him an instructor for officer training. When he volunteered for service in the Pacific, his unit had just set sail from Seattle when the atomic bombs were dropped on Japan. And when he hoped to get to Korea, instead he helped train the Special Force. This time, after about a month at the front lines in Korea—honing his skills as a patrol platoon commander in no-man's-land—he was called before his commanding officer, Lt.-Col. P. R. Bingham.

"Herb," the colonel began, "I've got a job for you."

Cloutier nodded.

"I can't tell you where you're going, but you're going to leave the battalion for a while. I want you to just take enough to put in your big pack. Good luck. And keep your feet and knees together."

"Geez, I'm going on a parachute mission," Cloutier thought. Later that night, in the darkness at Fort George Airfield, about fifteen kilometres south of the front, Cloutier and a British soldier named Hudson, with the King's Shropshire Light Infantry (KSLI), were hustled onto a transport aircraft; Hudson had no idea where they were headed either. Inside the DC-3, Cloutier's imagination went wild. He looked around for parachutes. He thought for a moment that he was headed north over North Korea for a jump beyond the Yalu River into China. When the Dakota landed at Pusan, Cloutier got even less information from the Americans (he later found out they were CIA) who met him and Hudson. Nor were any details of their destination revealed when he boarded a freighter headed out of Pusan harbour. It wasn't until morning, when the boat pulled into a port, that he found out.

"What's your name?" asked one of the Americans on shore.

"Cloutier."

"Rank?"

"Captain," Cloutier said. "Canadian army."

"Come with us," the Americans said.

"But where are we?"

"What the hell do you mean, where are you? You're on Koje."

Cloutier didn't want his ignorance of the place to show. He kept his mouth shut and took in the activity around him. At his first breakfast in a big US Army mess hall on the island, Cloutier saw all the Americans eating with their weapons on their laps or in open holsters. Then, en route to Gen. Boatner's quarters, he saw the compounds. Prisoners were packed into every corner. The anti-American signs, posted during Dodd's kidnapping, were still hanging everywhere inside the barbed wire. It wasn't until Capt. Cloutier actually met Gen. Boatner, however, that he learned he and Hudson were the advance party for a company of RCR and KSLI troops that would assist in the complete overhaul of the prison camp on Koje-do.

Gen. Boatner explained to Capt. Cloutier how he intended to resolve the Koje-do problem. He planned a three-step transformation of the camp: first, to control overcrowded POW compounds; second, to demolish inadequate existing compounds; and third, to move rebellious prisoners into new and smaller compounds, each holding no more than five hundred. His guiding rule for dealing with POWs was simple: "Prisoners do not negotiate!"

To demonstrate his tough stance, Boatner first had pillboxes built, armed and manned around the clock. He had guard towers at the corners of compounds moved back to give gunners a wider range of fire. He ordered the removal of all communist flags and offensive signs and the destruction of communist statues inside the compounds. Then Boatner put on a show of firepower. He rolled in trucks carrying quadruple .50-calibre machine guns to locations just outside the compounds, and he positioned twenty-two Patton tanks in full view of the camp inmates.

With equal precision, Boatner gave Capt. Cloutier whatever he needed in preparation for the RCR's role in phase three of Operation Breakup. When Cloutier found a location for the RCR campsite on a mountainside, Boatner had a unit of US Army engineers bulldoze the hillside flat for tents and an entire parade square. When the captain requested rations, the Americans delivered them in huge garbage pails, complete with heaters. When he went in search of replacement clothing and boots for his 150-man "B" Company, Cloutier found an American quartermaster who supplied 150 pairs of pants, sets of underwear and boots of various sizes. He even gave Cloutier a couple of two-and-a-half-ton trucks to haul the gear to his new campsite. The only hitch were the squad tents the Americans provided. They were ratty, ripped and looked bug-infested.

"I'm not putting a Canadian inside those," Cloutier told the quartermaster.

"It's all we've got on the island," the American said.

"We'll sleep out under ponchos before we sleep in those," Cloutier said. "The sight of them is sickening."

The quartermaster rang up the general and said, "We've got a Canadian here. He wants twenty squad tents."

"You give him twenty squad tents," the general's voice came booming back.

"We don't have them," explained the quartermaster.

"I didn't ask you whether you had them," stormed Gen. Boatner. "Get him the goddamn tents!"

The beleaguered quartermaster went all the way to Pusan to find Capt. Cloutier his squad tents. They arrived and were erected the night before Maj. E. L. Cohen and the 150 men of "B" Company (code-named Peterforce) arrived on Koje-do. The morning after the RCR arrived—Monday, May 25—they paraded to hear an address by Gen. Boatner. He drove up in his jeep, gathered the RCR soldiers in a big circle around him, stood up with his hands resting on a pair of pearl-handled pistols and said, "I'm Bull Boatner . . . I'm glad to have you Canadians on board here. I know you'll do a good job."

Then, according to RCR Cpl. Tom McKay, "He told us what he expected from us:

"'If you see somebody escaping and you're going to shoot, then make goddamned sure you kill him, because the hospital's full right now.'"

Further illustrating the limited control he had over the prison and the confused political state of the camp compounds, Boatner added, "'You would also be wise not to shoot the guy who is almost over the fence. Shoot the one who's trying to stop him. The first one may want to come over to our side.'"

It quickly became clear why this man's nickname was "Bull." The American camp commander drove his troops as hard as his quartermaster. When he laid out the dimensions and features of the new camp, he gave his engineers just days to build it. Each morning he was up at 5 o'clock, expecting to see that they were hard at work outside his quarters. It was rumoured that two of his engineers committed suicide while on Koje-do and that he sent one American commanding officer off the island for inefficiency. He used the Canadian campsite as a model for the rest of his units to live up to. When the RCR site was nearly complete, Capt. Cloutier commandeered some bags of slack lime and whitewashed everything in the camp— every rock, every pole. When Boatner saw this, he told his officers, "I want you to drive by the Canadian camp and if yours doesn't look as good as theirs tomorrow morning, you can get off this island!"

The fact remained, however, that the prisoners were still masters of their compounds. By day, they gathered "one hundred across and sixty deep" in view of their UN guards to march, exercise and sing patriotic songs. Each evening, they listened to political speeches and staged concert parties that lasted until midnight. In Compound 76, which housed most of the communist leaders, the trials and executions of purported anti-communists and traitors continued—fifteen bodies were found dumped at the compound gates in early June. Meanwhile, at Compound 66, the one the Canadians would soon be responsible for, the RCR troops began to realize just how powerful their opposition was. The inmates had fashioned stout clubs studded with metal. There were even rumours of Molotov cocktails made from kitchen-stove fuel. The POWs still controlled life inside the wire.

That changed on Tuesday, June 10, exactly a month after Gen. Dodd's release.

At 5:15 that morning, the loudspeakers outside Compound 76 began broadcasting orders for the prisoners to assemble—one hundred at a time—so they could be moved to the newly built compound sites. Nobody would be harmed if he cooperated. But nothing happened. Gen. Boatner commanded proceedings from a nearby hillside. In true Boatner style, the operation had been planned and rehearsed down to the last detail.

A flare exploded in the sky above the compound, which signalled both the US 187th Airborne with bayonet-tipped rifles and five Patton tanks to move forward. Tear-gas grenades were fired into the compound and the tanks battered down the posts and barbed wire to move into position. Paratroopers wearing gas masks and infantrymen holding flame-throwers followed each tank into position. The Americans were instructed not to fire first.

The prisoners began chanting in anger. They were armed with knives, sharpened poles and flails. As the Americans advanced, they were met by a volley of rocks and spears. Only the flame-throwers answered by setting the buildings afire.

"Then everything broke loose," Cloutier said. He had accompanied the 187th Airborne company commander into the compound, because he and the RCR would soon have to clear out Compound 66. Cloutier watched in horror as some prisoners who threw their hands up in surrender "were being killed by other prisoners. Where they got their weapons, nobody knew. But they fired first."

In one corner of the compound, about a thousand prisoners began pelting the paratroopers with concussion grenades and tear-gas bombs. The Americans converged on the group without firing a shot. When the prisoners attacked, the paratroopers repulsed them, using bayonets and rifle butts, "but as soon as a couple of American soldiers dropped," Cloutier said, "they just opened fire and anybody who even showed a sign of shooting anything, was taken care of." The arrival of an additional dozen tanks ended the mêlée abruptly. Thirty-one prisoners had died and 111 had been wounded. One American soldier had been killed and 14 wounded. Operation Breakup ended all resistance in the camp. It also pre-empted a mass prisoner breakout that had been planned for June 20. The 6,500 prisoners of troublesome Compound 76 were transferred without further incident to their new smaller compounds, separating communists from anti-communists. The worst, however, was not over.

The press and diplomatic corps had a field day with Koje. The communist dailies deplored Boatner's tactics as proof that the Americans treated prisoners inhumanely. Even the Canadian ambassador in Washington, Hume Wrong, berated the Americans and charged that a few decent troops and officers could have righted the mess in short order. Still, the greater problem for Canadian authorities was the use of Canadian troops as prison guards on Koje-do in the first place. It seemed natural to the Americans that guards at Koje-do "be UN commitment rather than purely American." And while they recognized the American order was perfectly legal, upper levels of the Canadian military staff didn't particularly like being associated with such an inefficiently run POW operation. What was worse, Canadian politicians, in particular the Louis St. Laurent Liberals, viewed the action as having an unfortunate effect on public opinion. The Canadian government seemed most upset about not being consulted first. However, the strongest diplomatic wording Canada's external affairs minister, Lester Pearson, used in a memo to the US State Department was Canada's "misgivings" over the decision.

Whether legitimate grievance or a tempest in a teapot, the concerns of the diplomats and politicians were furthest from Herb Cloutier's mind. Friday, June 13, was chosen as D-Day for "B" Company of the Royal Canadian Regiment to carry out its portion of Operation Breakup in Compound 66. All week long, banners had appeared inside the compound denouncing the Canadians as "satellites of American imperialists." And outside the wire, guards found a tomato-can label with the inner side "covered with Korean characters which proved to be notes for a compound lecture on Canadian Army organization, arms and equipment." The night before the RCR operation, the North Korean prisoners again staged a rowdy concert party and set fire to papers, apparently documents they didn't want their Canadian guards to find.

At 10 o'clock on the morning of June 13, the RCR men rolled up in front of Compound 66. They were joined by a company of King's Shropshire Light Infantry. The troops dashed to positions around the compound and formed columns at the entrance. The POWs had been instructed to emerge from the compound, strip off their clothes and file into waiting vehicles. Capt. Cloutier had gone inside Compound 76 three days before. He knew what violent reaction there might be. The RCR troops assumed their battle positions. However, no battle occurred. To everyone's surprise the POWs followed the orders to the letter. None was more relieved than the RCR soldiers.

"It took just ten minutes," wrote correspondent Bill Boss, watching from the sidelines, "for a detachment of the Royal Canadian Regiment to take over for their first active tour of duty as guards of the compound . . . Smart and business-like in their summer kit, the Canadians . . . formed a line on the graveled pathway leading to the barbed-wire enclosure as [the prisoners] filed out in yoked pairs to trucks waiting outside." By midday, the RCR had moved the 2,700 officers and 630 non-commissioned officers of the North Korean People's Army (NKPA) from old Compound 66 to the valley beneath the RCR campsite position for incarceration in new 500-man compounds. For six weeks, until they were relieved by another American unit, the Canadians fulfilled their custodial duties—twenty-four hours on and twenty-four hours off—alternating with the KSLI.

Guard duty was routine and mercifully uneventful. Each morning, the POWs would be brought out of the compound and marched to the ocean where they bathed and emptied their honey buckets. Then it was back to the compound where the RCR guards assumed watch duty. The toughest problems the guards faced were averting the theft of military clothing and keeping civilian prostitutes away from the enclosure.

"To be honest, we were all tickled pink to be there," George Mannion said. Like Cloutier, Pte. Mannion wasn't told where his unit was going. Because they crossed from Pusan to Koje-do in landing craft, Mannion figured it was an amphibious attack much like the one at Inch'on. "But by comparison to life in the front-line, [Koje] was an easy number."

"I won't forget it," agreed Capt. Herb Cloutier. "The only time I got in under a tent or opened and closed a door for a whole year was on Koje. In the front line it was living in bunkers and holes in the ground."

From the beginning of the war, UN Command enjoyed complete air supremacy over the battlefield in Korea. After only two months of the war, all but 18 of North Korea's 130 combat aircraft had been put out of action. Even when the Chinese entered the war, their Russian-built MIG-15 fighters were kept at bay by US bombers and jet fighters. Among the fighter squadron pilots flying Sabres were twenty members of the RCAF, who served in the US Fifth Air Force. Canadian pilots were credited with more than twenty MIGs destroyed or damaged.

However, sometimes the air supremacy was accompanied by carelessness. Soon after coming out of the front lines, "B" Company of the 3rd Battalion of the PPCLI suffered a rude awakening. They had set up an overnight bivouac close to one of the bridges that crossed the Imjin River. The following morning, the relative peace of breakfast was shattered when four USAF F84 Thunderjets screamed in from the south and mistakenly loosed several bombs on the UN encampment. The error cost a number of American troops their lives.

Such incidents emphasized the importance of knowledgeable observers near or over the battlefield. The Royal Air Force operated Auster observation planes to direct UN artillery fire at Chinese positions. Among their pilot-observers were two Canadians from the Royal Canadian Horse Artillery (RCHA)—Capt. Joe Liston, who was shot down and became a POW, and later, Capt. Peter Tees, who conducted 453 shoots and received the Distinguished Flying Cross, the first awarded a Canadian army officer since the First World War.

To improve the accuracy and reliability of close air support for ground troops, control and direction methods, used during the Second World War, were re-introduced in Korea. This involved a Tactical Air Control Party (TACP) that accompanied the forward infantry on the ground. A TACP consisted of a USAF pilot officer, a radio operator and a driver-mechanic in a jeep with a radio. From the ground the TACPs communicated with the infantry headquarters and directed fighter-bombers during air-strikes.

Further improving the scheme, a Forward Air Controller (FAC) was put in the air over the forward infantry positions. The US Fifth Air Force experimented with several different aircraft, but settled on the piston-engine T-6 Texan aircraft (similar to the Canadian Harvard two-seater, trainer aircraft). The USAF 6147th Tactical Control Group (TCG) was formed. The TACPs continued to accompany forward troop movements, but now air-strikes would be controlled via airborne FACs. Each Texan was crewed by a USAF pilot FAC, teamed with an army observer FAC in the second seat. Shortly after the 6147th TCG was formed, the prefix "Mosquito" was added to their radio call signs. The name stuck.

"I just happened to be in the right place at the right time," Lt. Geoff Magee explained. Although he'd applied for aircrew during the Second World War, Magee ended up in the navy. Even in 1952, in Korea with the 1st Battalion of the RCR, he still would have preferred air force. He hadn't been in Korea more than a few weeks, "when a signal came in to our unit asking for an officer to volunteer for service with the USAF, in some capacity. . . Suddenly, I was about to realize my boyhood dream of flying."

Before long, Magee joined the 6147th TCG at K47, an air base outside the city of Ch'unch'on. There, he was paired with USAF pilot Roy James and trained as an observer FAC in the back seat of a Texan. Magee served on 162 Mosquito missions, more than any other Canadian. His duties as an observer FAC included pinpointing targets for jet fighter-bombers, intervening during an attack to correct attack accuracy and, if needed, directing jets to emergency landing locations.

Each day's operation followed a similar pattern. A Mosquito crew— flying at 200 mph—approached a target from roughly 2,000 feet, while the fighter-bombers—flying at 600 mph—approached from perhaps 30,000. The T-6 observer chose the radio channel of the strike force (a different channel for each of the nationalities in UN Command). Making sure the high-altitude pilots could see the T-6, the Mosquito crew then dove on the target, marking it with smoke rockets. When the fighter-bombers attacked, the Mosquito aircraft stayed nearby to assess the damage and to ensure that each fighter-bomber returned to friendly lines safely.

As the war became more deadlocked and front lines more static, the Chinese picked up on the routine. They soon realized that a lone, essentially unarmed Texan aircraft over their position meant an imminent air strike. They also anticipated the Mosquito crew's return and descent for one last low-level pass after the attack, and they often answered with small-arms, machine-gun and 20-mm cannon fire. During a single day in one corps area, five of seven T-6s were hit by Chinese fire.

It was July 1, 1951, when Pat Tremblay, an infantry captain in the Royal 22e Régiment took off in the second seat of his T-6 with American pilot Elmer Witten at the controls. Tremblay had just completed five days of introductory observing from a Texan and was beginning his operational tour in the Mosquito group.

From their base at P'yongtaek, the pair headed north at about 1,000 feet. They passed over Seoul and its Kimpo Airfield. Then Witten spotted some hills and potential targets near the front lines and dove to take a closer look. As they were about to turn for home, Tremblay was nearly blinded by a flash of light as Witten's cockpit was suddenly shattered by machine-gun fire.

"Are you okay, Witt?" Tremblay yelled into the intercom. "Do we bail out?"

There was no response from the pilot in the front cockpit. His cap was tossed back against the pilot's seat. One hand lay limp on the control column. Then Tremblay barely heard Witten say, "Pat . . . try . . . fly . . . plane."

The army captain was petrified. Until that week, Tremblay's only airborne experience was as an army parachutist. Even though the Texan was equipped with dual controls, he had no idea how to fly the plane. He touched the control column and called to his partner, "Wake up Witt. Tell me what to do!"

Instead of a response, Tremblay only found a trickle of blood running by his foot. Witten might now be dead.

Despite the destruction to Witten's cockpit and potentially to the mechanics of the plane, Tremblay's hand on the column had settled the aircraft. It was flying straight and level . . . but north!

Gradually, Tremblay discovered that moving the control column from side to side dipped the wings accordingly. Then he found the foot controls and they lurched the plane left and right. Slowly, a degree at a time, he turned the aircraft around.

"Witt!" he yelled. "We're headed south!"

Again there was just the slightest hand movement from his pilot. The .50-calibre bullets that had hit the plane had broken Witten's spine and pierced his stomach. He was paralyzed below the waist and bleeding severely.

Tremblay continued to steer the crippled aircraft south. Soon he recognized the Imjin River. If the plane came down now, he sensed, at least it would be in friendly territory.

Again Tremblay noticed Witten's hand moving, this time in a circular motion. When the observer looked to the east, he saw Seoul and realized that Kimpo Airfield was nearby. The plane lurched again, only this time it was Witten who had made the plane turn. And descend. Witten had also managed to jettison the Texan's underwing rockets to avoid an explosion on impact.

The ground was coming up quickly as Tremblay again seized the back-seat control column, but by then it wasn't necessary. Witten had managed to bring the plane down dead centre on the runway. He couldn't steer the plane and it bounced off the tarmac, hit a boulder, tore off its landing gear and came to rest in a cloud of dust.

Tremblay couldn't believe he was still alive. He leaped out of his seat and pulled Witten free of the plane. Moments later, the fire brigade arrived and the T-6 blew up. Elmer Witten was maimed, but both he and his observer were alive. Witten would be awarded a Distinguished Flying Cross (DFC) and the Purple Heart. Pat Tremblay would be awarded the Military Cross and live to finish an illustrious tour with his home regiment, the Vandoos, in Korea.

In all, 50 Tactical Air Control Party airmen were killed during the war, 16 were reported missing-in-action and 31 became prisoners-of-war. As a unit, the Mosquitos were awarded three US Presidential Distinguished Unit Citations and two Republic of Korea Presidential Unit Citations. Twenty-one of its crew members were Canadian and among others recognized with DFCs were Lt. Geoff Magee, Lt. Phil Plouffe, Lt. Bill Ward and Capt. J. R. P. Yelle.

Jean-Paul St-Aubin's memory of the Koje-do uprising is not an exciting one. He never set foot on the island or faced angry communist POWs there; instead, he was on board a small ship en route from Kure, Japan, to Korea at the time of the crisis in Compound 76. St-Aubin, a private in a pioneer platoon, had been in Japan, where he volunteered to reinforce his outfit, the Royal 22e Régiment, on Hill 355. As the ship made its way to Korea, word arrived about the prison insurrection on Koje-do. For five days the ship circled the island in case Pte. St-Aubin and the rest of the 200 troops on board were needed ashore. The call never came. All St-Aubin remembers of Koje is the aggravation of bobbing around in the Sea of Japan for nearly a week, while surviving on "sausages that tasted like sandpaper and powdered eggs that tasted like sawdust."

Life in the front lines as a pioneer soon helped the young French Canadian forget the boredom of his nautical adventure off Koje-do. As a specialist in engineering and mining tasks, Pte. St-Aubin was soon bedding down on slabs of clay inside bunkers carved into Korean hillsides. Underground, he and his platoon mates burned gas that dripped from a stolen gas tank into a mess tin for heat; wood or paper fuel would create smoke and reveal their position. St-Aubin's taste buds soon got used to American C-Rations of ground meat and spaghetti, hamburger patties, chicken stew, or beans with pork that somehow all looked and tasted the same. The days and nights were accompanied by the constant serenade of guns—UN and Chinese—blasting each other's lines relentlessly. As a respite from life at the sharp end, once every ten days St-Aubin's platoon got a trip to the Mobile Laundry and Bath Unit.

"The only time our bunker received a direct hit," St-Aubin said, "was a day we had gone behind the lines for showers. There was nothing left inside my dugout when I got back. Pictures, everything . . . gone."

In fact, the nature of Pte. St-Aubin's daily work made the deafening shellfire and his subterranean lifestyle at the front pale by comparison. As a member of the pioneer platoon attached to the Royal 22e Régiment, the nineteen-year-old private's specialty was landmines—laying, mapping and retrieving Canadian mines and, when necessary, disarming Chinese mines.

When his regiment was rotated into a new defensive position on Hill 355, Hill 187 or an area to the west of the Sami-ch'on called the Hook, Pte. St-Aubin and the rest of his pioneer platoon were responsible for installing anti-vehicle and anti-personnel minefields. UN minefields were laid in accordance with strict rules: patterns were set; locations had to be approved by senior officers; they were grid-referenced on special maps; and they were surrounded by barbed wire with warning signs in applicable languages. On the other hand, clearing mines and booby traps was much less exact. The Chinese and North Koreans used a mixture of relics from the Second World War as well as those manufactured in Russia or China. Some had wooden bodies that made them impossible to find with metal detectors. Others were simply mud-covered grenades, their pins replaced with mud, so that when UN troops kicked what looked like a mud ball, the exterior would break away, allowing the grenade to detonate.

"Bounding Betsies [used by both sides] were the toughest to deal with," St-Aubin remembered. Also called "bouncing Betties," "each was about three inches in diameter . . . about eight or nine inches long . . . round like a can and on the end of a short post . . . and buried in the ground." What made these mines lethal was the bounding part. When tripped by wire or trap, a detonator would pop the mine several feet in the air before the mine exploded, scattering deadly shrapnel, waist-high, in every direction. Front-line troops referred to bounding mines as "de-bollockers" for obvious reasons.

Mapping out and maintaining a minefield was mandatory and a matter of life and death. Every infantry platoon commander relied on his pioneers to deliver him and his men through "friendly" mines. Whenever the shelling along the front lines let up, the pioneers ventured out of their bunkers to check the status of their fields the way a gardener surveys his vegetable patch after a rainstorm. First, the pioneers had to make sure none of the defensive mines had been tampered with by Chinese patrols overnight. Or, if Chinese artillery shells or mortar bombs had fallen into a Canadian-built minefield, new mines would have to be laid, broken barbed wire repaired and maps updated before a UN patrol went out into no-man's-land the next night.

"One night, we had to retrieve five bounding Betsies," Pte. St-Aubin said. It was customary—the Geneva Convention required it—that when a battalion left a line position to be replaced by another unit, any unregistered mines, such as those defending UN outposts way out in no-man's-land, be removed. "So my platoon commander, Hal Merrithew, and I went out in front of [Hill] 355 to get them. It was about 5 o'clock in the morning. Dark and very foggy."

The moment Lt. Merrithew and Pte. St-Aubin reached the outpost location, they got out a mine detector to track down and remove the Betsies. Despite being hundreds of metres in front of their own lines and working with their backs to the still-distant Chinese positions across the remainder of the valley, they felt protected by the darkness, the dense fog and, if need be, the cover of guns behind UN lines.

"It's a tricky business," Merrithew recalled. "You have to find these things in the dark, use a safety pin [to defuse them], then dig them out of the ground and bring them back with you. Lots of concentration."

"We suddenly lifted our heads," St-Aubin said, "and realized the fog had lifted. It was light now. And you could see the [Chinese] hill positions clear as day. The two of us were right in the middle of no-man's-land . . . Either [the Chinese] were sleeping or couldn't be bothered with us. We got back up the trail to our trenches very fast."

Jean-Paul St-Aubin didn't know why he was chosen to become a pioneer. The closest he'd come to handling military property was a stint with Veterans Affairs after the Second World War, packing veterans' medals and sending them through the mail. Even though handling bounding Betsies required an entirely different skill set and temperament, the army, at least in St-Aubin's case, had clearly matched the right person with the right job. Given the sort of roles Canadians were performing in this war—now a grinding war of attrition—talents and tasks had to be more logically matched. Moreover, the chemistry among small groups of fighting men—platoons and sections—became critical to a soldier's survival.

"From the moment you're put in charge of a platoon," Lt. Merrithew said, "you're trying to get a feel for your men . . . a feel for who will lead and who will follow." Unlike the Second World War, where soldiers were disciplined as a reflex to attack on command, Korea was not a matter of "going over the top. Korea was basically a defensive war . . . and you had to build your platoon on personalities you could rely on in any situation.

"You get some devil-may-care guys. Absolutely zero fear . . . You get other men who are afraid, but you can depend on them because they'll always do their job. The third type is cautious, hangs back on actions . . . So you have to build your platoon with the fearless, the meek and the cautious."

The jelling of Hal Merrithew's platoon began on the parade square at Valcartier, Quebec, in 1951, as he trained with members of the 1st Battalion of the Royal 22e Régiment. Some were permanent force soldiers and paratroops; others were veterans of the Second World War or reservists. When they arrived in Korea in 1952 as reinforcements for the front lines, the men of Lt. Merrithew's platoon were joined with members of the Vandoos' 2nd Battalion, men who were partway through their tour of duty in Korea, to form a mine-field repair platoon. It was their job, usually in the dead of night, to locate damaged barbed-wire barriers around Canadian defensive minefields and repair them before dawn.

Merrithew's platoon treated fence repair like a precision march. Each man in the platoon carried several strands of four-foot-long barbed wire. Every strand had a loop at each end. Finding a break in the minefield wire, one man took the broken strand and threaded it through the loop at one end of the repair strand. He handed the other end of the repair strand to a second man, who found the other broken strand in the main fence, threaded it through the eye at the other end of the repair strand, drew it tight and wrapped it back on itself to close the gap. Merrithew had prepared his platoon so com-pletely, his men could repair broken wire almost as quickly as they walked along the fence, entirely in the dark. He trained his men in pairs—the fearless with the meek—so that "every man knew every inch of every fence around the minefields and every gap through it."

Cpl. Roland Pearce was attached to Lt. Merrithew's troubleshoot-ing platoon in 1952. Just twenty years old, J. P. (as he was known) was average-size, soft-spoken and shy—one of those meek types Mer-rithew talked about—but because he had worked with explosives at the INCO mines in Sudbury, Ontario, for two years, Pearce was a natural candidate for pioneer training when he enlisted in 1950. He was bilin-gual, so he ended up with the Vandoos and arrived in Korea during the fall of 1951. He spent his first night in the front lines—Christmas Eve—in a frozen bunker near Hill 355. While all his pioneer work during his year-long tour in Korea was dangerous—patrols into no-man's-land, handling landmines and repairing minefield fence—none frightened Cpl. Pearce more than his mission on October 8, 1952.

It was a little after dark. Lt. Merrithew had arrived at the company command post, just behind the front lines on the flank of Hill 355. The platoon commander was going over the night's patrol plans with his commanding officer, Lt.-Col. L. F. Trudeau. It was to be a routine night of checking and mending minefield fences. The colonel took a call from a forward company.

"We've got a patrol in a minefield," the colonel said aloud for Merrithew to hear. He pointed out the location on a map.

"I know that field," Merrithew piped up.

"What'll we do?"

"I'll go in and get them," Merrithew said.

The colonel asked the lieutenant what he needed, and the two men quickly made arrangements for a protective party of infantry, stretcher-bearers and artillery cover, should the rescue group run into a Chinese patrol. When he arrived at the front lines, Merrithew's repair patrol was waiting. There were two of his regular pioneers among the platoon members—Cpls. J. P. R. Pearce and A. Dion. The latter, unlike J. P., was a big man—heavy-set and over six feet tall. He was also talkative and always willing to step forward.

"Merrithew asked for volunteers," Pearce said, "and generally if you look at me, I say 'Okay.'"

Minutes later, Lt. Merrithew, Cpls. Dion and Pearce and a medic with stretcher-bearers had moved down the forward slope on the friendly side of the minefield. It was so dark the rescuers couldn't even see the ground in front of them. They could, however, hear the moans of the wounded Canadian soldiers on the far side of their own defensive minefield. Following the sure-footed lieutenant through the known gap in the minefield, the group soon arrived on the enemy side of the field. Merrithew deployed the protective party toward no-man's-land and approached the spot where the Canadian patrol had unwittingly entered the minefield.

"Follow me," whispered Merrithew to his two pioneer corporals. "I'll take the first one." Despite the darkness, the lieutenant knew where the first mine was and was soon disarming it. He then directed Cpl. Pearce toward the second mine.

"I'll find it with the detector," Pearce said. He took the earphones, extended the probing arm and disc of the detector and listened. "It's no use . . ."

Instead of hearing periodic static indicating a mine in the soil, the detector emitted a continuous buzz. After months and months of steady shelling, the minefield was littered with shrapnel and the detector couldn't distinguish a single steel-cased mine amid the debris.

Pearce slowly dropped to his knees, pulled out his bayonet and began probing the soggy earth to find the second mine. It was a bounding Betsy. With Merrithew talking him through, Pearce surgically scraped away the dirt, inserted a safety pin and whispered back to Merrithew, "Disarmed."

Just beyond the second mine, Pearce found Pte. Joseph St-Germain.

"He didn't look badly wounded," Pearce said, "but when I checked closer, I knew he was dead."

Merrithew cautioned Pearce not to move the body. The mines in that field were spaced approximately five feet apart and it was possible St-Germain lay on top of a third mine. When Pearce had finished probing around the body, he and Dion carefully carried it out of the field.

As Pearce and Dion re-entered the field for the other casualties, Merrithew checked with the protective party commander. They heard noises in the darkness out in no-man's-land and figured it could be a Chinese patrol in the area. The lieutenant radioed back for "artillery fire and bursts of Vickers machine-gun fire to cover any noise we might be making in the minefield."

By now, Cpl. Pearce had disarmed another mine and, with Cpl. Dion, had advanced as far as a second wounded patrolman. Consoling the man as they went, the two corporals retraced their steps and carried him to safety. Next they found Pte. Richard Roy, barely alive. They got him out of the field, but Roy would die at the Regimental Aid Post within the hour. Deftly, methodically, the two young corporals moved in and out of the minefield, retrieving the wounded. They worked as effectively and rhythmically as if they were checking and mending broken wire.

The fifth and final patrolman, Pte. Albert Leclerc, lay farthest into the minefield. He wasn't badly wounded, but when Pearce reached him, both the rescuer and the casualty instinctively knew there was something wrong.

"My leg . . ." Leclerc whispered as he pointed down.

"Don't move," Pearce said.

Beneath Leclerc's outstretched leg, Pearce found another unexploded mine. Without moving either the man or the mine, the pioneer corporal found the deadly prongs that when tripped would detonate the mine. He gently inserted a safety pin, disarming the mine. Pearce then helped Leclerc to his feet. Having lain on top of a mine for more than an hour, the soldier was suddenly overwhelmed with fear. Realizing Leclerc was in shock, Pearce slung him over his shoulder and carried him out.

By about midnight, the rescue was done; the night's work, however, was not. Lt. Merrithew and his two corporals had to return to the minefield one more time, to remove the safety pins in the mines they had disarmed, re-activate the detonators and return the field to full defensive status. Their report showed that the Canadian patrol had miscalculated on the location of the gap in the minefield. The first man had walked well into the field without incident; so had the second. But the third had stepped on a mine, killing him and one other soldier. The other wounded were knocked over by the concussion of the exploding mine or the shrapnel that ripped into them at point-blank range. As well as killing St-Germain and Roy, the night left lasting impressions.

"I didn't sleep at all that night," says Roland Pearce. "I came back to my dugout, but just couldn't sleep . . . I kept seeing those wounded guys out there."

Both Cpl. J. P. R. Pearce and Cpl. A. Dion were later awarded the Military Medal. For his efforts, Lt. H. O. Merrithew was decorated with a Military Cross. What lingers in his memory are the words of one of the young patrolmen his platoon carried out of the minefield that night. "Take your time, sir," said the soldier in broken English. "I know you'll save me." Hal Merrithew also remembers (but breaks down explaining) the skill and efficiency of the two corporals he paired up for the mission—the fearless one and the meek one. "I had never seen such a dark night in all my life . . . We had to do everything by feel. But there were two good men. And they got the job done."

IN THE
KILLING ZONE

T ED ZUBER didn't see the Chinese sniper homing in on his position. The RCR private was situated in a bunker that had once been a UN observation post called Ronson. It over-looked no-man's-land in an area known as the Hook, so named because it jutted hook-like into the Sami-ch'on valley. This forward outpost had been so badly shelled during the months UN troops had used it, it had caved in and been abandoned by regular riflemen. The damage meant that Zuber's field of view was limited to a few hundred yards. He had a blind spot on his left.

Zuber's partner, Pte. Al Craig, sat a few hundred yards to Zuber's left and a little lower, covering Zuber's blind spot. He too was dug in. He had spotted the Chinese sniper creeping toward Zuber's position, but couldn't get a clear shot at him.

Craig and Zuber had been paired in sniper training when their Royal Canadian Regiment moved off Hill 355 in early November, 1952. Their instructor, Sgt. MacPherson, was a veteran sniper from the Canadian campaign to liberate Holland in 1944–45. He had trained them with sniper scopes on Lee-Enfield, single-shot, bolt-action rifles. Their RCR colonel had told them they would be useless to the battalion unless they could "put six out of ten rounds into a two-cent book of matches at 500 yards." Zuber and Craig had each

hit the mark with at least eight shots. They had gone on to learn cam-
ouflaging, sight optics and stalking.

Now Pte. Zuber was being stalked and didn't know it.

The two RCR marksmen had rigged a temporary field phone
linking their two positions. Finally, Craig wondered what was taking
Zuber so long to react. He rang his partner. "Ted, you see the son-
ofabitch?"

"Where?" answered a startled Zuber.

"Why are you letting him move up on you like that?"

"What're you talking about?" Zuber said. He had seen another
Chinese soldier jumping up and down in a trench farther away, but
Zuber figured that soldier had probably been ordered to draw fire in
order to expose the Canadian position to Chinese sniper fire. Still,
Zuber was oblivious to the sniper in his blind spot. "I can't see him at
all," he admitted to Craig.

"Let me tell you exactly where he is," Craig said.

As trainees, Zuber and Craig had not only taken the course
together, but also MacPherson, their instructor, had told them "to
eat, sleep and shit together . . . so you'll find out how each of you
thinks, so you know what not to expect from each other." So, although
he couldn't see a thing in front of his spot on Ronson, Zuber trusted
Craig's word without even thinking.

"I think he's taking up a firing position . . . about 125 yards to
your front. A bit to the left. Not quite 11 o'clock."

Zuber trained his Lyman-Alaskan sight toward the spot.

"I'm going to shoot the guy in the trench."

They both knew that the Chinese soldier leaping up and down in
the distant trench would only be momentarily visible, so Craig wasn't
likely to hit him. Zuber realized what Craig was up to and prepared
himself.

"Ready?" Craig said.

"Go!"

Craig fired at the man in the distant trench. The Chinese sniper
lifted his head to see where the unexpected shot had come from, and

in that instant Zuber found the sniper in his sights and killed him with one shot. It was one of five kills Pte. Zuber would make as a sniper during three months on the Hook position.

Far from being a pathological killer, Pte. Ted Zuber was merely a soldier who had adapted to soldiering in what would turn out to be another year of attrition along the front lines. Had he not joined up to go to Korea, Zuber might have followed up his apprenticeship in Kingston, Ontario, with a career in commercial photography. Or he might have gone home to Montreal to pursue his hobby as a sketch artist. As it was, he applied his photographic knowledge to gunsights and scopes, and his artistic ability to sketching field drawings of terrain and Chinese army positions for the intelligence section of his regiment. He was riding shotgun for the battalion, and the job seemed to reflect his aptitudes and personality.

"The army made us polish the insole of our boots . . . press our boot laces . . . polish the backside of our brass . . . starch all of our uniforms," Zuber said. "And while I was comfortable with the need for military discipline . . . I didn't want any part of it. I somehow grasped that the sniper section was the only place in the infantry where I could work as an individual."

No one soldier working alone was going to win this war. Ted Zuber knew that. By now, most knew that this war was not winnable. Nor did it seem negotiable. Since July 1951, representatives of opposing military commanders had been meeting off and on to reach an armistice. While the leading figures involved never suggested they would abandon the talks in favour of military escalation, neither did they seem ready to surrender any part of the battlefield to the other side. The pattern was clear to troops of all armies in Korea. Defensive front lines would remain unchanged. They would be dug deeper. The war was deadlocked.

Mao Tse-tung had ordered his officers to engage the Americans "in positional warfare, where bloody fights were waged with little exchange of land." There would be no victory, just endless skirmishes between groups of soldiers in trenches and out in no-man's-land, "where lessons for war from 1917 were more applicable than those from 1944."

By the time UN Command had consolidated its forward position along the imaginary Jamestown Line in the fall of 1951, the commanders of the Commonwealth Division sent patrols into no-man's-land every night. Unlike the South Korean ROK Army patrols, whose general philosophy was to advance, find the enemy and fight it out, each Canadian patrol had a different strength and a different mandate.

A fighting patrol, usually platoon-size (about thirty men), would attack an outpost, capture (or "snatch") a prisoner or create a diversion to keep opposing troops off balance. An ambush patrol of fifteen to thirty men would set a trap in an area through which Chinese patrols were sure to operate. A recce patrol included an officer or sergeant and three or four riflemen, and their task was to retrieve information on routes, enemy defences or its movement patterns; they were sometimes the bait for a larger ambush patrol. An escort patrol worked with engineers or pioneers while they carried out their tasks, and a standing patrol worked out in front of a company position to give early warning of any Chinese activity in the region.

In this static war, information was power. On the surface, at least, patrolling was designed to get information by whatever means—spying on Chinese soldiers, capturing them and, if need be, engaging them. Most platoon commanders realized patrolling was also designed to keep up their soldiers' fighting pitch during the lulls in ground warfare. No one who was responsible for the safe return of soldiers from a night patrol dared let his men fall into a false sense of security or, as PPCLI platoon commander Bob Peacock noted, "No patrol is ever routine, unless you want it to be your last."

Peacock's No. 6 Platoon set out one night in the fall of 1952 to establish a forward patrol base on Bunker Hill, a small hill some 400 yards in front and to the right of Hill 355. The only protection that Bunker Hill offered were the remnants of fire positions and shallow trenches. The platoon was assisted by a Forward Observation Officer, stretcher-bearers and the battle adjutant, Maj. R. F. Bruce, acting as patrol master that night. The patrol went like clockwork. Peacock's group arrived at Bunker Hill a little after nightfall. Canadian fighting patrols passed through en route to their appointed rounds, and things fell silent for about an hour.

"Suddenly, heavy fighting broke out close by in front of an American forward position," Peacock wrote. "The Chinese had launched a silent attack without any artillery support, probing the gap between the Americans and ourselves . . . [Then] we were raked by heavy machine-gun fire which our American neighbours had brought into action . . . Luckily we were fairly well protected in our shallow slit trenches. Maj. Bruce narrowly missed being a casualty as he was in the open taking care of personal matters when the machine-gun fire hit our position. He said later the experience had given him a different view of routine patrolling."

John Tomlinson was rushed to Korea as a reinforcement for the 1st Battalion RCR in the summer of 1951. As a nineteen-year-old private, Tomlinson felt he had plenty of attributes for the job. He had joined the regular army in 1950, taken paratroop training and become a signaller in a demonstration platoon that was used to train officers. In fact, at Camp Borden's School of Infantry, he became part of a movie cast shooting a warfare training film, "I think it was called 'Infantry Platoon in the Attack.'

"There were three or four cameras and a director on a vehicle beside us," Tomlinson said. "We start off walking down a road . . . come under fire and go to ground. The lead section comes up into firing position and engages the enemy. Then the section commander discovers it's a machine-gun nest, so word goes back . . . The platoon commander gives his orders . . . So we'd do a right flanking attack, engage the enemy in a fire fight. The two rifle sections would sweep through and capture the position . . .

"Except in war it doesn't work like that. There's a bit more confusion. It isn't daylight. And when the platoon commander stands up, he gets a bullet between the eyes. And there's no guarantee when you've finished, the forty men you started out with will still be there at the end."

Few of his patrols at the front in Korea went according to the script either. During a company patrol across the Sami-ch'on valley toward Hill 166, Pte. Tomlinson was part of the platoon headquarters, fifty yards behind a fighting patrol. As it climbed the forward slope of the Chinese-held hill, the leading patrol became plainly visible, even in the dead of night. In the resulting exchange of fire, the vanguard sustained numerous casualties and the entire company had to make a hasty withdrawal. Tomlinson hasn't forgotten the emotional and physical exhaustion of that night:

"I never wet my pants in fear, but there was a lot of adrenaline flowing . . . Out in the middle of that valley, no-man's-land doesn't belong to anybody. And when you suddenly come under fire, I don't care if you're in a parking lot in downtown Toronto with no lights and somebody's firing at you . . . it's a feeling of high excitement."

Patrolling, or the prospect of patrolling, brought out the best and worst among infantrymen when their turn came. Not unlike nervous military aircrew, who traditionally urinated on the tail wheel before taking off on a combat mission, anxious troops could experience everything from sweaty palms to hives to vomiting before a patrol. Sometimes the personal upheaval was psychological, such as the day John Tomlinson and "C" Company of the RCR were rotated back into the front lines in March 1952. Tomlinson was paired with a bunker mate who had never patrolled before. He suddenly found the recruit polishing a .303 bullet.

"What're you doing?" Tomlinson asked innocently.

The man kept rubbing.

"Why are you polishing a rifle bullet?"

"I'm going to shoot myself . . ."

Tomlinson thought the soldier was kidding.

"Promise you won't tell?" the man said.

"Sure," Tomlinson laughed, "if you give me your beer ration." And he sat down and began undoing his bootlaces.

Moments later, the recruit loaded his rifle and fired. The breach of the rifle was right beside Tomlinson's ear and he jumped back in astonishment. The frightened man had blown a hole in his foot.

Because most patrols were mounted at night, fear of the dark was common. Jim "Scotty" Martin, an RCR platoon commander with the 1st Battalion, had a corporal whose childhood fear of darkness lingered into his tour of duty in Korea. It was a detail that Martin picked up along the way and jotted down in a notebook he kept on the men in his platoon. Martin also noted that Cpl. Vic Dingle "was a bit dogmatic . . . had pretty strong opinions . . . that the troops called him 'Crow' because of his dark complexion," and most important, "that he was a good section commander." On May 23, 1952, he proved it.

Lt. Martin led a fighting patrol with five additional pioneers that night. The objective was to establish a firm base on the far side of the Sami-ch'on valley that would allow the pioneers to set booby traps around several Chinese mortar positions on Hill 156. Before he could establish the firm base, Martin's patrol ran into a Chinese patrol. In an instant, it seemed, the night lit up with machine-gun fire, rifle fire and grenade explosions.

"We go to ground," Martin said. "It's obvious I can't set up a firm base, so we draw off the hill. But as the fire opens up, we're all diving for cover and I get hit in the leg."

Because of the adrenaline pumping through him, at first Martin didn't realize how serious the wound was. He had enough of his wits about him that he avoided shooting his pistol in the dark, and instead heaved fragmentation and phosphorus grenades in the vicinity of the Chinese patrol. What was left of Martin's patrol gathered at the base of the hill. One soldier was dead. Three others were wounded. The pioneer platoon had already begun to retreat. The patrol got word to pull back, and then Martin realized "a third of my calf muscle is sticking out the side of my leg" and he could barely walk.

That's when Vic Dingle, Martin's senior corporal, rose to the occasion. He suddenly sensed that his platoon commander was relying on him. At that moment—fear of the dark or not—survival of the platoon depended on him. Dingle quickly organized the retreat. Each section was to act as a firm base for the other as it withdrew. It took the rest of the night, but with Martin hanging off his shoulder,

Dingle got the remainder of the patrol home to its company position. At dawn, as Martin was loaded onto an evacuation helicopter bound for a MASH unit, he learned that the pioneers who had been with him on the patrol took a short cut and walked right into a minefield; five more were wounded. It was a patrol "that just didn't click." However, an alert and apparently fearless Cpl. Dingle probably saved it from being a disaster.

If patrolling itself was stressful, patrolling on a winter's night added to the discomfort. By this time in the war, most infantrymen had thrown away the Department of National Defence handbook on Korea with its claim that winters in South Korea were "a chilly version of British Columbia's." In the middle of Korea, just above the 38th parallel, the cold could be Arctic and the wind-blown snow could verge on white-out. Moreover, army-issue parkas were not an asset because the swishing noise of nylon rubbing on nylon was nearly as loud as a man's voice in an open field.

Cpl. Jack Noble won't forget his turn on patrol one January night. Normally a machine-gunner with No. 11 Platoon of the RCR's "D" Company, Noble went out this night to back up a fighting patrol sent out to bring back a Chinese prisoner. As the leading section of the patrol reached the Chinese side of the valley, an RCR soldier stepped on a Chinese mine. The snatch attempt was immediately called off.

Through much of the rest of the night, the RCR fighting patrol tried to draw the fire of a pursuing Chinese patrol, while Noble and a couple of medics brought back the wounded. They made litters with their rifles and carried the men in slings. The temperature dropped so quickly that night, Noble's feet went numb with the cold. He took off his boots and walked in his sock feet so that at least the friction of his feet rubbing on the frozen ground might revive the feeling in his feet. The medical group got back safely, but the soldier had lost a foot to the Chinese mine. Cpl. Noble had nearly lost both feet to the cold.

The troubles hadn't ended for that night's mission. When the members of the fighting patrol finally reached the gap in the UN minefield to re-enter the RCR company position, they were stopped in the darkness.

"Halt," shouted one of two Canadian sentries on duty at the gap.
The fighting patrol halted as ordered. Now an irreversible
sequence of events had begun, and its successful outcome depended
on everyone following procedure to the letter.

"Advance one and be recognized," continued the sentry.

That was the signal for a person in the dark to take one more step
forward and announce the first half of a double-barrelled password,
such as "Blue Bonnet" or "Betty Grable" or "Nuts and Bolts." The
patrol leader advanced a step, but there he hesitated. He had forgotten the night's password.

By rights, the sentries could now open fire. They would not be held
responsible. It wouldn't be the first time a Chinese patrol had tried
to penetrate the UN front line this way. Some, they said, could even
speak perfect English. The safeties came off the sentries' weapons.
They also hesitated.

In the nick of time, someone else in the RCR patrol blurted out
the right first password.

The sentries cursed loudly, more to relieve the tension than to
condemn the patrol. Then there was nervous laughter all round and
a retreat to the bunkers for a toddy of rum.

When the Korean War began, a soldier's most trusted tool in the
field was his firearm, whether a Lee-Enfield rifle, a Bren gun or, if
he traded liquor for it, an American .30-calibre carbine. However, by
the time negotiators began talking peace and the United Nations
armies reached the vicinity of the 38th parallel, the soldier's most
trusted tool was his shovel; instead of surviving *on* the hills at the
front line, a soldier was expected to survive *in* them.

When the battlefield was constantly shifting, soldiers dug slit
trenches for command posts, ammunition pits and latrines. Most
trenches were temporary. When the fighting reached a stalemate at
the Jamestown Line, they dug trenches and pits and latrines all over
again. But they also dug holes to live in. These cubbyholes were
either adjacent to the fighting positions or on the reverse side of the
hill being defended. They were permanent. Indeed, the progress of

the war (and the peace) was soon reflected in the depth and permanence of the soldier's living quarters in the front lines.

Bunkers began life as slit trenches. Open to the great outdoors, these three-to-five-foot deep trenches allowed in rain or searing sunshine during the summer, or snow and freezing cold during the winter. Excavation of a trench ended when the excavator hit rock. That's when sandbags, piled on top of one another, gave a trench the desired overall depth and protection. However, the real spur to renovate a trench resulted from another natural phenomenon.

"Open slits made irresistible traps for every wandering snake or field mouse and insects that leaped, wriggled or crawled," L/Cpl. John Dalrymple wrote. "In the evening, after evicting the more obvious of intruders, [a soldier] would settle down to vainly search for dreams on a rustling palate of rice straw, assorted spiders, homeless beetles, five-inch praying mantises and displaced but industrious ants. One night of this would make an ardent convert for the Home Improvement League."

A roof was the earliest addition to the evolving bunker. Tree limbs or scavenged timbers provided the rafters and a groundsheet pegged at the corners offered a temporary water-resistant ceiling. The flotsam and jetsam of war—ration crates and ammunition boxes—became furnishings. Sometimes a sleeping ledge could be cut into the side of the trench with rice straw for warmth. In winter, an old tea kettle loaded with glowing charcoal made a small furnace that threw a bit of heat without any tell-tale smoke or glow to reveal the position.

When a visit on the hillside turned into a long-term stay, the roofed-in slit trench could be ripped apart and expanded into a full-sized bunker or "hootchie." Occupants would dig back deep into the hillside and roof their bunker with heavy logs. Above that, soldiers wove together a cushion of branches, twigs and straw mats, topped by a rubber groundsheet, loosely packed earth and greenery to camouflage the location. Inside, three or four bunker mates built an earthen ledge for dry sleeping, a couple of openings for standing guard, a cupboard carved into one wall for ammunition and rations and a fireplace at one end with a concealed chimney made of bazooka bomb cartons.

"We used to make our own beds with machine-gun belts," Bud Doucette said. Of his 127 days in action with the RCR in Korea, L/Cpl. Doucette spent most of them defending one hill or another as a machine-gunner. To make daytime sleeping hours more comfortable, "We'd weave the used machine-gun belts together, hang them up and sleep on them," much like a hammock.

"We were a long way from civilization," Charlie LeBlanc recalled. A Cape Breton farmer, Cpl. LeBlanc arrived in Korea as a section leader in Able Company of the R22eR. While manning Hill 355, LeBlanc and his bunker mate Ken Snowden converted wooden ammunition boxes to tongue-and-groove flooring in their bunker. That impressed his colonel, but not the sign he'd posted over his bunker. "It said 'Charlie's Shortime Inn.' He told me to take it down."

Aside from the aforementioned insects, the only living creatures that enjoyed life in bunkers were the rats. Despite the use of rat poison, rat traps and general hygiene in the trenches and bunkers, rats thrived. They chewed everything from leather picture frames to gun belts. They crept into sleeping blankets. They dug themselves into every nook. Not only were they unsanitary, they bore something lethal—haemorrhagic fever, or Songo fever. The disease originated in mites living on the rats; when the mites bit a soldier on the neck or wrists, his blood would begin clotting, which clogged his liver, causing him to die of his own body poisons.

"There was no cure for it,"medic Cosmo Kapitaniuk said. As far as he knew, the Japanese had encountered it during their Amur River campaign against the Russians in the 1930s. It was generally understood that eight men in ten died when infected by the disease. "Whenever a guy showed symptoms, they evacuated him immediately by helicopter . . . There was this secret American lab south of the 8055th MASH unit . . . It was off limits even to us."

"I thought I had leprosy or something," said Don Flieger, a Service Corps corporal who worked at Kimpo Airfield near Seoul. For amusement (and safety) at night, Flieger and his buddies would sit on the edge of the runway, spot rats with flashlights and shoot them with their 9-mm pistols. In February 1952 he developed a rash that turned into blisters. When he arrived at the special American MASH unit, "I had a temperature of 104 . . . The blisters had broken and started to bleed. I was terrified." If it weren't for the eight complete blood transfusions Flieger underwent over the next two months en route home, he probably wouldn't have lived.

In response to the threat of insect bites and diseases, the brigade began equipping its front-line soldiers "with paludrine pills, anti-louse powder, anti-flying insect aerosol bombs and anti-mite oil—the latter messy for it must be smeared on pants cuffs, shirttails and neck bands."

The "Chino bunkers," as some front-line infantrymen referred to them, had two other nemeses. Monsoon rains, which sometimes lasted for weeks, placed additional weight on bunker roofs and caused them to collapse, trapping their occupants. PPCLI platoon commander Bob Peacock pointed out that "in August 1952, we lost eleven of fourteen bunkers in a single day . . . A minimum of ten inches of rain fell in a twelve-hour period . . . The roof of our platoon HQ bunker suddenly dropped on the four of us, burying us in sandbags, logs, mud and other debris. We were fortunate to get out alive with nothing more than cuts, bruises and the loss of some personal equipment and clothing."

The bunker's other mortal enemy was the Chinese army's guns. A combination of their Russian-designed su76 high-velocity assault guns, their 152-mm howitzers, their 122-mm artillery and their mortars could deliver relentless fire across no-man's-land at any time. Because the United Nations' air forces controlled the airspace over the front, the Chinese dug their battery positions deep into hillsides or tunnels so that they could fire with maximum protection. A Chinese artillery and mortar barrage signalled several things. First, it generally meant a new gun unit had arrived at the front and was "registering" or homing in on a UN target. Second, it often forewarned of an imminent ground attack. In either case, if the Chinese artillery and mortars chose a "time-on-target" barrage, in which shells from various positions all landed on the target at the same time, the explosions often made short work of the UN's bunkers and command posts, no matter how well constructed and fortified they might be.

Where fifty Chinese shells in a day were notable in the autumn of 1951, the average had reached 2,500 in the Canadian area a year later. In fact, the Chinese inflicted their heaviest bombardments between mid-1952 and mid-1953, consequently, "the heaviest casualties of the war were incurred in the last year of the conflict." The proportion of killed to wounded—normally one-to-ten—in this period was one-to-two.

Correspondents interviewed front-line troops about life under fire. Some visited their bunkers between barrages. They all tried to put phrases such as "shelling," "under artillery fire" and "bombardment" into perspective. "The soldier sits in his dugout or his slit trench and is shelled. What happens?" asked Canadian Press correspondent Bill Boss. "The whistle-whine of the approaching missile sends an involuntary sharp tug of destruction on his heart . . . Lying in that hole, or caught out in the open on patrol . . . with messengers of death and injury raking to and fro about him, now close, now far, now sprinkling him with dirt, now spinning jagged bits of shrapnel whirring through the air, he counts his chances. Life, so real right now, could finish in a flash."

On September 1, 1952, "C" Company of the RCR sustained four casualties due to artillery fire. The following day, "A" Company lost nine men as a result of a salvo of mortars that also knocked out a Lord Strathcona's tank, injuring its crew of four. Three days later, Lt. Cyril Harriott, who had struggled for months to obtain a posting to Korea, reported to Able Company; within minutes of his arrival in the front lines, Harriott was killed when an incoming shell exploded at his position.

"The first night I was on the hills in a bunker I was shit scared," Ed Ryan said. After joining the military in 1951, Ryan found himself at Currie Barracks in Calgary, where the Princess Patricias discovered his talents as a hockey player. He figured he'd sit out the war on a players' bench at the Calgary Corral, but as the need for front-line replacements increased, Pte. Ryan ended up on a draft to Korea to reinforce Baker Company of the PPCLI.

"I always figured I should come back with a V.C.," Ryan mused. "But then one night it was raining and mortars were coming in . . . [Normally, they] would have hit the ground and the shrapnel would have just cut us to pieces. But the mortars just embedded into the soft soil and everything was blowing up around us. I started calling for my mother: 'I want to come home!' I was so scared."

Dave Baty was a PPCLI reinforcement too. On a day late in May 1952, as his Able Company moved forward from a reserve position toward the front lines, "the Chinese must have spotted us. And their shelling was quite accurate . . . It was their 122-mm artillery.

"The first thing they hit was a fuel dump," Baty said. "When they saw they'd hit something—all the flames and that—they really poured it on . . . I got hit trying to find cover . . . Shrapnel got me on the back and legs and arms. But I don't think I'd be here if the shells weren't hitting rice paddies. If they'd landed on the road, I'd be a dead man."

There were amusing near misses too. When "B" Company of the RCR rotated onto Hill 159, No. 6 Platoon built an outhouse, complete with sandbag fortifications, right in the middle of the platoon area near the hilltop. On this particular day, during a break in the action, Pte. Art Browne made his way to the outhouse. His friend, Cpl. Russ Cormier, watched in horror as a Chinese self-propelled shell crashed into the outhouse and exploded deep in the outhouse pit. In the seconds before the shell hit, Browne had stood up and pulled up his boxers. When the smoke and dust cleared, Cormier saw Browne standing uninjured but with his pants down around his ankles. He was shouting: "Missed me! Missed me, the buggers!"

Even tank crews of the Lord Strathcona's Horse felt vulnerable to the Chinese guns. During the Second World War, Phil Daniel was with the 1st Hussars armoured regiment, and in Europe "if you were fired at three times, you would move . . . In Korea, we used to get fifty shells every day at noon . . . but up in those hills you couldn't move. Where could you go? You were dug in. You were trapped. You sat and took it."

Just after 9 o'clock on August 20, 1952, Sgt. Daniel's tank was hit by a Chinese shell. All five crewmen were in the tank at the time. With the explosion, "everything turned red," Daniel said. "I was knocked out by the shrapnel. The driver [Tpr. L. G.] Neufield was killed. But we were in such an awkward spot, we had to wait until noon before they could get ambulances in to us."

When the Petit brothers—Claude and Norris—got to Wainwright's advanced training area with the PPCLI in the spring of 1952, they experienced forced marches, bivouacking in the wilderness and war games. In the middle of one exercise, soldiers in small circling aircraft "dropped bags of salt on us from the plane" to simulate mortars and shells falling on troops in battle. Neither of the Metis brothers from Duck Lake, Saskatchewan, seemed fazed by salt bags falling from the sky. But the real thing was different.

One afternoon, shortly after "C" Company of the Princess Patricias moved into a counterattack position behind the Hook in November 1952, Pte. Claude Petit was manning one end of a stretcher full of supplies for members of his No. 8 Platoon. Re-supplying up and down the reverse slopes went on during daylight hours. So did Chinese shelling.

"All of a sudden the shit hit the fan," Petit said. "Mortars were coming in and they kept coming up the hill toward us."

The other man holding the stretcher was hit between the shoulder blades in his back. He passed out on the spot. Petit and a nearby medic grabbed the man and pulled him into a bunker, where they bandaged him and administered morphine.

"What the hell?" said Petit suddenly. He was looking down at his bloodied hands.

"You're hit someplace," the medic said. And he cut open Petit's coat to reveal wounds on his shoulders. What the medic also found under the private's coat was a recently arrived experimental bullet-proof vest. It, instead of Petit's stomach, had been cut to pieces by flying shrapnel.

"They weighed about sixty pounds," Petit said. "But I never took that bastard off again, while I was up there."

One of Claude Petit's fellow Patricias, Butch MacFarlane, considers himself even more fortunate. One midday, MacFarlane, a Bren gunner with "B" Company, sat with several other members of his No. 5 Platoon near platoon headquarters behind the Hook. They had paused among the stacks of barbed wire and piles of iron stakes (used to string wire in front of no-man's-land) to eat their C-Rations.

"All of a sudden there was this awful whack, just like somebody smacked an anvil with a maul hammer," MacFarlane said. "We all scattered. Then, when nothing happened, like a near-sighted bear, we all came back looking to see what had happened . . . Sticking out from among all these iron pegs was the tail fin of a Chinese mortar. They didn't pull the pin out. It didn't explode . . . The shrapnel from the iron pegs alone would have ripped the hell out of all of us."

As the static war in Korea evolved, so did tactics. Joe York, a corporal in the RCR assault pioneer platoon, remembers taking a course using huge searchlights, several kilometres behind the lines, to bounce beams of light off the clouds at targets on the Chinese side of the valley. The resulting "artificial moonlight," while helping UN gunners pinpoint Chinese positions, also unexpectedly revealed UN night patrols. One platoon commander described the explosion of light in no-man's-land like suddenly "being centre stage at Radio City Music Hall in New York."

In the earliest days of the war, most Canadian soldiers considered their British tin-hat helmets clumsy and useless. Instead, they used toques and balaclavas. In Korean trench warfare, new bulletproof vests, like the one that saved Claude Petit's life, and a strong, snug-fitting helmet were becoming regular infantry apparel. In fact, during Operation Trojan, Commonwealth troops were given American helmets as part of a deception to give Chinese spotters the impression that US units had moved onto Hill 355. In addition, UN troops were told to wear shirt sleeves down and buttoned. Signallers were to use American radio procedures, and troops were to use mostly American weapons. UN Command hoped the deception would tempt the Chinese into probing the new lines, thus increasing the potential for snatching Chinese troops as prisoners. The strategy worked until Canadian gunners fired their Vickers medium machine guns. The sound was easily recognized by the Chinese; the next morning Chinese loudspeakers across the valley were heard "welcoming Canadians" to the front.

Earl Simovitch and his combat engineers group discovered another aspect of the static war, "when they brought in a prisoner [who] told us they were digging a tunnel under our lines." Pte. Simovitch had grown up in Winnipeg before the war, but moved to Minneapolis to become an architect. As a foreign student working in the US, he became eligible for the draft. He dutifully reported and wound up in Korea in 1952 as a camouflage and demolition specialist with the 65th Engineer Combat Battalion. The Americans were on hills adjacent to the Commonwealth Division in an area they called the Iron Triangle.

"We found out the Chinese had dug a tunnel maybe a couple of thousand yards [under no-man's-land]," Simovitch said. "The Turks were near that section and they could hear the digging but didn't know what the hell it was.

"They found an air vent on a shaft that may have gone down hundreds of feet. It was concealed by whatever shrubbery was left . . . I got together composition C and napalm in a large canister, but when I got to the front lines I started puking. I had been in a confined space preparing these demolitions. My head was pounding . . .

"The patrol went up, dropped the explosives down the vent. There was a thirty second delay. Then I heard this massive rumble. It seemed the whole top of the hill lifted," effectively collapsing whatever tunnels lay underground. Simovitch received a Bronze Star (rare for a Canadian in the US military) for his service in Korea, but the memory of the destruction and life lost in those sorts of actions stayed with him.

By the autumn of 1952, the monsoon rains that had flooded many UN Command bunkers and washed away the brigade's Teal Bridge across the Imjin, had ceased. Rebuilding was going on. Reinforcements were filtering into front-line positions, although most Canadian infantry platoons were operating understrength. Increased Chinese shelling suggested that an offensive was brewing. Consequently, the officers at various company command posts began sending out more fighting patrols, ambush patrols, recce patrols and snatch patrols, to bring back prisoners with information. It was common knowledge that "the prize for a Chinese prisoner was a week's R & R in Tokyo."

Four RCR troops went out on a lay-up patrol or snatch in early September. Signaller George Mannion, wireless operator Don Moodie, Cpl. Karl Fowler and patrol leader Lt. Russ Gardner crossed no-man's-land to the Chinese-held Hill 227. They spent nearly sixty hours behind Chinese lines reconnoitring a kitchen area where about twenty soldiers were camped.

"It was the scariest thing of my life," said Pte. Mannion, who packed around the fifty-pound radio set during the mission. "For two days and three nights we hid in the grass watching these Chinese . . . Some guys are gung-ho. I'm not. I was glad the lieutenant didn't decide to grab a guy then . . . All I could think of was 'Christ, I hope we've got the right password when we get back.'"

A few nights later, Gardner and Fowler led a larger snatch patrol back to the same area. They found a Chinese telephone wire near the kitchen and broke it. It wasn't long before a Chinese soldier came looking for the break in the line, whereupon the RCR patrol seized him and brought him back alive. According to fellow patrolmen, "It was the oldest trick in the book," but as important, it netted Gardner the Military Cross and Fowler the Military Medal. Moreover, information gleaned from the prisoner confirmed a build-up of Chinese troops and munitions and a move in the direction of Hill 355.

Two other encounters early that fall flagged a significant Chinese build-up in front of the Canadians' defensive positions. On September 27, Lt. Dan Loomis led a fighting patrol to Hill 227 to seek out Chinese positions and strength. The patrol suddenly found itself pinched between a machine gun on the hill and an ambush patrol in the rear. In the firefight that took place, seven of the patrol's twenty-three soldiers were wounded, including Loomis, who took shrapnel from a Chinese grenade. He still managed to extricate his patrol by leading it "single file through an old minefield that had been laid during Operation Commando" the year before.

The second engagement on October 1 followed reports that a forward outpost—named Vancouver—had been overrun by Chinese forces. Lt. Andy King led a relief party to the outpost, where he found two men dead and the rest buried in the rubble of the command post. King organized the evacuation of the position while directing fire on an unexpectedly large Chinese force, which mysteriously vanished as quickly as it had appeared.

The anticipated assault against Hill 355 was about to materialize.

The summer and fall of 1952 had been eventful for Capt. Bob Mahar. He had come to Korea from the RCR's base at Petawawa with the 1st Battalion. He'd gone onto Hill 355 with the regiment in August. By October he had moved from second-in-command to Charlie Company commander. After months of army rations, a food package had arrived from his wife. Mahar had always had access to eggs and flour, but not the final ingredient for his favourite dessert, lemon meringue pie. In his wife's package was a box of powdered lemon pie filling.

"I was back at 'B' Echelon in the officers mess," Mahar said. It was the afternoon of October 23, and he'd begun "to make lemon pies for me and anyone else who wanted them. And just as I got to take them out of the oven, the shit hit the fan up front."

Chinese guns had been pounding the Canadian positions intermittently all month. Then, in late October, the frequency and focus of Chinese shelling changed dramatically. In one day, spotters counted about 1,600 shells hitting RCR positions, primarily on the saddle ridge between Hill 355 to the east and Hill 227 to the west. This small

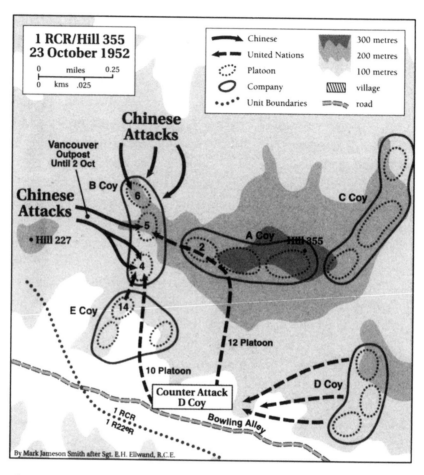

1 RCR/Hill 355
23 October 1952

0 miles 0.25
0 kms .025

Chinese — 300 metres
United Nations — 200 metres
Platoon — 100 metres
Company — village
Unit Boundaries — road

Chinese Attacks

Vancouver Outpost Until 2 Oct

B Coy
Chinese Attacks
Hill 227
C Coy
A Coy
Hill 355
E Coy
14
12 Platoon
10 Platoon
Counter Attack D Coy
D Coy
1 RCR 1 R22eR
Bowling Alley

By Mark Jameson Smith after Sgt. E.H. Ellwand, R.C.E.

plateau, soon to be occupied by "B" Company of the RCR, was the same spot the Vandoos had defended so doggedly in November 1951.

"For four days they just laid the boots to us with every gun they had," Capt. Herb Cloutier recalled. Back from his assignment earlier in the year with "B" Company (the so-called "Koje Commandos"), the RCR captain had recently organized "E" Company, an additional unit of riflemen. It occupied the draw immediately to the south of "B" Company as the bombardment continued. "I never saw anything like it. Hill 355 I think was [reduced to] 350 by the time they got finished shelling."

When Platoon Nos. 4, 5 and 6, of Baker Company, went onto the saddle position, after dark on October 22, L/Cpl. George Griffiths remembered "a lot of the trenches and bunkers were caved in . . . The first night I was beside a machine-gun with a rifle. We were just shooting into the dark."

Some of their fire found its mark. When the sun rose the next morning, Griffiths and his platoon mates spotted the bodies of several Chinese soldiers who were cut down trying to lay Bangalore torpedoes in the Canadian defensive wire. In the few bunkers that remained habitable, the thirty-four men of the three forward platoons tried to find cover underground and "lived that day on soda biscuits and jam."

The heavy shelling didn't let up. That afternoon, the command post for No. 6 Platoon caved in under the pressure and the platoon commander, Lt. Russ Gardner, took shelter with Sgt. G. E. P. Enright of No. 5 Platoon, whose commander, Lt. John Clark, acted as runner between the platoon areas and the company headquarters. No. 5 Platoon rifleman, Cpl. Les Butt, left his two-man bunker when a shell explosion outside the bunker flipped him from his back to his stomach. He joined seven others from No. 6 Platoon in a more substantial shelter, where Cpl. R. R. McNulty, a Second World War veteran, kept up morale by telling jokes and making the men laugh. Instinctively, however, everyone knew an attack would come soon.

"That evening, I took a standing patrol down a little trail toward [former outpost called] Victoria," Scotty Martin said. It was just a probe in front of the "E" Company position into no-man's-land, "when the Chinese time-on-target barrage began. Fire was coming down on all three forward companies to the extent that the hills just disappeared. We ran back as fast as we could."

Just after 6:30, with daylight gone and their guns registered on "B" Company's position, the Chinese gunners opened up for ten full minutes, followed by fire left and right of the saddle area for another forty-five minutes.

From the neighbouring "E" Company position, platoon commander Dan Loomis was counting the orange flashes as Chinese shells and mortar bombs exploded. He stopped at 700, because "before it was over, visibility was less than an arm's length due to the heavy pall of black fumes which also caused everyone's eyes to water."

The Chinese had chosen to cut off "B" Company from the rest of the regiment.

At No. 5 Platoon position, rifleman George Griffiths was counting Chinese soldiers—not orange flashes. "My war was only on the two feet of ground I was standing on, and they were coming in [at a ratio of] ten to one."

"I heard all this noise . . . Bugles blowing and yelling and screaming," Jim McKinny said. As a lance bombardier with the Royal Canadian Horse Artillery, he was stationed up Hill 355 at a forward observation post. To get a better look from his trench, he took out a set of donkey ears, a kind of periscope he used behind the protection of a parapet to register locations and angles for the artillery command post behind the lines. "I realized that the Chinese were overrunning the position."

None of the RCR commanders understood how so large a Chinese assault force could appear so quickly on their doorstep. Despite all efforts to stop the onslaught—machine-gun fire, Bren-gun fire and grenade-throwing—the No. 5 Platoon position was losing ground quickly. In his immediate area, Lt. Gardner ordered a retreat up the hill toward the No. 2 Platoon position of "A" Company, but en route the group was hit by a mortar barrage. Gardner only survived by playing dead until the vanguard of Chinese troops had passed over him. Meanwhile, Lt. Clark and his group fought until their ammunition was expended; then he and his surviving group made their way toward "A" Company too.

When medic Cosmo Kapitaniuk reached the Advanced Dressing Station behind the RCR's position, the wounded were already coming in, and he spent the night—some five trips in an ambulance—transporting RCR wounded to the American 8055th MASH unit. "Chest wounds, abdomen wounds, leg wounds . . . It's a wonder some of those guys were still alive."

Twice that evening, Capt. Cloutier tried to lead a signaller and several troops from "C" Company to reconnoitre the whereabouts of "B" Company survivors and to determine Chinese gains, "but there was so much dirt flying," Cloutier said, "we were driven back to our bunkers." About the same time, the No. 4 Platoon commander and "B" Company commander, Maj. E. L. Cohen, arrived at battalion headquarters behind the lines to report that their positions had been overrun. Any Canadians left in the "B" Company area had either been killed or taken prisoner.

The Canadian response wasn't long in coming.

At the RCHA forward observation post, L/Bdr. Jim McKinny was both listening to wireless exchanges from the battlefield below and reporting troop movements. He heard the RCR commanding officer call for "D. T. fire" and took the grid reference where the fire should be aimed.

"That's on top of you, sir," McKinny radioed.

"Yes," he answered. "And make it damn fast."

McKinny's relayed grid reference to bring fire down on Baker Company's position had double significance for the young volunteer from Saskatchewan. He knew his cousin, L/Cpl. Gerald McKinney, an RCAMC medic, was in action with the 1st Battalion of the RCR. What L/Bdr. McKinny didn't know was that in removing injured infantrymen from the battlefield, his cousin had been captured that night and spent the rest of the war in a Chinese POW camp in North Korea. L/Cpl. Griffiths, from No. 5 Platoon, also captured that night, was well on his way across no-man's-land by the time the Canadian 25-pounder artillery pieces began firing into the saddle position below Hill 355.

"From 6 o'clock that night [October 23] until 6 the next morning we were firing," Bob Bunting said. A bombardier at No. 2 Gun with "A" Battery, Bunting can recall few more hectic times in his artillery career. "All night, it was angle of sight, elevation and charge directions from the OP to the command post to the battery positions . . . The whole regiment joined in . . . The barrels of our guns were so bloody hot, the paint was just burning off them."

"It sounded like bees buzzing over our heads," said Herb Cloutier of the RCHA's continuous firing. In fact, the Canadian shelling was so precise that it halted the Chinese advance and prevented any resupplying of the front-line Chinese storm troopers. At the height of the

RCHA barrage, a South Korean monitoring the Chinese wireless communications heard a Chinese commander claim, "I am boxed in by artillery fire. I can't get reinforcements forward."

The temporary stalling of the Chinese offensive gave Canadian troops valuable time to regroup. A counterattack was organized from the "D" Company position to the rear of Hill 355. Capt. Bob Mahar received instructions for "C" Company's role in the counterattack when a pioneer officer delivered a package containing a lemon meringue pie he'd left baking at the officers' mess the afternoon before; his orders to relieve "D" Company were written on the bottom of the pie plate. Meanwhile, recce patrols led by Maj. Cohen and Lt. Clark into the "B" Company position from the east, and Capt. Cloutier from the south, helped retake the "B" Company area. By 3:30 in the morning of October 24, Hill 355 was back in Canadian hands. It was during this counterattack that some Canadian troops discovered what they had been up against that night.

"I jumped into one trench," Cloutier recalled, "and there was a Chinaman with explosives strapped to his back. But before I could fire, his own people blew him up . . . One of them was wearing goggles . . . anti-gas goggles. That frightened us, because we suddenly realized they might be [attacking] with gas . . .

"And all night long, out in the dark, you could hear them dragging away the bodies of their dead . . . Next morning, we found all kinds of bandages and blood and bodies," out in the former outpost positions. The Chinese had used the heavy bombardments not only to destroy Canadian defensive locations, but also to secretly move hundreds of troops forward into bunkers in the middle of no-man's-land. That's why the attack on "B" Company was so rapid and overwhelming. That's why the casualties, sustained mostly by Baker Company, were so high—18 killed, 35 wounded and 14 taken prisoner. Spotters in helicopters the morning after the battle counted in excess of 600 Chinese bodies in the valley. UN Command estimated that about a hundred RCR troops had defended the base of Hill 355 against two Chinese battalions, or about 1,500 men.

For defence of Kowang-san, Military Crosses were awarded to Capt. Cloutier and Lt. Clark, while Sgt. Enright was awarded a Military Medal. The greatest praise was reserved for the Canadian artillerymen. Capt. D. S. Caldwell, the Forward Observation Officer with the RCHA, was also awarded a Military Cross. Soon after the battle, the RCR commander Lt.-Col. Peter Bingham presented the RCHA commander, Lt.-Col. Teddy Leslie, with the VRI (Victoria Regina Imperitrix) cipher, the RCR regimental crest, for display on their gun shields. There's some disagreement whether the presentation was a jab for bringing RCHA shells down on Canadian positions, or as a badge of honour for the defence of Kowang-san.

"No question," Herb Cloutier concluded. "Artillery saved our bacon. That's all there is to it."

On November 1, 1952, the Royal Canadian Regiment turned over Hill 355 to the 1st Royal Australian Regiment with the following notification:

"This is to certify that Kowang-san has been handed over slightly the worse for wear but otherwise defensible."

The same day that Canadians turned back the Chinese at Kowang-san, Republican presidential candidate Gen. Dwight D. Eisenhower spoke to a partisan crowd of 5,000 during a whistle-stop in Detroit. He criticized the Truman administration for making the American public "wait and wait and wait" for peace. He promised, "I will go to Korea," and in so doing bring about an end to the war. Two weeks later he trounced his Democratic opponent, Adlai Stevenson, 442 electoral votes to 89. By December 2, 1952, the president-elect arrived in Korea and listened to his generals' aggressive plan to win the war militarily. Instead, Eisenhower would continue the Truman policy of seeking a negotiated solution.

In fact, the peace negotiations were still bogged down on voluntary repatriation of POWs and had regressed into "an institutionalized propaganda forum." All the while, the symbolic searchlight illuminated the skies over Panmunjom as it had for a full year. Soldiers such as RCR platoon commander Bert Pinnington, himself wounded in a shelling on Hill 355 and petrified that the next one would kill him, watched "the searchlight all the time, beaming straight up in the air . . . Guys being killed week after week, month after month . . . And these donkeys are discussing peace." It made Pinnington wonder, "Why are we here? What are we fighting for? I thought I'd be charging up hills and doing really dramatic things. But instead I was sitting in a hole . . . waiting."

Pinnington had been one of 1,197 Canadian casualties in Korea to that point.

In the early-evening hours of New Year's Day, 1953, RCR sniper Ted Zuber had come in from a successful daytime mission. He had taken out a Chinese sniper in the area in front of the Hook. Most in his battalion felt it was tit for tat, since the night before, Cpl. John Gill, an RCR section leader bringing in his patrol back through a UN defensive line, had been killed by a Chinese sniper. Pte. Zuber settled down in the tunnels beneath the Hook position to sleep.

Also in the tunnel that night were a combat engineer named Connors and two South Koreans who had been assigned to work with him. At that moment, the threesome were resting. Connors had lit a candle and begun reading a paperback, *The Perfumed Garden*. Meanwhile, a fourth man, a signaller named Doug Rainer, had been given permission to take a cigarette break in the tunnel. He sat next to the sleeping Zuber.

About twenty new recruits were also in the area as part of a reinforcement draft from Canada. The replacements had just begun preparing their weapons for the night's postings. One of the new men was told to prime a box of a dozen grenades in the tunnel. Around midnight, one of the grenades he had primed slipped from his hands. The grenade had a four-second fuse. Instead of shouting an alarm or tossing the grenade farther down the tunnel, the recruit panicked and ran out of the tunnel.

The explosion decapitated one of the Korean workers and severely wounded the other in the chest. The engineer had his leg broken in two places. The signaller had part of his foot blown off, and Pte.

Zuber took shrapnel up and down his legs and in the buttocks. Oddly enough, when Pte. Zuber gained semi-consciousness, he was able to see in the tunnel. The body of one of the Koreans had sheltered Connors's reading candle and it was still burning, providing a bit of light in the smoke-filled tunnel.

The Regimental Aid Post was already busy when the wounded arrived from the tunnel. The medical officer was working over sawhorses. Pte. Zuber, on a stretcher, was placed on the bunker floor next to the wounded South Korean labourer. A medical corporal approached, saw that Zuber's pants were bloodied and asked, "What is it?"

"I think I'm okay," Zuber said, and he pointed to the Korean. "What about him?"

"Oh, Christ," said the medic, realizing how serious the Korean's chest wound was. He immediately knelt down to investigate.

"Hey!" shouted the medical officer to the corporal. "Our own first!"

There was no argument. The corporal got up from the Korean, moved to Zuber and said, "Forgive me."

Zuber was conscious enough to be horrified. Horrified for the dying South Korean. And horrified for the dilemma facing the young corporal. The two Canadians listened to the wheezing sound next to them; it slowed and then ended as the Korean labourer stopped breathing.

There was little time to grieve because, for Zuber, "emotion was a luxury we learned to give up in the front lines." Later, at a Norwegian MASH unit, Zuber remembers a doctor smirking as he probed the wounds in Zuber's buttocks. They took eighteen pieces of shrapnel from the bones in his legs and the flesh of his backside.

Three weeks later, sniper Ted Zuber was back in the line. The RCR war diary reports he "unleashed poetic justice today when he killed two Chinese [snipers]," one of whom was carrying the identification tags of Cpl. Gill, the RCR soldier killed on New Year's morning. In the killing zone, the best a soldier could hope for was to even the score.

A BIT OF HOME

B Y NOVEMBER 1952, Pte. Len Peterson had been away from his home in southern Alberta for eight weeks. The last time he had walked down familiar streets in Olds, he had been on embarkation leave. After that, his 3rd Battalion of the Princess Patricia's Canadian Light Infantry had pulled up stakes from their advanced training camp in Wainwright and shipped out for Korea aboard the USNS *Marine Adder*. During its first weeks in the line, Peterson's battalion assisted the British Black Watch regiment on the Hook and then began settling in for its first Korean winter. To warm himself during one daytime break, Peterson wrote a letter home to a girl he'd known in high school. He hoped he might get a response.

Before long a letter arrived at his No. 8 Platoon position in Korea. Peterson wrote back. This time he enclosed a few snapshots—pictures showing the countryside, the dog that had become the platoon mascot and living quarters in tents and bunkers. Generally shy and quiet, Peterson asked his school chum in Olds, Rose Marie Stumpf, to write some of his platoon mates and to send pictures from home. Soon letters were arriving for Peterson as well as for Joe Tonkin, Bill Reid, Pat Fontaine, Carson Hutchens and Johnny Birjuit.

The letters contained news from home, what young people their age were doing, as well as word on what was hot in books, records and movies. Enclosed were snaps with comments on the back: "How do you like my new spring outfit?" "My kid sister and I sunbathing."

And "This is a pale mauve formal I'm going to wear for graduation."
By the time sixteen-year-old Rose Marie graduated from high school, in the spring of 1953, she had been dubbed "The Sweetheart of the PPCLI" and her picture was on display in the tents and bunkers of many members of the Princess Patricias 3rd Battalion. Rose Marie had written more than 500 letters and, back home in Olds, she was being besieged by newspaper reporters from Calgary and Winnipeg for the inside story on becoming the Korea forces' pin-up.

"It's up to us to do something for the boys," Rose Marie responded. "After all, they are over in Korea fighting for us."

In spite of Rose Marie's hugely successful one-woman letter-writing campaign, the more formal support system for Canadian troops was, for most of the war, basic. Previous to the Korean War, civilian organizations, known collectively as Auxiliary Services, had provided for Canadian soldiers by sending such things as scarves, writing paper and cigarettes. By 1949, the armed services themselves had decided to take charge of the "welfare" of troops abroad. That left traditional service providers, such as the Canadian Red Cross Society, the Royal Canadian Legion, the Knights of Columbus, the Salvation Army and the YMCA, generally out of the picture. A year into the war, the British Navy, Army and Air Force Institute (NAAFI) and the United Service Organizations (USO) were assisting Commonwealth and American soldiers. Welfare of Canadian origin, however, was "conspicuous by its absence."

When they arrived, magazines were out-of-date. Pocketbooks were sometimes available through the NAAFI library, and writing paper could only be found in some American ration boxes. The brigade got the latest newsreels and films from the Americans, although Canadian film projectors were regularly broken. Scarcest of all were made-in-Canada cigarettes, beer and such things as playing cards and cribbage boards.

When these problems were raised in the House of Commons in late 1951, the St. Laurent government responded. By New Year's Eve the same year, Minister of National Defence Brooke Claxton and an entourage from Parliament were in Korea inquiring into the welfare being provided to the troops at the front.

On his return, Claxton promised that his department would provide such services as current motion pictures, tape recordings of CBC Radio programs, a daily ration of twenty free cigarettes, spot news delivered in cables, magazines and newspapers, recreational facilities at the Commonwealth leave centre in Tokyo and sports equipment for field games.

Not long after Claxton's announcement, a North Star transport aircraft landed at Haneda Airport in Tokyo. On board, along with tires, generators, spare parts and parkas, were some rush containers labelled "welfare supplies." Inside was "hockey equipment . . . no shoulder pads, but there were elbow pads, shin pads and skates. I can't remember if there were jocks," Eric McClymont said.

An all-round athlete, McClymont had been an excellent swimmer, middleweight boxer and star shortstop for the Carleton Place Esso softball club in Ontario. However, from his boyhood in minor hockey right through to his first days at Camp Borden with the Royal Canadian Regiment hockey team, McClymont most enjoyed lacing on the blades to play hockey whenever he could. So why not behind the lines in Korea in the winter of 1952?

"When the gear all arrived," McClymont said, "the way we picked the team was—if the skates fitted, you played . . . So we made up a team to play the Vandoos." On the appointed day, players, spectators, dignitaries and photographers arrived at a spot along the frozen Imjin River for the afternoon contest. The engineers had scraped the river's ice surface. They had even erected boards and goal nets. On the riverbank overlooking the impromptu arena was a freshly painted sign that read "Imjin Gardens."

The game began with officers posing for a ceremonial face-off. The RCR players lined up in regimental hockey sweaters (flown in specially), as did the R22eR team. Then out came a couple of referees in their striped jerseys to drop the puck and begin the game. To suggest neutrality, they weren't from either infantry regiment, but "they didn't know shit about hockey," McClymont said.

"We had the two Stewart brothers . . . kind of like Mutt and Jeff, one big guy, the other a little short ass. We had a guy from Timmins named Dube on defence. Another defencemen was Gerry Enright . . . We had a really quick winger, company quartermaster MacPherson . . . and Sgt. Major Britton played goal . . . It began really just as a day of fun, but it turned crazy. It was a dirty hockey game to tell you the truth. There was no love between us and the Vandoos."

Not long into the first period, a few elbows were thrown, then a few stick slashes. With the boards about waist-high, a well-placed hip-check could actually propel an opponent over the boards and into the snow beyond. The bumpy ice surface made passing and shooting pretty unpredictable. As the game progressed, so did the intensity. And the crowd grew too. Paul Rochon was one of many R22eR soldiers trucked to the riverbank to watch what he remembers as "a very pushy game." As the audience cheered on the Vandoos' side along the boards, a couple of American helicopters hovered overhead with airborne spectators leaning out and snapping photographs.

"We played close to sixty minutes," McClymont said. "After one period, you took a ten-minute break to get your skates off to give to somebody else to play. I happened to be lucky. I played the whole game . . . Oh, was it dirty . . . But, you know something, I can't remember the final score. It was just great fun."

The Canadian defence minister had also promised "films of special interest" to the troops in Korea. Screenings of such annual sporting institutions as the Grey Cup final, the Canadian Open Golf Tournament and the Stanley Cup finals would be flown in. Claxton's department ultimately delivered those "welfare" packages too. For soldiers who were in Korea around the end of the war, there was a bonus. Not only did the films arrive, but so did a few of the sports celebrities who appeared in them.

"The year we won the Stanley Cup, I was contacted through the Red Wings organization and asked to go to Korea," recalled wartime hockey player Red Kelly. "I said, 'Sure.'" The big defenceman from southern Ontario had been in the NHL with Detroit since 1947, and while not particularly flamboyant, Kelly was a fan favourite in the six-team league of the early 1950s.

With Kelly's consent, the Department of National Defence began organizing the junket, which also included Regina Roughriders' star half-back Ken Charlton, Calgary radio sports commentator Henry Viney, Regina sportscaster Lloyd Saunders and sports columnist for the *Toronto Telegram*, Bob Hesketh.

"Red was the star attraction," according to Hesketh, whose daily "News on Sport" column covered everything from the Olympics to CFL football to the Toronto Maple Leaf road trips. "The idea was to go over [to Korea], show films of the Grey Cup and the Stanley Cup, meet some of the troops and have question-and-answer periods."

Before they headed overseas, each member of the group received National Defence guidelines about do's and don'ts in Korea. Each received an advance of $100 spending money. Each one got death and dismemberment insurance. Each got anti-tetanus and anti-typhoid shots. Each packed the prescribed sixty-six pounds of baggage with "lots of civvy clothes," Hesketh said, "but they all stayed in the bag," because the army issued them khaki uniforms for their entire stay in the Far East. Hesketh nicknamed the group "The Rover Boys" in the columns he sent back.

The sports celebrity junket got off to a noteworthy start when, after seventeen hours aboard a Canadian Pacific airliner from Vancouver to Japan, the men landed at their first Tokyo hotel in search of a quiet night's rest. Kelly, a deep sleeper, bedded down on a set of floor springs and mattress, while Charlton and Hesketh took in the hotel's dinner and entertainment and then retired late. They all were wakened at dawn by the vibrations of their hotel rooms. Kelly looked at the overhead chandelier swaying like a tree limb in a stiff breeze. Hesketh went to the window, spotted a large bird bath losing its contents and shouted to the big footballer in the next room, "Hey, Charlton?"

"Yeah?" called back a groggy voice.

"We're having an earthquake!"

"Yeah?" Charlton said again. "Ain't that interesting."

Although the locals told them that there was no damage and that it was just a slight tremor, the Canadians agreed, it seemed "more like the Frisco quake of 1908."

Partly because sports was common knowledge to all of them, but also because they were thrown into this new experience together, everybody in the troop tour got along. Henry Viney, a short heavy-set man, loved his cigars and often wore his cowboy Stetson so that everyone would know he was from Calgary. Since he'd made a similar trip before, Viney seemed to take command of things. Tall and always smiling, sportscaster Lloyd Saunders, in Hesketh's words, "was a good time waiting to happen." Saunders had bought a camera and snapped shots of everything and everybody. For footballer Ken Charlton and hockey star Red Kelly, both from small towns, travelling outside North America was a first, but the appreciative troops made the entire group feel at home.

At each location behind the lines in Korea, whether inside a tent, a mess hall or a Quonset hut, the military outfit that was hosting the visit set up rows and rows of chairs and a movie projector for the sports films that Briston Films had made available for the trip. That's when "Sergeant" Viney leaped into action as emcee, cracking jokes and introducing each member of the entourage. Charlton then did a running commentary for the Grey Cup films and Kelly offered play-by-play of the Stanley Cup excerpts, simply referring to himself on screen as "Number four, there."

Generally, enlisted men and NCOs saw the show first, followed by the officers, but "at every stop," Charlton said, "we'd sit around after the presentation over a beer and answer questions about sports and what was happening back home in Saskatchewan or Ontario."

"Red must have shaken hands with about 500 of them," Hesketh wrote, "even the Canadiens fans . . .

"There's been no theme to the things they wanted to know. As many about the [Toronto] subway as about the Maple Leafs. The Brown Derby, the Royal York Hotel, where's the mail? have all been chucked at us. A soldier named Morrison, who used to live next door to Sid Smith of the Leafs, asked us to be sure to let him know about it. Bruce Taylor, who used to play hockey with Eric Nesterenko when the Nester used to hide his skates at the Taylor house because his parents didn't want him to play hockey . . . And another soldier from Brantford who wants us to phone the *Expositor* so that his friends will know he has left the country . . ."

Hesketh joked about the group's "cauliflower ear" to emphasize the hours upon hours the visiting celebrities listened to young soldiers' stories and questions about home. What struck the *Tely* sports reporter most were the "thousands of little kids . . . who had no home. They were the camp kids. They followed the soldiers and the soldiers fed and clothed them . . . Kids who were living in the wreckage, thieving and living hand-to-mouth."

After travelling by jeep in Korea, broadcaster Lloyd Saunders said, "Never again will I complain about Saskatchewan's roads, roads that I thought were the worst in the world. Korea's, and I use a bit of Korean slang, are No. 11, meaning impossible." Because water was always in short supply and not very appetizing, Ken Charlton remembers "cleaning my teeth with beer." For Red Kelly the lasting impression was "seeing Canada among other countries, participating, playing a role . . . I had seen a bit of the world . . . and it made me more aware of the world and Canada. It's one of the reasons I ran for Parliament later on" in the early 1960s.

Army-sponsored welfare was always welcome, even if highly organized and short-lived. Having Red Kelly and Ken Charlton narrate films of the Stanley Cup or the Grey Cup was a definite crowd pleaser. Perhaps the most delicious distractions from the war, however, were those the troops least expected. In the words of one quartermaster sergeant, "Ever since they joined the army, [Canadian soldiers] have been rationed things—so many boots, so many shirts, so much food—so we had the idea of producing something of which we could give them just as much as they wanted."

Maxwell "Duke" Poyntz came to Korea with the RCR in 1951. A long-time quartermaster, Poyntz had served in the Canadian army occupation force in Germany, where he ran the recreational services of the McNaughton Club. He'd earned the nickname "Duke" because he was often seen in Oldenburg driving a glistening Mercedes-Benz car. Behind the lines with "B" Company of the 2nd Battalion RCR in Korea, Duke drove a jeep and became the regiment's unofficial social director. In his first days behind the lines, Poyntz organized a nine-man section with the sole job of manufacturing recreational venues. The group managed to obtain the first motion pictures since the men had left Pusan. They brought a US army show through. They built volleyball courts, baseball diamonds and a horseshoe pitch in every company area. They dammed a stream into a sizeable swimming and bathing hole. Pooling their financial resources, Duke's section of do-gooders bought $500 worth of Korean silks, kimonos and other souvenirs for resale at cost to the unit.

Still, Max Poyntz's crew is best remembered in Korea for its culinary initiative. Armed with well-scrubbed packing cases as pastry boards, empty beer bottles as rolling pins and empty ration tins as dough cutters, the privates and corporals in Poyntz's unit began manufacturing doughnuts for the troops. With no bookkeeping and no access to unit rations, the group managed to procure 200 pounds of flour, 150 of lard and 60 of sugar, two cases of powdered milk and two of powdered eggs for the daily production line. Each day, the tent known as Duke's Donut Dive served up as many as 6,000 doughnuts—including jelly, iced, cake and slab—along with fresh coffee, cold chocolate, lemonade or eggnog. What's more, it was all for free.

A little later in the war and a little closer to the front lines, near the Kansas Line north of the Imjin River, off-duty Canadian troops found escape in a large mess hall at "A" Echelon known as Peterson's Paradise. The building, made possible by Maj. Jack Peterson, who was second-in-command of the 2nd Battalion RCR, was constructed of materials liberated from deserted villages, including wooden poles and beams and a straw-thatched roof. The way reporter Bill Boss described it, "Peterson's Paradise is close enough to the front to be shelled, yet far enough away to let a guy get away from it all for eight hours."

"Immediately after the dawn stand-to," wrote Cpl. Ron Trider of the 2nd RCR, "those chosen for a day's rest made their way to the jeep-head to board trucks which took them to the rear. Each draft had approximately seventy-five men to visit Paradise. As they debussed, they were met by the battalion's bugle band which tooted and thumped at them with great enthusiasm."

Behind the bugle band was an array of signs welcoming the shaggy troops: "Are your boots polished?" asked one. "Is your brass shining?" asked another. And then another concluded: "There's no excuse. This way to barber shop and shoe shine." For the affordable sum of fifteen cents in Korean won, plus ten cents for a shampoo, the visiting soldiers could get coiffed by Koreans, whom Cpl. Trider described as "the descendants of Geronimo . . . using hand clippers that pulled and skinned and scalped.

"At the showers, heads and bodies were scrubbed and scoured with a vengeance, then rinsed with steaming hot water pumped out of the polluted Imjin River. Even the fellows who didn't consider showering a priority, tolerated it without complaint. Dirty socks and underwear were dropped in a pile in exchange for clean items worn and discarded by the previous visitors to the showers."

Inside a shrapnel-torn mess tent, Pte. Ross "Steamboat" Bonham served up steaming porridge, three poached eggs and buttered toast. Breakfast was served at tables with chinaware and tablecloths. (No one knew where the tablecloths came from, but rumours hinted at some connection between Peterson's Paradise and a boxcar of white bed linens that had gone missing between Fort Lewis and Wainwright.) For men accustomed to eating out of mess tins on groundsheets placed on the edges of trenches, explained Peterson, "I know once in a while a man enjoys sitting at a table, having waiters look after him. So we have bowls, plates, cups and glasses. And the tables are served by four Korean houseboys." The process was repeated during a lunch of soup, fruit juice, roast dressed turkey with all the trimmings and supper of steak and onions—grilled to order—and apple pie and coffee.

During the afternoons, visitors to Peterson's Paradise could spectate around an outdoor boxing ring, or catch up on correspondence, read or watch movies (usually westerns, unless the padres were absent) in the thatched theatre full of seats made of cartridge cases spray-painted blue. On occasion, entertainers, musicians or comedians visited the theatre. Ron Trider recalls one occasion when a US Army band featuring former members of the USAAF Glenn Miller band performed. Despite the upbeat performance, the American musicians, used to playing outside the combat zone, were clearly worried about the potential for being caught in a Chinese shelling attack.

"A small barrage of Chinese/Russian rockets struck in the vicinity," Ron Trider said. "When the first salvo crashed into the area, the band stopped playing and scattered. The Canadian audience fought their impulses to run for cover and called for the band to return and continue the concert.

"One Canadian headed for a tent-covered dugout whose occupant had recently been rotated out of the lines. The visitor had been invited to share a few beers [that] the host had been hoarding for a couple of weeks. As his visitor reached the tent, another rocket struck nearby. The band's drummer quickly followed him into the dugout. . . The three had an enjoyable visit, except perhaps for the host, who watched his entire beer ration disappear."

A few weeks later, the mess hall and theatre at Peterson's Paradise suffered a direct hit—an event Cpl. Trider described as "Paradise Lost."

The parade of celebrities behind the front lines in Korea was a who's who of entertainment from the 1950s. Some Canadian troops managed to attend shows sponsored by the USO featuring such performers as Bing Crosby, Bob Hope, Betty Hutton and Piper Laurie. Marilyn Monroe is purported to have performed "in a tight-fitting dress with no undies," while Jack Benny's deadpan humour proved too subtle for most military audiences. In contrast, a performance by American country-and-western singer Elton Britt was so engrossing that during the show two Chinese soldiers surrendered to UN forces at the concert.

Canadian "B" Echelon positions were visited by such shows as Jerry Gosley's Smile Show, CBC Radio performer Carol Carr, the Fun Revvers and the Sweet Cap Variety Show, which featured veteran actor-singer John Pratt. In late 1951, American comedian Danny Kaye passed through Canadian positions both to entertain and to be filmed as part of a campaign to promote blood donations back home.

During the performance of a British concert party, the show on stage suddenly found itself competing with a show in the front row. A member of the R22eR had pulled out his harmonica and was playing along with the stage band. In an attempt to be accommodating, the piano player in the band invited the amateur harp player on stage to do a solo, whereupon the Vandoos soldier stole the show. Following the harmonica number, the audience shouted, "Encore!" After each new number they shouted louder. It was all the British musicians could do to finish their program.

On the other hand, Vancouver-based singer Lorraine McAllister had no trouble captivating the troops every minute she spent in Korea. In December 1952, she and her accompanist, accordion player Karl Karleen, arrived for a two-week performing tour behind the lines. In Tokyo and Seoul she stopped traffic, "because she was the first blonde woman many of the people there had ever seen." During one of her first performances—singing requests over a wireless set from the headquarters of "B" Squadron of the Lord Strathcona's Horse—she sang and Karl played through the receiver of every Canadian tank along the front line. There wasn't a position she wouldn't visit. She even fired a shell from a 25-pounder artillery piece of the Royal Canadian Horse Artillery just behind the lines.

"We came in with the dessert," McAllister said of her appearances. She and Karl Karleen would time their visits to hit the mess hall or recreation hall just as troops were finishing their meal. "Then the show went on . . . . I'm like radar. I send out beams. The men respond. And then I play accordingly."

Part of that radar sensitivity was knowing that the troops enjoyed her feminine presence. Unlike other performers, McAllister did not wear khaki. Even when being jeeped from one location to another, she wore a strapless evening gown with a parka thrown over her shoulders. "The men want to feel they've got a Canadian girl around," she said, "so I've got to look like one."

UN troops were great audiences. Whether in a Quonset hut or an open-air amphitheatre, the soldiers crowded in and lapped it up. They never tired of the standard songs of the day. Lorraine McAllister always got requests for "Alouette," especially from the francophone soldiers. Wherever the Sweet Cap Variety Show performed, John Pratt was always expected to sing "You'll Get Used To It," a song written by Jewish-Canadian refugee Freddy Grant and which Pratt had made famous during the Second World War while entertaining troops in the *Meet the Navy* show. There was Rosemary Clooney's "Come On-A My House," Patti Page's "Tennessee Waltz" and the Weavers' version of Leadbelly's 1931 song "Goodnight Irene." Another tune requested by Canadian troops was a Korean song of unrequited love called "Arirang." But by far the most requested song in Korea was Hank Snow's "Movin' On."

Until April 1950, Clarence Eugene Snow, from Brooklyn, Nova Scotia, had been little more than a regional performer. Self-taught on a Hawaiian guitar his mother bought by mail order, Hank, "the Singing Ranger," tried his hand at touring in the 1940s, when he travelled across the continent sharing the stage with a trained horse named Shawnee. His breakthrough occurred when his tune "Movin' On" hit the country-music charts in the US in the spring of 1950. The song went to number one in July, stayed on the country-music charts for fourteen months and carried Hank Snow's popularity to the Grand Ole Opry in Nashville. Riding that wave and watching the industry around him, "in March of 1953, I volunteered to go to South Korea, joining a succession of Hollywood stars and entertainers who went there regularly, bringing a little bit of home to a lot of homesick boys."

Snow led a country-music troupe that included his back-up band, the Rainbow Ranch Boys, Ernest Tubb and his Texas Troubadours, vocal duet Annie Lou and Danny Hill, and Opry comedian Doc Lou

Childre. Throughout their three-week tour of Korea, the country-and-western artists experienced snow and rain, jeep and transport travel and every conceivable venue, from the huge Ernie Pyle The-atre in Tokyo, to a warehouse behind the lines called the Rice Bowl, to the deck of a hospital ship off Inch'on.

"Just as we were arriving alongside the *Haven*," Snow recalled, "somebody yelled that a helicopter was approaching. We watched as it descended towards the stern of the ship with wounded in its plastic pods. About 75 feet off the landing pad, the chopper motor cut out and it crashed heavily onto the deck. The wounded were removed and quickly rushed off. We were shaken but proceeded to entertain the wounded, the bedridden and the ship's crew."

On land, the war was never far from the edge of the stage. On one occasion, the troupe played outdoors before an audience of 5,000 soldiers who were nestled into the hillsides of a horseshoe canyon. The performers were told that the Chinese were close enough to be watching too, and while the troops weren't the least bit distracted by distant gunfire, "we gave them the fastest show of our tour.

"As well as 'Movin' On', the song most frequently requested was 'My Mother' which I wrote in the 1940s. It seemed to have special meaning for the boys. And as I sang it again and again, the tears flowed down their cheeks. I offered to write a personal letter to the soldiers' mothers. I expected about 400 addresses, but I ended up with over 7,000 letters to send when I got home. I signed each letter with love, happy to provide a link between the soldiers and their homes."

While Hank Snow's "mail-out of love" left a huge impression on sons and mothers for years to come, he may not have realized his immediate impact on the war in Korea. Nearly every military outfit borrowed the melody line from "Movin' On" and created its own version of the Hank Snow hit. The US Marine Corps altered the lyrics to say:

I've been here twelve months too long,
I'm beginning to like the weather.
I beat the odds, I'm goin' home.

Among the Canadian versions was one that criticized their American comrades-in-arms:

Hear the pitter patter of ten thousand feet
It's ole 1st Cav Div in full retreat.
They're movin' on, they'll soon be gone.

Besides providing a tune Korean War soldiers could sing and march to, Snow's signature song worked its way into army lingo too. Whenever a unit was forced to make an unscheduled retreat, to disguise the fact on radio sets, soldiers would often say, "Let's pull a Hank Snow!" and few, if any, Chinese eavesdroppers would ever know what it meant.

On the heels of Canadian showman Hank Snow, another home-grown troupe made its way to Korea. Since 1947, loyal listeners of CBC Radio had tuned in weekly to hear the booming voice of Herb May announce: "It's the Wayne and Shuster Show." When the show's producer, Jackie Rae, received a letter from the Department of External Affairs inviting Johnny Wayne, Frank Shuster and their radio show ensemble to entertain Canadian troops in Korea, it seemed the right thing to do.

"We took a page from Bob Hope, who was also in Korea at the time," explained Frank Shuster, who knew the value of performing to troops overseas. "Soldier audiences are the best in the world. They're so happy to see somebody from home. No matter what you do, it's great, as long as you bring a touch of home."

Creating entertainment for military audiences was nothing new to the two comedians from Toronto. From December 1942 to September 1943, they had headlined *The Canadian Army Radio Show*. Then for six months they toured a stage version of the show across Canada, raising money for the welfare of Canadian troops overseas. After D-Day, Wayne and Shuster were the first Canadian army entertainers to go into Normandy with a show entitled *The Invasion Review*.

Their show and personnel in Korea would be a composite of their *Canadian Army Radio Show* days in 1944 and their hit radio show in 1953. Their producer was also no stranger to a theatre of war. Jackie Rae had flown RCAF Spitfires over the English Channel during the Second World War and had been decorated with a Distinguished Flying Cross by King George VI in 1943.

"We recorded the [radio] show weekly at the CBC studios on McGill Street [in Toronto]," Rae said. "We were going to be [in Korea] for six or seven weeks, so we planned to record the shows on acetate," and send them back for broadcast. With that in mind, Rae brought along CBC on-location technician Don Bacon and CBC announcer Herb May, as well as ad agency representative, Cam James, to act as party manager. Producer Rae booked an ensemble of musicians and performers that would meet the requirements of the regular radio show as well as give the troops a stage production worth seeing. The rest of the Canadian Concert Party, as the military described them, consisted of band members Lew Lewis (saxophone), Vic Centro (accordion), Jim Reynolds (trumpet), Ted Roderman (trombone), Harry Nicholson (drummer), as well as dancer Zena Cheevers and singer Terry Dale.

"I was thrilled to be able to go," Terry Dale said. At age seventeen, she had already been the regular band singer in Vancouver's Cave Supper Club. She later moved to Toronto to join Art Hallman's orchestra as its vocalist. Wayne and Shuster noticed her and hired her for their radio show. She was twenty-six when they invited her to help them entertain troops just behind the front lines in Korea, but "when you're young like that, you aren't afraid of anything."

On March 28, 1953, armed with multiple inoculations for tropical diseases and the Canadian government handbook on Korea, the entourage boarded a Canadian Pacific Airlines DC-4 for Tokyo.

Twenty-four hours later they arrived at Haneda Airport and received Canadian army-issue uniforms. The men wore them, but, like Lorraine McAllister, Terry Dale and Zena Cheevers figured the soldiers didn't want to see women dressed in khaki, so most of the time they shed the uniforms in favour of street clothes off stage and evening gowns and heels on stage.

During their first few days in Tokyo, the Canadian entertainers adjusted to the climate, the people and the time zone. The band members never forgot the Miranuchi Hotel rooms, which Lew Lewis said, "contained toy furniture. I'm not a big man, maybe five-foot-seven, and I had to bend down to shave. Don Bacon and Herb May were six-foot-four, so when they lay down on their beds, the end of the bed came under their knees."

The Wayne and Shuster troupe gave its first performance in Tokyo to an American audience at the 6,000-seat Ernie Pyle Theatre, which was so large the Canadian ensemble felt "like a bunch of gnomes on this huge stage." The Japanese backstage crew spoke no English, but was so professional that a diagram was direction enough. They easily understood lighting and curtain cues for Wayne and Shuster's classic sketch about the murder of Julius Caesar in the Roman senate, called "Rinse the Blood Off My Toga." It parodied the successful late-40s radio detective drama "Dragnet."

"My name is Flavius Maximus," Wayne would say à la Sgt. Joe Friday.

"Dum, da-dum, dum," the band instruments would respond.

"I'm a private Roman eye."

"Dum, da-dum, dum. Dum."

"My licence is IXIVLLCCDIXMV." Wayne would wait for the laugh and finish with, "Hard to remember, but it comes in handy as an eye chart."

At the end of the first week in April, the Canadians boarded a Royal Australian Air Force DC-3 for Seoul, where they were met by British Army officers who escorted them to their home base for the next few weeks behind the lines in the British sector. Terry Dale and Zena Cheevers stayed in a wooden trailer with bunk beds, and on their first morning in the camp an officer's batman came knocking with tea, fresh bread and jam. Meanwhile, the men in the troupe were assigned to tents dug into the ground; they were sandbagged for protection and contained cots, sleeping bags and Arctic stoves to take the chill off those early-spring nights.

The entertainers' performing areas were equally basic. Most often it was a glorified Nissen hut (that the British called the Drury Lane Theatre). When on the road, the Wayne and Shuster Show was packed into a couple of jeeps. On arrival, band members and troops would place planks on forty-gallon oil drums for a stage, with a tarpaulin or canvas canopy for the sun or rain. Troops would assemble on the nearby hillsides and the show would begin. Most times, the show opened with bandleader Lew Lewis walking out on-stage playing a jazz riff on his sax. Trumpeter Jimmy Reynolds followed. Then Vic Centro on accordion and Ted Roderman on trombone joined them. Finally, drummer Harry Nicholson came out, cymbal in hand, sat at his drum set and the band played its first number.

When Herb May introduced the stars, Johnny and Frank were generally met with thunderous applause. Dashing on stage, Wayne and Shuster launched into banter (borrowed from their *Canadian Army Radio Show* days) about life in uniform: "Army life is very strict. Lights out at 9 o'clock. Women out at 10 o'clock." They lampooned everything from food, to weather, to themselves: "We're the only people fired at deliberately by both sides." A recurring situation depicted Shuster as the lowly private down in the dumps about the war and his lot, and Wayne, his commanding officer, passing the buck. The chatter between them was crisp and full of army jargon. But inevitably, the memorable moments were the ones that no one expected. On one occasion, C.O. Wayne gave Pte. Shuster an order.

The beleaguered private refused.

"That's an order, private!" Wayne barked. He pulled an imaginary pistol from his belt and pointed it at Frank's head. "Do it or else."

Just then a nearby British artillery battery fired a round.

Without missing a beat, Wayne looked at the imaginary pistol and did a double take to the audience.

Shuster smiled smugly and said: "Missed!"

The improvised bit brought down the house.

Following a Wayne and Shuster sketch, Herb May introduced the female contingent of the ensemble. Zena Cheevers presented a nearly gymnastic dance routine that included Spanish dancing, jazz dancing, cowboy dances and even baton-twirling. Then band singer Terry Dale, in strapless gown and high heels, would walk on stage offering to help Johnny and Frank in a sketch.

"No, Terry," one of them would say. "Just sing."

She would sing "Don't Sit Under the Apple Tree" and "whatever was popular in 1953. I remember singing 'Till There Was You' and one song in French for the Vandoos. They loved it. They were a smashing group. I'd never seen so many handsome men in my life. They were so gentlemanly."

The Vandoos' hospitality extended well into the evening and, for Wayne and Shuster, into unknown territory. At the officers' mess, the colonel of the regiment introduced Frank and Johnny to the concept of chugalugging liquor. The two Canadians were teetotallers, or as Shuster often said, "I'm the only guy from World War II who never had a drink."

The Vandoos' commander would not be refused, and before a few chugalugs were over, the two comedians were under the table. However, what soon became more alarming to Shuster than his fuzzy mental state was the whereabouts of his partner. Wayne was suddenly missing. The colonel ordered a search party, but it found no trace of the Canadian funnyman. It wasn't until some hours later that another R22eR officer reported a stranger in his quarters, a man he confessed looked more dead than alive. When Frank was called to the officer's tent, he found Johnny passed out, in the fetal position, not dead, but dead drunk.

The troupe's itinerary was usually kept secret and audiences were thrown together quickly. Princess Patricias' private Art Marion remembered being rounded up "at three o'clock in the afternoon and trucked right out of the front lines. It was all kept quiet, you know, so the enemy wouldn't hear about it . . . because all it took was one bomb in there with all those people in one spot . . .

"It was great entertainment, because for us anything was entertainment. Didn't matter whether it was two wrestlers or entertainers, we loved it. But I remember [Wayne and Shuster's] crazy jokes and the girls in those flimsy clothes. Boy it just drove us nuts!"

The Wayne and Shuster troupe performed nearly forty separate shows, often two and three a day. Still, the Canadian Army organizers built in enough time with each appearance to allow the performers to mingle with the ordinary soldiers, whether medics, riflemen, engineers, Service Corps troops or Mobile Laundry and Bath Unit workers. As in the sports junket with Red Kelly and Ken Charlton, the Wayne and Shuster Show members sat with soldiers to talk about home, took down phone numbers to call back home and received letters to be posted in Canada.

"Most of the soldiers never spoke about the war," Terry Dale recalled. "They were always upbeat . . . never talking about the futility of it all. The worst they admitted was being homesick. I remember visiting this one fellow in a field hospital. They told me quietly he was going to lose his leg that day."

"Those kids in Korea were so young," commented producer Jackie Rae. "That really bugged me. I was angry at first . . . I'd forgotten how young I was. I was eighteen and flying operations [in the RCAF over Europe in 1941]. It seemed so useless."

To most members of the troupe, it appeared no matter how hard they tried to be a distraction for their audiences, the war was always close by. The women performers were warned never to walk barefoot because of the danger of insect bites and haemorrhagic fever. On one occasion, air raid sirens sounded in the performers' home-base camp; everybody got under cover, but when they emerged, all they found were propaganda pamphlets that had been dropped by a pilot (nicknamed "Bed Check Charlie") in a single-engine Chinese airplane. Though it didn't stop a single show, artillery fire could always be heard in the distance.

"We were circulating with soldiers after a show," Lew Lewis recalled. "And we had a request from an American unit to squeeze in an extra show for soldiers in a nearby MASH location. So we offered our apologies we couldn't spend more time at this little soirée and we got in our jeeps, went to the hospital and played another show . . . After the hospital show, we heard that the area we had just left had been shelled and a couple of guys were killed. We missed it by minutes."

That wasn't the only close call. During time off, several Wayne and Shuster Show cast members took side trips to the front lines—some authorized, some not. Lew Lewis visited the hill from which the searchlight teams tried to illuminate Chinese patrols at night; during his jeep ride up the hill, Lew was repeatedly instructed to duck down, just in case. Herb May, a former RCAF instructor, took an unscheduled flight over no-man's-land in a UN spotter plane. One afternoon, not knowing Jim Reynolds's whereabouts, front-line forces suddenly discovered him taking snapshots from a hilltop; he had unwittingly walked through a minefield to get there. What's more, despite attempts to prevent his retracing his steps, he recrossed the minefield, miraculously without incident.

On a day off, Terry Dale asked, "Can I get up close to the front to see what's going on?"

A British officer eagerly obliged, driving her to the jeep-head.

"What have I gotten myself into?" she thought when she got to the front lines. She was wearing a bright yellow scarf and imagined the Chinese saying, "There she is! Shoot her!"

Inside a forward observation post, the soldiers offered her tea and a look through their binoculars. When they spotted a Chinese tank across no-man's-land, they told her, "We'll blow it up for you."

At first amazed by it all, the young woman watched in horror as the soldiers radioed and brought down fire on the tank, blowing it to pieces. She recognized that they were just showing off, but then "I realized the seriousness of it all. I felt sorry for both sides in the war, because of the killing that was going on . . . I grew up in a hurry over there."

The Wayne and Shuster entertainment mission to Korea left behind a lot of smiles on both the entertainers' and their audiences' faces. Lew Lewis never forgot teetotalling Johnny Wayne getting

Larry Moore

National Archives of Canada/PL-50111

National Archives of Canada/PL-50000-A

Following the August 1950 call for volunteers, (top, l–r) Ray Morgan, Red Butler, Ken McOrmond and brothers Vern and Roland Roy headed out of Sudbury, and Larry Moore hopped on his Harley to race to Toroonto's Chorley Park to enlist. RCAF instrument tech-nician Bill Tigges (back row, 3rd from left) was part of a tribute to the late Mackenzie King; the North Stars flew over Parliament Hill on their way to Korea.

If the Liberty ships bound for Korea were "tin cans," then the sleeping arrangements were definitely sardine-like.

At sea, Canadian soldiers tried to ignore the roll of the ship with the roll of the dice.

Training at Fort Lewis, Washington, was water-logged: days of rain, mud around the barracks, endless ponds to ford prompted one private to write "we are growing webbed feet."

On Nov. 21, 1950, a westbound troop train carrying members of the Royal Canadian Horse Artillery collided with an eastbound passenger train near Canoe River, B.C. The modern steel Transcontinental smashed through the old wooden coaches of the troop train, killing 17 soldiers and injuring 52.

Troops of the 2nd Battalion Princess Patricia's Canadian Light Infantry were outnumbered eight to one as they defended their positions at Kap'yong with Lee-Enfield rifles in April 1951. Their stand earned them the US Presidential Distinguished Unit Citation.

" MOVE ON, MOVE ON –
THEY'RE NOT FIRING
NOW ! "

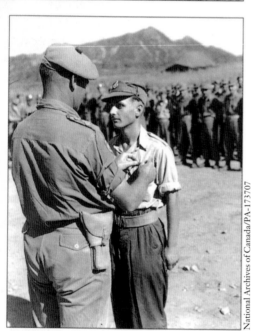

Pte. Wayne Mitchell felt almost as nervous receiving his individual D.C.M. for meritorious service at Kap'yong, as he did in the battle itself.

To offset the stresses of leading his Royal Canadian Regiment platoon, Don Stickland (inset) sketched cartoons, such as this incident during the battle of Mount Kakhul-bong.

In the fall of 1950, Royal Canadian Navy sailors used nothing more sophisticated than dinghies, steady hands and time-fused demolition charges to clear sea lanes of contact mines.

In the plotting room aboard HMCS *Cayuga*, (above left) navigator Andrew Collier shows senior UN officers the way up river to Chinnampo. On Dec. 5, 1950, the Dunkirk-like mission successfully evacuated the Eighth US Army and (above right) burned the port leaving nothing of use for the advancing Chinese forces. *Cayuga*—218—is later dubbed by her crew "the galloping ghost of the Korean Coast." (Inset: Bill Davis).

Don Hibbs (on guitar) described this impromptu concert with his buddy Pte. White in a Ginza beer hall in 1951 as "'The Old Mill Stream' by Tex White and Buffalo Hibbs."

Night training of mortar platoons. For four days and four nights in Nov. 1951, mortar troops of the R22eR defended forward infantry positions with 15,000 bombs; in the process they burned their mortar barrels beyond repair.

Sherman tanks of the Lord Strathcona's Horse make their way north from the Pintail Bridge over the Imjin River; the co-driver inside this lead tank, Tpr. Roy Stevenson, would later earn the Military Medal in action at Hill 355.

An orphan taken in by members of the RCR, Willie Royal learned military routine and an appropriate vocabulary; after the war, he became a librarian with a wife and family in Suwon, South Korea.

Few Canadians gave as much time to the war effort as Canadian Press war correspondent, Bill Boss, who brought "the good, the bad and the ugly" to homefront newspapers.

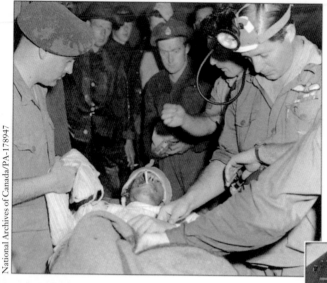

In the spring of 1951, Dr. Frank Cullen was a long way from Toronto Western Hospital where he interned. In Korea he worked at this regimental aid post, sometimes with no more light than a miner's lamp on a head band.

Cosmo Kapitaniuk volunteered for Korea to be a medic, to fight the communists, and to save souls with his Christian message.

Canadian soldiers were entitled to one *Asahi* beer per man per day. Shortly after this special shipment of Carling's arrived on the reverse slope of Hill 355, Chinese artillery opened up and blew it to pieces before a drop was drunk.

Some mornings, Canadians found Chinese propaganda signs just beyond trench sentry positions.

Herb Cloutier was sent as the advance man for a top-secret operation which turned out to be the clean-up at Koje-do, the main POW camp for captured North Korean and Chinese communist soldiers.

RCR "B" Company troops practise anti-riot drills before marching into Compound 66 to search, interrogate and redistribute communist POWs.

An RCR Orders Group is briefed prior to a night fighting patrol on June 21/22, 1952; present are (l-r) G.F.B. Ritchie, J.L. Mazerolle, J.P. Doran, G.F. Macpherson, R.H. Mahar, E.G. Bauld, D.E. Holmes, D. Desroches and B.C. Robinson.

The morning mist helps conceal RCR soldiers repairing defensive barbed wire, struck by Chinese bangalore torpedoes during the night.

CBC radio reporter René Lévesque interviews Lt. John Barrett north of Imjin river.

Defusing Chinese box mines with detecting equipment was one thing in daylight, quite another at night.

Her bow ripped back to the first guns from running aground, HMCS Huron sat through the armistice in drydock in the summer of 1953.

National Archives of Canada/PA-194124

National Archives of Canada/PA-188736

Not memorable hockey, but playing on the frozen Imjin River helped Canadians forget the war.

Canadian entertainers were never far from the front in Korea. Former WWII entertainer John Pratt still sang "You'll Get Used To It."

Lorraine McAllister (with accordionist Karl Karleen) sang *en français* to these Vandoos in the field.

Wayne & Shuster brought their entire radio show, including band singer Terry Dale.

NHL's Red Kelly (2nd from right) and CFL's Ken Charlton (far left) brought Stanley Cup and Grey Cup film highlights; with them were sports reporters Bob Hesketh (kneeling), Bob Saunders, Korean houseboy Johnny and Henry Viney.

Pat Fontaine and Carson Hutchens read letters from Rose Marie Stumpf, "the Sweetheart of the PPCLI."

Korean civilians sometimes asked for payment to be photographed; after Canadian engineer Ernest Beattie photographed these orphan children, his unit paid them royally.

Although the source is the American army newspaper, members of the Lord Strathcona's Horse—Allan Minette, Gerald Patenaud, Roy Temple and Henry Greveling—relish news of the armistice.

En route to the Canadian Field Dressing Station with Red Cross worker Ina McGregor (background) are former POWs (l-r) Paul Dufour, George St. Germain, Joseph Binette, Ernie Taylor, Len Badowich, Jim Gunn, Barry Gushue and Victor Percy.

A convoy of ambulances with Canadian POWs arrives at Freedom Village on Aug. 5, 1953.

Ji,m Lynch

Sporting his RCR scarf, POW James Pelletier waves to the welcoming committee at Freedom Village on Aug. 5, 1953.

Ji,m Lynch

Back in South Korea, ex POW George Griffiths gulps down his first western food in 10 months; it's so rich, it makes him sick.

Ji,m Lynch

For the first time since being captured by the Chinese in May 1953, sniper Jim Gunn is surrounded by friendly faces— Red Cross workers (l-r) Ina McGregor, Pam Whitehead and Mildred Herman.

On July 27, 1997, Korea veterans unveiled their own Wall of Remembrance. That day Bill Allan saw a dream come true.

At the wall, sisters Barbara Differ and Hazel Regan found closure and a witness to their brother Bill's death in Korea.

One cenotaph at a time—here at Field, Ont.—Korea veterans such as David Graham campaign to have war monuments re-dedicated.

drunk. When he left Tokyo, musician Jim Reynolds was carrying his trumpet in a brown paper bag and a couple of bottles of souvenir liquor in his trumpet case. Jackie Rae had packed a foot-thick bundle of soldiers' letters, which he faithfully posted when he got back. And when Terry Dale was asked to return her army-issue uniform, she intentionally neglected to return the shoes, because "they were the most comfortable shoes I'd ever worn."

An image that stayed with Frank Shuster from Korea was the wild applause he and Johnny received, even when they were backstage. "It was wonderful," Frank Shuster recalled, "just the recognition of being good at what we do."

THE LAST
STATISTIC

I F HE'D HAD IT HIS WAY, Ernest Beattie would have spent the
Korean War in Ottawa taking photographs of intelligence data
for the Canadian Army. As a welder in the Royal Canadian
Electrical and Mechanical Engineers (RCEME) corps with plenty
of hobby photographic experience, he had applied for the job. Instead,
because the army needed welders to repair equipment in Korea, in
March 1952, Beattie was shipped overseas. No matter. Along with
regular kit and his welder's gear, Beattie carried his 35-mm camera.
During his tour in Korea, in fact, he aimed his camera more often
than his rifle. He took hundreds of pictures—of the boat trip over,
the train ride across Japan, the RCHA gun emplacements around
his workshop, a fire that consumed the kitchen one day, vehicle convoys crossing the Imjin and, as often as not, Korean civilians.

Outside his RCEME encampment south of the Imjin River, there
was an area his unit used as a garbage dump. Broken parts, boxes,
tins and leftover food were regularly hauled by truck and dumped
there. Just as regularly, a group of small children would emerge from
nearby caves to pick through the waste. These orphaned Korean boys
could make do with anything left by the Canadian soldiers. Sometimes they would just build a fire with the junk left behind and feast

on the food scraps. Beattie had photographed them several times.

"Just before Christmas," Beattie said, "we decided to give the kids a special gift."

The engineers had uniforms cut down so that they would fit the boys. Arrangements were made to transform the RCEME mess hall into a Christmas Day party, complete with decorations, gifts and a full Christmas dinner. On the special day, several members of the Provost Corps were dispatched to round up the boys without explanation. The provosts brought the children into the RCEME compound, told them to strip off their old clothes and pushed them into the showers of the Mobile Bath Unit.

"The kids looked terrified," Beattie said. "They thought they were personally going to be cooked for somebody's dinner, They had never had warm water poured over them."

When the children emerged from their showers, they were giggling, but now squeaky clean. Next, they were dressed in their tailor-made uniforms, complete with caps, shirts, pants and boots and paraded into the engineers' mess hall. A table had been set and placed on a riser at the front of the room in their honour. They feasted on turkey, potatoes and all the trimmings and were presented with other Christmas gifts, while the RCEME soldiers sat before them watching, cheering and waiting on the children hand and foot. It was a Christmas neither the soldiers nor those boys would ever forget.

Unlike most others, the orphans that Beattie's unit adopted that Christmas had a brief respite from their grinding poverty. Life was tough and cruel for most Korean civilians as the war raged around them. While Canadian troops were always warned that thievery was common among Korean children, most soldiers felt sympathy for the orphans who foraged in garbage pits and along roadsides to survive. During the winter of 1952–53, when he was rotated on and off Hill 355 and the Hook, RCR machine-gunner Jack Noble saw his fair share of suffering. As he and his platoon mates shivered through the January cold, he couldn't imagine the cold that the Korean children had to endure.

"We used to use gasoline to wash our guns," Noble said. "One night, I stole some gas and put it in small cans that the kids could burn to keep warm in caves dug in the hills. It would burn pretty near all night . . . But something happened this night. The gas burned out. And this little fellow froze.

"I carried lots of wounded—some with intestines falling out, an arm half blown away, or their faces crushed in—but it didn't hit me like this kid. It was tougher than losing a friend in battle."

The war was grinding on, halfway through its third year. Since United Nations Command had solidified its defensive positions at the Jamestown Line, northwest of the Imjin River, in late 1951, the front line had not moved. There had been the changing of the guard in Washington. Eisenhower had come to Korea and gone home again. The peace talks dragged on. The inertia affected morale all the more. Canadian soldiers nearing completion of a tour of duty kept one eye on their work and the other on the searchlight at Panmunjom. Each man wondered whether he might become the next, and maybe the last, statistic of the war.

Sometime during the early evening of January 8, 1953, a corporal, nearly at the end of his tour, was assigned to a reconnaissance patrol in front of the Hook position; he asked his friend, Bernard MacDonald, to take his place. Like the corporal, Pte. MacDonald was a Maritimer. "Tunny," as MacDonald was known, came from a big family—five boys and five girls—from Antigonish, Nova Scotia. Prior to the war, he had worked as a blacksmith, delivered groceries and even travelled to Calgary to compete in cowboy rodeos. By age twenty, MacDonald had joined the Royal Canadian Regiment and gone to Korea. At six foot four, MacDonald was likely the biggest man in his platoon, but he never took advantage of his size. He took pride in sending his pay home to his mother. He liked his platoon mates and "everybody liked him."

On January 8, after dark, No. 7 Platoon—consisting of platoon commander Lt. Dan Loomis and Cpl. Robert Floyd, Pte. Bill Allan and a number of others, including Tunny MacDonald (in place of the corporal)—prepared to move out. Their job was to reconnoitre an outpost forward of the Hook once occupied by Chinese troops. First, UN artillery batteries laid down fire on the position. Then RCR machine guns raked the outpost. Loomis's "sneak and peek" patrol followed.

"We did a sweep through the position," remembered the lieutenant. "Some went to one side, some to the other . . . We got to the other end, consolidated the position and were beginning to withdraw . . . and there was an awful bang!"

"We heard an explosion," Bill Allan said. "We thought it was a grenade or a shell or something. Someone said it must have been a mine . . . So, we hurried back to our firm base position . . . And the sergeant called the roll to make sure everybody was back. But it was a cold night and everybody was coughing and grunting . . ."

"I was the last in," Loomis said. "And I said, 'Everybody accounted for?' 'Yes sir.'"

"Next morning, we go to breakfast," Allan continued. "And Tunny doesn't show . . . And we started thinking about the roll call and whether Tunny had been accounted for . . . And then we remembered that explosion . . . So I went out on the next patrol and we found him, his rifle set up on the parapet, his body halfway in the trench. He'd been hit in the head . . . We brought him in . . . We were all upset . . . It was the toughest death I've ever gone through."

"In a way," Loomis said, "I lost two soldiers that night. The corporal blamed himself because Tunny MacDonald took his place and was killed."

Dealing with the troops' end-of-war apprehensions was common among platoon commanders. Each approached the problem differently. Lt. Herb Pitts had come straight from Royal Military College, in Kingston, Ontario, to Korea in mid-1952, as a reinforcement to the 1st Battalion of the PPCLI. Almost immediately, Pitts led recce and escort patrols; he worked as reinforcement to the RCR when they defended Hill 355 in October; and by November he was with the 3rd Battalion PPCLI on counterattack preparation and rehearsal for occupying the Hook at the far southwest end of the Commonwealth Division front lines. The toughest task was developing esprit de corps and earning respect from his men, particularly from those who'd been there longer.

"I was a reinforcement," Pitts said. "So my bonding had to be almost instantaneous with the group. My association with men in Korea at that time tended to be rather short. But there is a bond that builds quickly among soldiers in circumstances like that, and it depends entirely on credibility, knowledge or skill. If you know your job, you'll get support. Trust is extremely important."

Like Loomis, Pitts found himself facing men in his platoon who were getting close to the end of their year's service. One more patrol seemed an unnecessary risk. His response to the problem was impartiality; everyone had to fulfill patrol duties on a rotation basis, including himself. Pitts felt that "in the Canadian Army tradition, you can make your directions stick in ways other than saying 'I order you to.' I believe you lead by example," and as a result, at one point, Pitts was out on patrols three and four nights a week.

The young lieutenant's leadership skills were tested late that November, when his new commanding officer, Lt.-Col. Herbert Wood, called him to the command post behind the Hook.

"I would like you to take a volunteer wiring group," Wood explained, "and train them to lay barbed wire in front of our position in as fast a time as possible."

Pitts accepted.

"You'll report to the engineers," Wood continued. "And you'll find thirty men . . . They've been assembled, volunteers from across the battalion."

Word had spread about the mission. When Herb Pitts arrived behind the lines at the training site, he also found two men from his own platoon among those ready, willing and able to take on the job. Pitts took that as a vote of confidence and began bonding this new unit to the task ahead. During the intense period of training over the next few days, Pitts decided that the volunteers should spend as much time together as possible—tenting together, eating together in the engineers' kitchen and talking about everything and anything, not just the assignment.

Trained by the 23rd Field Squadron of the Royal Canadian Engineers (RCE), the wiring party would have to lay concertina wire as quickly and quietly as possible across hundreds of metres of exposed hillside in front of the Hook. The position might be under fire; the ground, already freezing, might be snow-covered and treacherous. The operation would have to be completed in two nights, and it would have to be done over ground that had previously been mined. For the task, Pitts divided his team into three groups of ten men, each under a corporal. The standard for laying triple-roll concertina wire fence was 100 yards in ten minutes in daylight. After two days of training, a team led by Cpl. Frank Mullin was able to lay the 100 yards of wire in the dark in nine minutes!

"Throughout the training," Pitts said, "we were sort of kidding that whoever maintains the best times will get to lay the wire closest to the enemy lines. It was the carrot. You've done the best, your team deserves the honour."

On November 30, the first night of the actual operation in the valley in front of the Hook, a convoy of trucks arrived behind the forward position and dropped off the load of stores, wires and iron pickets. With them were scores of Korean porters who would haul the materiel forward for the three wiring parties. Lt. Pitts made one last check with his C.O. to confirm the wiring objectives and then led a quick recce trip forward to the wiring position so that his three section commanders would know where they would be working.

It was just after 10 o'clock when Cpl. Mullin's party—the one winning the right to be first—headed down the pathway into no-man's-land to begin the operation. Lt. Pitts was in the lead. Cpl. Mullin was next, followed by Pte. Jacob Batsch, and a radio operator. The rest of the section of men, laden with wire and pickets, was behind.

In the darkness, Lt. Pitts heard someone slip and fall behind him. Concerned about the noise, he turned to Mullin and said, "You lead on. You know where the start point is."

Pitts turned, pulled out of the line and retraced his steps to discover that the radio operator had fallen on slippery ground. He hadn't taken three steps when there was an explosion at the head of the column.

Pitts turned to see Cpl. Mullin horizontal in the air and falling to the ground. Mullin had stepped on a bounding Betsy; it had leaped into the air, exploded and severed his head from his body.

The next man in the column, Batsch, slumped to the ground. Pitts caught him as he fell and asked, "What's the matter?"

All Batsch could do was cough out a last breath.

The lieutenant pulled back the flaps of Batsch's parka to see that a piece of shrapnel from the mine had punched a hole in the private's chest. Pitts got on the radio. "Get two stretchers down here. I've got two casualties."

What Herb Pitts feared most was the reaction of the rest of his wiring party. Most were new arrivals in Korea. Most had not yet heard a shot fired at close range. Suddenly, minutes into their first operation, they were looking at the corpses of two men killed in front of them. What was worse, when the lieutenant moved back up the line, he found that the Korean porters had stopped, obviously scared and ready to run. Pitts found the supervising Korean officer and told him, "You keep these people here. This job's got to be finished."

"I don't know if I can control them," the man said.

"You control them, or I'll report you."

The Korean officer pulled out his pistol and began threatening the porters. Eventually, with the two casualties moved back, the line of labourers calmed down and the group advanced into the valley. Within a few hours, the rest of the wiring party—the Canadian volunteers—had laid 1,800 yards of concertina wire without further incident. Two nights later they repeated the process, only deeper into the valley and closer to a Chinese outpost.

"The job was completed," Herb Pitts summed up. "We had re-wired the critical area, at the expense of two soldiers, with a bunch of men who were strangers to each other and to the war . . . The men took the risk that the C.O. and I expected us to take . . . I don't know what makes men put their trust in one another. But after five or six days together, training and conducting the two operations, [the wiring party] all dispersed to various parts of the battalion. It's a tribute to our young soldiers," and the trust Herb Pitts inspired. He was later awarded the Military Cross for "his coolness and leadership" during the operations.

The fortunes of other patrols in front of the Hook were equally capricious. Lt. Peter Worthington (now a prominent journalist) commanded a platoon in "D" Company of the 3rd Battalion of the PPCLI. One winter morning his recce patrol had to probe a dike-like feature, known as Pheasant, near the Chinese side of the Sami-ch'on Valley. UN Command wondered about a potential build-up of men and munitions beyond the dike. Because it was a daytime mission, "I had the guys wear pajamas over top of their battle dress," Worthington said. "Snow had fallen, so with their white flannel pajamas on, they would blend into the landscape."

Besides the possibility of being spotted in daylight, there was the added danger of mines. The Sami-ch'on River was flooding and the only way to Pheasant was through a UN minefield. Worthington didn't have any mapping for the field with him, but coached his fourteen-man patrol through it.

"I just told the guys, 'Cross the minefield. Go ahead!' very nonchalantly," Worthington said. "It never occurred to me. I was so caught up in my training—you know, keep the officer in the middle—that halfway across I realized if the lead man steps on something, how would I ever explain? But I was so confident."

The patrol reached Pheasant without incident. Finding no evidence of Chinese troops, they set a course to return to UN lines via the defensive system of the neighbouring Royal 22e Régiment position. Here again, Lt. Worthington was well into the manoeuvre when he wondered about "the Vandoos suddenly looking up and seeing all these guys they didn't know about, dressed in white pajamas and coming through their lines. But we got away with it.

"It was like a narcotic," Worthington said. "It was exciting, an exhilarating feeling, when you're frightened and you survive. There's a tremendous feeling of having come through something unscathed."

Christmas of 1952 brought more tension and surprises. The PPCLI company on the Hook was standing-to all Christmas Eve night. There were real fears that the Chinese, knowing it was a religious holiday, might mount an offensive. Sentries in the forward trenches heard noises out in the darkness. Artillery and rifle fire were called down in front of the position. As dawn broke, Lt. Worthington was told by his platoon, "There are Chinese out there. They're all standing. Should we shoot?"

"Hold your fire," Worthington said.

The growing light revealed a line of fir trees full of decorations and with presents laid beneath them. Chinese patrols had hung Christmas trees in the Canadians' defensive barbed-wire fences overnight.

The lieutenant got on the radio to his battalion headquarters.

"For God's sake, don't let your troops go near them!" HQ said. "They could be booby-trapped!"

"It's too late," Worthington reported. Like children, his men were already scampering down the trails through the minefields and bringing back what the Chinese had left under the fir trees.

Inside packages, the PPCLI soldiers found glass figurines of pigs and dogs. Some found bags of tea with peace slogans attached. There were war diaries with inscriptions reading "Stop the Imperialist War" and quotations from Mao Tse-tung. There were safe conduct passes encouraging the Canadians to give up the war. Some soldiers found postcards, with stamps already on them, ready to mail to their families explaining why they were surrendering.

"Gather up the material," HQ told Worthington. "The troops can't keep any of it."

Lt. Worthington passed the message along to his men. The Chinese presents were all handed over to Canadian intelligence officers—all except the one each man, including Worthington, saved for posterity. The cheering effect of this incident was remarkable; so much so that Christmas night, a PPCLI patrol on reconnaissance passed by the Pheasant dike feature in no-man's-land and left behind gallon cans of ham chunks with lima beans (C-Rations the Canadians hated) as a return gift for the Chinese. Of course, fraternizing with the enemy was strictly forbidden, but Worthington figured it wouldn't blunt his men's fighting instincts.

"In fact, on Boxing Day, the next morning," Peter Worthington said, "there was a great scramble. Two Chinese were spotted out in the open beside their trenches fixing wire and everybody grabbed rifles and began firing at them . . . It hadn't affected their fighting ability at all."

The relative lull at the front (and the resulting complacency of Canadian military leaders) concerned one company commander with the 1st Battalion of the R22eR. Maj. Harry Pope, a Vandoos veteran of the Second World War, had come to Korea in mid-1952; he would serve a full year's tour with the 1st R22eR, then serve another six months with the 3rd Battalion and later be awarded the Military Cross.

In its position that December 1952, "C" Company of the R22eR faced a relatively inactive front, where, according to Maj. Pope, there were "a few shells fired at our tank every two or three days—with the loss of two or three of my men." Frustrated by having to sit and take it, the major often took a turn as gunner in the company's lone tank, firing back at Chinese positions.

Some of Pope's initiative rubbed off on his men, when "one of my signallers, Pte. J. A. A. F. Deschesne proposed to me that he go in broad daylight with another signaller to the enemy side of the Sami-ch'on to see what was to be seen there. I admired this aggressive spirit and the example it gave to the rest of the company.

"I warned the adjoining companies and I asked the FOO to hold himself ready to massacre with his twenty-four guns any enemy showing a disposition to annoy the patrol. I asked Lt. Rutherford to follow the patrol with his tank gun . . .

"There was no reaction from the enemy. Even when Pte. Deschesne and his colleague, on the other side of the river, 200 yards from the enemy position and 2,000 yards from ours, stamped out 'Merry Christmas from "C" Company' in the snow, the enemy did not react."

Maj. Pope's regimental commander had equally clear ideas about defending the indefensible hills of Korea. Lt.-Col. J. G. Tony Poulin was also a career soldier, because when he graduated from Quebec's Laval University in 1939, "I wasn't hot enough at figures to become an accountant . . . to be a doctor you had to go into the country and deliver babies in snowbanks . . . and lawyers were a dime a dozen." He served in Africa, Italy and Holland in the Second World War and just before Christmas 1952, he arrived in Korea to prepare for the arrival of his troops.

The 3rd Battalion of the R22eR would soon move onto the Naeoch'on feature, a saddle-like rise on the left flank of the much-prized Little Gibraltar (Hill 355), but not before Poulin gave the position a fighting chance. First, he overhauled defensive works, of wood, tin and sandbags, that "stuck out of the earth like hot dog stands," making them easy targets. Poulin ordered all defensive positions dug flush to the ground and camouflaged. Next, he reconfigured his defensive fire, protecting immediate approaches with beefed-up Bren gun and .30-calibre Browning machine-gun pits, and protecting dead ground with 60-mm and 81-mm mortars.

Finally, he worked with one of his pioneer officers, Lt. Jerry Bowen, to increase the firepower of his defensive minefield. Four five-gallon drums full of napalm were fitted with detonators that were connected electrically to a platoon command post. When ignited, each drum, buried just underground, could spread deadly fire over fifty yards of frontage. Once the prototypes of "Tony's Torches" were developed, Poulin was asked to display several for a visiting chief of staff.

"I have a feeling these might be against the Geneva Convention," Lt.-Col. Poulin commented after the demonstration.

The chief of staff turned to Poulin and said, "Is there any difference between this and napalm dropped from an airplane?"

"No," Poulin answered.

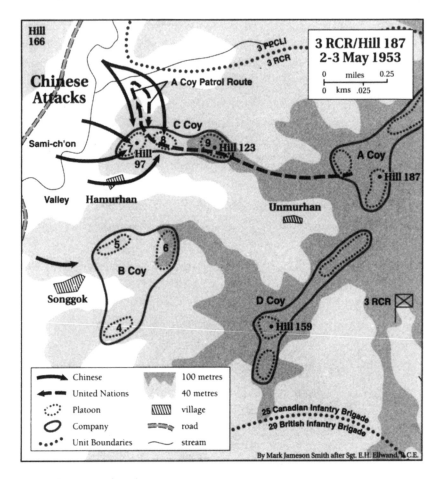

"Then, go ahead!"

Fortunately for Chinese ground troops, their commanders never directed a major attack on the Naeoch'on feature while Lt.-Col. Poulin and the R22eR were there. The napalm mines were never detonated to defend Canadian troops either.

The Chinese did, however, probe another Canadian front-line position in the spring of 1953, and the defenders had none of the sophisticated defences that by that time were protecting Hill 355, the Hook and the Naeoch'on feature. Instead, the ground surrounding the UN-held position, known as Hill 187, was exposed, less fortified and wide open to observation by the Chinese from Hill 166, just across the Sami-ch'on River valley. On April 20, when the relatively green 3rd Battalion of the Royal Canadian Regiment moved onto the position, the troops felt quite vulnerable.

Typical of the topography along the Jamestown Line, the highest ground, Hill 187, had three finger ridges radiating into the Sami-ch'on valley. Closest to the Chinese, "C" Company of the RCR was directed onto the northernmost finger, which included two smaller rises—Hill 97 (flanked by No. 7 and 8 Platoons) and Hill 123 (occupied by No. 9 Platoon). The second finger was manned by "B" Company's No. 5 and 6 Platoons. The third finger, dominated by Hill 159, would become the reserve area for "D" Company. Meanwhile, "A" Company would occupy the original Hill 187, farthest from the Chinese lines. Generally, the hills were steep-sided; the gullies between them were out-of-sight and the slopes were covered in brush and long grass, offering hostile patrols too much concealment.

"Many of us expected a bombardment or a firefight on May 1, the Communist May Day," Eddie Nieckarz recalled. Flown to Korea as an RCR reinforcement for the 3rd Battalion, Nieckarz had discovered the dark side of war early; while training in Japan he had witnessed a "dud" mortar bomb explode nearby, killing an instructor and trainee. He had done wire patrols in front of the Hook in the dead of winter, but the next two days with No. 9 Platoon in "C" Company were to be "a benchmark for the 3rd Battalion" and Nieckarz himself.

"When we rose from our sleep in the late afternoon on May 2," Pte. Nieckarz said, "we took our chop-chop, C-Rations, and were ready to begin our nightly watch. Patrols began getting ready to go into the valley."

Lt. K. L. Campbell, commander of the 3rd Battalion, had called for the usual number of reconnaissance patrols to be strengthened to fighting-patrol status. In addition, there were standby patrols organized as back-up in case a fighting patrol ran into trouble. The Chinese were cutting the defensive wire in front of "C" Company's position, and the stepped-up patrolling was supposed to curtail that activity.

Lt. Doug Banton was assigned standby patrol duty the first week of May 1953. Formerly a student at Ottawa's Carleton University and now an officer in the regular army, Banton was described by some as "a keener." He expected troops in his platoon to wear brass that shone brighter and boots that were polished better than any other soldier's in the regiment.

"I'm going to win the Victoria Cross in Korea," he told Pte. Terry Meagher when they trained together at Camp Wainwright. Later, Banton even offered Meagher a transfer into his operational platoon, suggesting "somehow I would figure in his Victoria Cross."

After dark, that Saturday night, May 2, the beefed-up recce patrols prepared for the night's routine duties along the northerly finger of Hill 187. Lt. Banton's standby patrol was also getting ready in the No. 8 Platoon area, as Lt. Gerry Maynell hustled his sixteen-man fighting patrol from "A" Company through the "C" Company crawl trenches to the forward slope. Maynell was one of the few Americans in the RCR, and that night his job was to ambush Chinese intruders.

"I escorted Maynell's group to the gap in the minefield," Ed Hollyer remembered, a second lieutenant and commander of No. 7 Platoon at the northwesternmost edge of the Canadian defences. Lt. Hollyer watched them move safely down the dirt path toward no-man's-land and returned to his platoon position. It was about 8:30. The night was moonless and black.

"A favourite trick of the Chinese," recalled then-RCR platoon commander Dan Loomis, "was to come right into our minefields and ambush us on our own routes."

As the patrol threaded its way through the minefield, one of Maynell's men thought he heard movement inside the field. Another motioned the patrol to stop when he thought he spotted movement among a number of haystacks off to the left. When the patrol arrived at its appointed ambush position, more movement was heard, this time to the rear. A flare was called for, and as it lit up the area, all was revealed.

"The Chinese had camouflaged themselves in the haystacks," Loomis said, "and then ambushed the RCR patrol."

The Chinese opened up at close range with their burp-guns, and the two opposing patrols exchanged grenades. Some seconds later, there were explosions and casualties on both sides. Maynell received a mortal head wound and Cpl. J. C. McNeil assumed command, attempting to lead the patrol back to the gap in the minefield. There, they were confronted by another Chinese ambush and another exchange of fire began.

By now, Lt. Banton's standby patrol, at the No. 8 Platoon location, was alerted and about to head toward the gap in the mines to rescue Maynell's patrol. At the platoon command post, Banton spotted signaller Ralph Verge, who was armed with an American carbine rifle he'd traded a liquor ration to get from a G.I. The weapon was light and semi-automatic.

"Can I have your carbine?" Banton asked.

"Yes sir," Verge said right away.

Banton grabbed the rifle and ammunition. Then he and his standby patrol disappeared down the path into the dark. Within minutes, Banton's section met the first survivors of Maynell's shattered patrol, who told him that the Chinese were in the gap. Banton and his men pressed on and ran right into the ambush. Despite the beating his patrol was taking, Banton stood his ground near an opening in the barbed wire. He began calling to Maynell's men to come to him through the gap.

"Lt. Banton broke two rules of the battlefield," Pte. Terry Meagher wrote. "Never stand when you can sit. Never sit when you can lie down. Lt. Banton was cut down in a minute and lay by the barbed wire . . . The keener did what he had always done—he got there first. It was not spectacular. It was no way to win a Victoria Cross."

Now the remnants of two RCR patrols were scattering across the forward slope in front of the Charlie Company sector. Ahead lay their own minefields with no clear way through, and behind them the Chinese—some said as many as 400—troops closing in.

With every grenade explosion and gunfire burst, Ed Hollyer could see the fighting going on below his No. 7 Platoon observation post, "but I also saw that the Chinese were forming up on either side of my position, right inside the minefield."

"Then, all these stragglers started coming up," Len Badowich said. The lance corporal from Manitoba had recently been given responsibility for a section of about a dozen men in No. 7 Platoon. "And one of my guys—he was from Nova Scotia—he goes out and starts carrying wounded guys up the hill . . . There are lots of heroes in war, but to get a medal you've got to be seen by the right people. This guy should've got a medal."

There appeared to be five separate Chinese forces moving against the "C" Company RCR position that night. First were the probing patrols that now dominated the area around the Canadian mine-fields. Next came section groups to gap the wire. Following them were trench destruction groups. Then, snatch groups of platoon size were ready to move in and take prisoners. Finally, a force of company strength lay in reserve. The main assault phase was apparently triggered by the artillery and mortar barrage that began at about 10 o'clock.

"Never saw or heard such a concentration of shelling before," Father Walter Mann wrote. Attending wounded at a Casualty Clearing Station at the time, the Catholic chaplain felt "the shells were never going to stop coming in." At the "A" Company position, Cpl. Jim Cruden said, "It looked like daylight from the explosions." In the "B" Company area, Cpl. Russ Cormier recalled "shells came down like rain."

"In the eerie light of exploding shells, I could see the heads of soldiers slightly above the protection of sandbags," said Eddie Nieckarz in the "C" Company sector. "But if you wanted to live, that wouldn't do. You had to get into the bug-out hole at the back of the slit trench," and that's where his section leader, Pte. Danny Welling-ton, ordered Nieckarz and several others to gather, so that he would know "where we were when the attack started.

"Then the bombardment increased at a tremendous rate, two or three explosions every second. Our hearts were racing. We were scared . . . At one time, Danny started to say 'Hail Marys' and we prayed with him . . . Nobody else wanted to be section leader because you had the responsibility of looking after other people . . . but all night long, Danny kept moving through our section and kept everyone alert."

Jim Gunn ran miles that night, although not where he expected. As a sniper assigned to the forward trenches of Charlie Company, Gunn would normally have been using an American m-i carbine with an infra-red scope, or his Lee-Enfield rifle with a sniper-scope attached. However, with incoming artillery shells and mortar bombs, Pte. Gunn and his partner, Pte. O'Connell, decided to dispense with the scopes. They wrapped them in a poncho and hid them in the back of the trench. (They knew there was no protection for captured snipers under the Geneva Convention.)

When the bombardment stopped, the two snipers could hear Chinese troops on the hill below them. They tossed their remaining grenades down the hill. The shelling resumed and the two got down in a corner of their trench.

Next thing they knew, the Chinese trench destruction troops and snatch groups were pouring into their trench. The Chinese shouted as they fired their burp-guns and lobbed concussion grenades into the Canadians' trench system. Hit in the legs, O'Connell was bleeding badly. Another grenade knocked Gunn down and out. When he awoke, he was surrounded by a section of communist troops, yelling at him.

A Chinese soldier began pulling at O'Connell.

"No, no," Gunn said. "He's dead!"

O'Connell was left for dead, but survived. Gunn was taken prisoner.

Also corralled in the confusion near the No. 8 Platoon position was Cpl. James Pelletier. One minute there were explosions forcing the young section leader down in his trench; the next it was quiet and a Chinese soldier stood over him with a burp-gun aimed at his head.

"Lay down your arms," the Chinese soldier said in English. He was wearing a surgical mask over his nose and mouth.

Wounded in both legs, Pelletier obliged.

"This way, quickly," the man said, and even offered a hand to pull Pelletier from the trench.

Chinese shelling was most intense on the far left flank of the Canadian lines, in Lt. Hollyer's No. 7 Platoon area. The explosions smashed the communication trenches and shattered what little protection sandbags and timber offered at the gun positions. Section leader Len Badowich remembered thinking, "They're gonna come after this ends. They're gonna come." And they did. Even as the last Chinese shells exploded on No. 7 Platoon, Chinese soldiers came screaming through the smoke and dust. L/Cpl. Badowich just aimed his Bren gun and kept firing at the shadows hurtling toward him, but all along the forward slope, Chinese troops were swarming the trenches. There was hand-to-hand fighting, but the Chinese burp-guns and concussion grenades were winning out.

Line communication was now dead between No. 7 Platoon and "C" Company headquarters, but RCR signals officer Lt. L. G. Côté had a wireless radio.

"I want fire down on our own position," Lt. Hollyer said over the wireless.

"What did you say?" responded his C.O.

"The Chinese have overrun us," Hollyer shouted. "I want fire down on our own position!"

RCR section leaders spread the word through as many trenches as No. 7 Platoon still held. Concentrated UN fire would soon be exploding all over their sector. Orders were to take cover. It seemed an eternity, but within five minutes, brigade headquarters had coordinated a hail of artillery and tank shells, mortar bombs and machine-gun fire down on Hill 97, where what was left of No. 7 Platoon was hunkered down, awaiting the firestorm.

"As quickly as the trucks unloaded the ammunition, we were firing it," remembered gunner Bert Picotte of the 81st Field Regiment (RCHA). Canadian artillery batteries, directed by FOO Lt. George Ruffee, fired 3,400 shells and "the ground never stopped shaking."

"They were all DFSOS tasks," said tank Sgt. Phil Daniel. He and three other tank commanders in "B" Squadron of the Lord Strathcona's Horse knew it meant "Defensive Fire and SOS or fire down on our own positions." The four tanks were quickly on the move to take up counterattack positions, but because the Chinese shelling was so intense, two tanks were cut off and Daniel's tank lost a track. Sgt.

Daniel evacuated the tank and began removing shells; it would have to be destroyed so as not to fall into Chinese hands. Fortunately, within minutes, a recovery tank had made it through and repaired the broken track.

"When we got into position," Daniel said, "the stuff was still coming in. You couldn't put your head up over the hill for the machine-gun fire . . . An unbelievable night."

Despite the devastating UN fire on the No. 7 Platoon position, the situation was nearly lost. When he called for a short pause in the shelling, Hollyer ventured out and saw his trenches "filled with casualties . . . The Chinese were rolling the dead and wounded over the lip of the hill where litter bearers were hauling them away." When another wave descended on the position, Hollyer called for additional DFSOS shelling and led a handful of survivors toward the No. 8 Platoon area on the east side of Hill 97.

As he rallied what was left of his No. 7 Platoon section to pull back, L/Cpl. Badowich was intercepted by Chinese troops and captured. Cpl. Ernie Taylor, who had come up from "A" Company to work as a stretcher-bearer, was captured when he mistook a Chinese soldier for a wounded Korean Service Corps labourer. Pioneer officer Lt. Gordon Owen was also captured in the No. 7 Platoon area. Later, he and Len Badowich were able to laugh about it. However, when they met as POWs behind Chinese lines, Badowich looked incredulously at Owen, who was covered in blood and manure.

"What the hell happened to you?" Badowich asked.

"I took refuge in the shit house."

At one spot along the communication trench, near Hill 97, the members of No. 7 Platoon had dug a latrine pit and placed a log for a seat at the edge of it. For protection, the troops had built up the sides with sandbags.

"I jumped in there [during the battle]," Owen explained. "Every time they came around the corner, I shot back with my 9-mm pistol. Then they threw in potato masher grenades at me. They weren't that powerful but they'd splatter . . . I could've held out forever, but my gun jammed!"

Gunn, Badowich, Taylor and Owen were among seven taken prisoner in the battle around Hill 187. Elsewhere, the news was just as disheartening. Twenty-six RCR troops had been killed and another 27 injured; 4 Katcom (Korean Augmentation to Commonwealth) soldiers were dead, 14 wounded and 4 missing. Continued fire on the infiltrated areas of "C" Company's lines during the early-morning hours of May 3 eventually drove the Chinese out of the Hill 187 area. By first light, Dog Company had moved to relieve Charlie Company. Fr. Mann's mass had very few troops in attendance that Sunday morning; during the day, May 3, the former No. 7 and 8 Platoon positions were being restored and blanket patrols had begun the clean-up.

Sgt. Larry Edmonds came down from his "B" Company position to find "the medics were taking bodies out of the fields. They were tagged and wrapped in the blankets. And they were all laying out there."

"I remember [Pte. W. F.] Lucas's body was the first I came across," Terry Meagher said. "I picked up part of his jaw bone and put it back in place. Then we loaded him onto the helicopter."

When they emerged from their slit trench, Eddie Nieckarz and the survivors of No. 9 Platoon found their section leader, "Danny Wellington, lying in a forward trench with a little speck of blood in his eye . . . He was dead. We got a stretcher and placed him on it and four of us carried him to the rear slope . . . I counted only eleven people walking off the hill from our platoon and I wondered where in hell everyone else was . . . The last thing I did on Hill 187 was cry."

If there was a positive derived from the battle of Hill 187, it was that the 3rd Battalion RCR survivors believed they had come through their baptism of fire. Because they had bled together, many felt they had been drawn together as brothers. More important for some, they had not bugged out or fallen back; they had shown personal and group courage. Like the PPCLI at Kap'yong, the R22eR on the flank of Hill 355, and the 1st and 2nd RCR on the forward slope of Hill 355, the 3rd RCR had ultimately held its ground.

For meritorious service on Hill 187 that night, Cpls. McNeil and Pero and L/Cpl. Julien received the Military Medal. Military Crosses were awarded to Lts. Hollyer, Côté and Ruffee. The battle of Hill 187 was the last major Canadian infantry engagement of the Korean War.

In contrast to the stalemate Canadian soldiers endured on the Korean peninsula in the spring of 1953, Canadian seamen were chalking up significant victories along the Korean shoreline. The precedent had been set when HMCS *Cayuga* spearheaded a Dunkirk-like mission relieving UN troops at Chinnampo during the first winter of the war. Royal Canadian Navy destroyers—three at a time—never stopped front line operations off the east and west coasts of North Korea. They maintained blockades, fulfilled escort duties, searched sampans, junks and coastal islands for infiltrators, cleared coastal waterways of mines and patrolled the shoreline in search of "the white wisps of steam" from Communist Forces supply trains.

The very nature of North Korea's eastern coastline—dominated by the Taeback Mountain range—forced railway builders down to the shoreline to survey and construct the country's north-south rail lines. That made every supply train chugging down the coast to the 38th parallel a target for UN navy gunners. From as early as July 1952, when the American destroyer *Orleck* blew apart two trains in two weeks, United Nations naval vessels regularly sought out and fired on North Korean rail transport. The activity took on such a high profile that any ship destroying or disabling a Communist Forces train earned membership in "The Trainbusters Club."

HMCS *Crusader* was the first Canadian ship admitted to the club. On October 26, after four months of her first tour in North Korea waters, the destroyer's gun crew spotted a train as it emerged from a tunnel south of Songjin. From 10,000 yards offshore, the ship's 4.7-inch guns scored direct hits on several of the train cars. The next night, Cdr. John Bovey, the ship's captain, took *Crusader* closer to shore and attacked another southbound freight. In less than two hours, her Canadian gun crews had destroyed all freight cars, coaches and the locomotive.

That was just the beginning. In April 1953, off Tanch'on, North Korea, *Crusader's* gunners destroyed three complete supply trains in less than twenty-four hours. The next month, HMCS *Haida* made two train kills in one patrol, and by Dominion Day, 1953, HMCS *Athabaskan* had destroyed two trains. Of the twenty-eight supply trains officially recorded in The Trainbusters Club, RCN ships and gunners accounted for eight.

Fog along the coast prevented the *Athabaskan* from scoring a ninth train early in July, the last month of the war. The same fog helped take HMCS *Huron* right out of the war. During her first tour in Asian waters in 1951, *Huron* had fulfilled routine assignments—carrier screening, mine removal, boarding and searching of junks. On *Huron's* second tour in 1953, she was re-assigned to the "Sweet Adeline" patrol on July 7—protecting Yang-do, an island immediately off the east coast of North Korea. Just an uninhabited outcropping in the Sea of Japan, the island had suddenly become an important piece of real estate in the ongoing peace talks at Panmunjom. UN commanders sensed that the Chinese wanted Yang-do, so it had to be patrolled by UN warships at all times.

The Sweet Adeline required *Huron* to navigate a circuit up and down the strait between Yang-do and the mainland. Less than half a mile wide, the narrow waterway presented numerous hazards. The shoreline of the island itself was rugged and inhospitable; no accurate charts of Yang-do existed. Obscuring fog frequently settled onto the strait and floating mines were often set adrift there. Finally, the mountainous coast of the mainland offered North Korean gunners a dominating view of the strait; in 1952, shore batteries south of Songjin hit HMCS *Iroquois* broadside and killed three crewmen.

Huron began the southbound leg of the circuit in the daylight hours of July 2, but this time the fog worked to the ship's advantage, covering her passage. At midnight, as the watch changed and the ship turned to begin its northbound leg, the weather deteriorated. Fog reduced visibility to less than two miles in the strait and wave action complicated navigation. The ship was operating under "blind pilotage," or by its various radar systems—Sperry Radar, Radar 293 and ASDIC. As the middle watch began, the captain, Cdr. R. Chenoweth, retired to his cabin, and Lt. Cdr. T. J. Thomas assumed command on the bridge. He ordered *Huron*'s speed reduced to twelve knots.

The second officer in command, Lt. G. H. Emerson, was below in the operations room; he was responsible for determining the ship's course, using radar. Emerson informed Thomas that *Huron* should alter course to a heading of 050 degrees, roughly northeast. He then called for the range and bearing of Yang-do.

"Eighteen-hundred yards and dead ahead," said George Guertin, who was reading the Sperry Radar.

Emerson sensed that the ship was slightly off course and the island could be a problem. He called the bridge and requested a further change in the heading to 030 degrees, a sharper turn north. Thomas felt that heading would put *Huron* on line with the island. However, visibility was now down to 600 feet in the night fog, so he ordered the change.

With his watch ending, radar operator Guertin moved to the Radar 293 system, which was fixed on more distant features. Guertin's replacement at the Sperry system, Dale Chaddock, picked up the readings on the land ahead: "Seventeen-hundred yards . . . Sixteen-hundred yards . . ."

As *Huron* came about to the new heading, Lt. Emerson instructed the Sperry operator to range on a point of land about three-quarters of a mile away. The original piece of the island that Guertin had reported was closer than that, and at twelve knots the destroyer would cover the distance in less than three minutes. The only other detection system on board, the ASDIC system was searching for mines not rocks.

Guertin and several of the others in the operations room sensed a collision was imminent and "I put my arm around this brass voice pipe to brace myself."

"Land dead ahead!" was called almost simultaneously by the ASDIC operator and two lookouts, who spotted Yang-do's rocky cliffs emerging from the fog in front of them. The shoals of the island were already under the ship's bow. It was just past 12:30 a.m. and HMCS *Huron*'s participation in the Korean War was about to end.

"I was in my hammock," recalled ship's electrician Bill Johnson. He had just come off the first watch and was drifting off to sleep, "when everything started swinging."

"She was just shuddering and banging as the vibrations went through the whole ship," says L/S Neil Goodwill. Most men in his section of the ship had been asleep, but were instantly thrown from their hammocks. "And there was one big charge to the mess deck."

"I got thrown on my ass," says L/S Glenn Wilberforce. Being so far below decks on duty as a mechanic in the engine room, he didn't know what had happened and "I thought we had hit a mine."

HMCS *Huron* was firmly aground on Yang-do.

Typically, the hull of a Tribal Class destroyer was not thick steel, so a successful refloating of the ship depended on the structural and plate damage. A recce party went over the side to investigate in the dark. The front ninety feet of the destroyer's hull, right up to her first guns, had been punched in by the shoals. As well, the extended ASDIC dome on the underside of the hull was jammed into the rocks. And what everybody feared most: it wouldn't be long before the fog lifted, exposing the destroyer and her entire crew to the eight North Korean batteries known to be active on the mainland. Weapons were unlocked from storage and lookouts posted along the ship's forecastle in case the North Koreans attempted to board the ship.

"Our immediate job was to lighten the bow as quickly as possible," George Guertin said. He and scores of other sailors began the task of transferring as much weight as possible toward the stern of the ship. All forward ammunition was removed, including shells in the magazines of the Bofors guns. The ship's two anchors were lowered and their cables jettisoned. Storage lockers, compartments and even freezers, everything that wasn't nailed down, was removed from *Huron*'s forward holds. "I remember a bunch just taking the piano outside on deck. . . and all of a sudden it wasn't there . . ."

"A few seamen and stokers just heaved it overboard," Glenn Wilberforce said. ". . . It was always out of tune, and the officer who played for church on Sundays wasn't very good anyway."

As *Huron* got heavier at the stern, word was spreading of her plight. The USS *Missouri* and a flotilla of UN warships were soon dispatched to the area, and American helicopters hovered overhead. All night long the destroyer's crew worked feverishly to lighten *Huron* enough to power herself off the island. First they tried to pull the ship off using one propeller full-speed astern, then the other and then both together. Finally, "we got as many people as possible on the quarter deck and we actually started jumping! We jumped her off the island!"

By sunrise, HMCS *Huron* was free of Yang-do and still afloat. However, when Cdr. R. Chenoweth brought the destroyer about to head back to sea, it was clear that forward motion would put too much strain on the weakened bow and bulkheads; some of the ship's hull plates began flapping in the surf. And so, *Huron* began an ignominious journey back to Japan (some 600 kilometres away) steaming backward at an agonizingly slow speed of three knots.

The Canadian destroyer reached the port of Sasebo on July 20 and was immediately pulled into drydock. Evaluation of damages and repairs to her hull kept her there until October 25, nearly three months after the armistice was signed, which, ironically, yielded Yang-do to North Korea. (Following an inquiry into the grounding, three officers—Chenoweth, Thomas and Emerson—were disciplined.)

Adding insult to injury, not long after arriving in Sasebo, *Huron's* crew awoke one morning to discover a huge hanging mural (rumoured to have been created by seamen aboard the destroyer *Iroquois*) depicting a ship, her bows bent over into a garden patch, with a caption that read: "The Invaders of the Rhubarb Patch . . . First to go ashore in North Korea, ship and all."

During the final week of July 1953, peace in Korea was at hand. After a lot of posturing, the repatriation issue was resolved. Despite a clash between six divisions of Communist Chinese Forces and six Republic of Korea Army divisions alongside the US 3rd Division in mid-July, the demarcation line between North and South Korea was agreed to. Even though, during June and early July, UN gunners had hurled 4.5 million shells at the Chinese and Chinese gunners had answered with 1.5 million shells, the two sides signed a peace agreement.

On the morning of July 27, 1953—two years, two weeks and three days since the two sides began peace negotiations—the UN and communist delegations filed into a newly constructed Peace Pagoda at Panmunjom. One last-minute glitch had been eliminated just hours before: the communists had nailed two large blue and white peace doves over the pagoda entrance, but UN Command refused to sign the armistice until the "communist propaganda symbols" were removed. They were quickly painted over. At precisely 10 o'clock, the senior UN delegate, Maj. Gen. William Harrison, and the chief of staff of the Korean People's Army, Nam Il, entered the building. Each man sat down and signed his name eighteen times to the armistice documents. Not a word was exchanged between them and just as swiftly the two exited. A ceasefire would go into effect twelve hours later.

Neither side seemed wholeheartedly committed to the peace. Even as the ink dried on the two representatives' signatures, Chicago *Daily News* reporter Keyes Beech said he could hear "the boom-boom-boom" of distant artillery fire. During the day, UN Thunderjet fighter-bombers pummelled what North Korean airfields remained, and just twenty-four minutes before the actual armistice, an American bomber dumped its load north of the 38th parallel. At 10 o'clock that night, the firing at each other ended.

"I was spared!" That's all Eugene Bourassa could think of. When he joined the Princess Patricias in 1951, all he could think of was the poster on Sherbrooke Street in Montreal. It showed an airborne soldier in a beret. The caption read: "Does this hat fit you?" But this day, two years later, Bourassa only thought of his wife, "as flares [from the Chinese side] lit up the sky like daylight."

On Little Gibraltar, from which countless Canadian riflemen had fired countless rounds down into the valley against the Chinese, this night, PPCLI machine-gunner Charles Barker aimed his Vickers into the sky. All along the front, "the British, the Americans, we all lit up the sky with tracers and flares."

"You couldn't hear yourself think," recalled L/Cpl. Bud Doucette of the RCR. He was under orders to remove side arms and unload them, remove magazines from rifles and defuse hand grenades at 10 o'clock. But before then, it seemed "everybody was trying to get rid of all their ammunition, so they wouldn't have to take it home, I guess."

"Front line lit up just like a grandstand performance at the [Canadian National] Exhibition," Fr. Walter Mann recorded in his diary. "Rested peacefully tonight."

The next morning, the Catholic priest wandered around a number of forward UN positions shaking hands with officers and sharing the delight of the regular soldiers that the shooting war was over. He couldn't stop looking across no-man's-land where "Chinese could be seen roaming around the hills . . . and waving a great array of colourful flags," 400 yards away.

Having survived the Chinese assault on Hill 187 just weeks before, RCR Cpl. Russ Cormier looked out from his front line position to see "literally the sides of their hillsides opened up with tanks and guns pointing at us that we didn't even know were there."

There was "a human sea" of Chinese soldiers looking and waving back. Along with flags and banners were loudspeakers that heralded the peace and brotherly love, and even invited UN troops into the valley to meet them. Some Canadians obliged. What struck PPCLI platoon commander Robert Peacock was "the psychological effect of seeing the masses of Chinese coming out of their trenches and dugouts.

"There was a lot of nervous laughter," Peacock remembered, "about the relative strengths and a lot of pride in what we had been able to do against so numerous an enemy."

"Before this, few of us had ever seen more than a very few Chinese soldiers together at one time," Lt. Don Stickland wrote. At the time of the armistice, his platoon in "B" Company of the RCR was located across the Sami-ch'on valley from four hills nicknamed Matthew, Mark, Luke and John.

"From the position called John," Stickland explained, "flew a red flag. It appeared to have a white peace dove embroidered on it. Planted around the summit, just below the flag-topped peak, was a large banner. It was about fifty feet long and ten feet high and proclaimed in large letters 'Long Live the Peace!'"

According to the terms of the armistice, UN soldiers had forty-eight hours to vacate their battle lines. They had to disassemble pickets and barbed-wire fences, remove mines and military equipment, demolish trenches and bunkers and leave the area entirely. They were to pull back four miles and ultimately create a buffer, or demilitarized zone, along the new border between North and South Korea.

"We didn't return home immediately," Don Stickland wrote, "as was the case with Canadian troops in other wars. In fact, we didn't return home for Christmas either. But when we did return to Canada, we shared . . . our vivid memory of the awesome sights and sounds of that special night when the guns stopped firing. The war in Korea was over. We had survived."

THE OTHER SIDE
OF THE HILL

N APPARENT MIRACLE took place at Panmunjom on April
20, 1953. It was the first day of Operation Little Switch—
nearly two weeks of prisoner releases at a crossing point along
the 38th parallel known as "Freedom Village." The armistice itself was
still three months away; however, Chinese and United Nations peace
negotiators had agreed to an early exchange of sick or wounded prisoners. Among the first of those repatriated was a Canadian infantryman who had been listed as missing-in-action and presumed dead for
more than a year.

Paul Dugal, a lance corporal with the 1st Battalion of the Royal
22e Régiment, had disappeared during a patrol to Hill 169 on the
night of June 23, 1952. The mission to ambush a Chinese patrol
and bring back a prisoner was itself ambushed and forced to retreat.
Members of his platoon reported Dugal killed in action, but his
body was never found. He had been captured. Suffering from severe
head wounds, Dugal had spent three months unconscious in a Chinese
prisoner-of-war camp. Then, bedridden for the rest of his internment, Dugal had secretly kept a diary, which contained among other
things, the names of fifteen other Canadian POWs, whose fate in
combat had previously not been known.

Not only was his own arrival across the Bridge of No Return from Panmunjom to Munsan historic, but since Dugal was the first Commonwealth POW released, his diary revealed the general nature of conditions and treatment inside Chinese prison camps for the first time in the war. For his initiative and determination, L/Cpl. Dugal was awarded the British Empire Medal. For his trouble, his head wound had done irreparable damage; Dugal suffered from epileptic seizures until his premature death in Canada a few years later.

Publicly, Dugal was only allowed to reveal the names of fellow POWs he'd seen on "the other side of the hill." In a debriefing session with the commander of the 25th Canadian Infantry Brigade and Canadian intelligence officers, however, he described where Canadian POWs were being held, how they were being interrogated and how their Chinese captors were attempting to indoctrinate them.

Until that time, the only data about United Nations POWs had come from American soldiers liberated during MacArthur's invasion of North Korea in the fall of 1950, and their experiences had been horrific. Eyewitnesses reported that North Korean captors often shot POWs, especially if they were wounded and unable to walk. Those who survived initial capture were stripped of their boots and uniforms and marched north to overcrowded civilian prisons or commandeered schools. Between the start of the war in June 1950 and June 1951, nearly half the 5,176 US servicemen captured by North Koreans died in captivity.

Dugal's debriefing revealed a new POW reality.

Most, if not all, Canadian prisoners-of-war were captured by Chinese, not North Korean, troops. China was not a signatory to the Geneva Convention, which guaranteed standards of hygiene, medical care, food, accommodation and supervision for prisoners (standards that would have meant preferential treatment over Chinese soldiers). Moreover, China's view was that "United Nations prisoners taking part in this unjust war were war criminals and that if they were captured their captors had the right to kill them." In practice, however, the Chinese applied their so-called "lenient treatment" policy, which considered POWs as "victims of the ruling classes, students who were to be educated and pointed towards the truth." As such, POWs were to be fed, given medical treatment and neither robbed nor abused. For the Chinese communists, prisoners-of-war had a distinct propaganda value when kept alive.

Pte. Ken Dawe remembered the Chinese informing him about their practice of leniency when he was captured on October 26, 1952; but he didn't have time for qualitative assessment. By about 8 o'clock that night, Dawe and thirteen other RCR riflemen defending the "B" Company area of Hill 355 had been surrounded, captured and herded into a Chinese bunker. With him were Pte. Don Orson, Pte. Elmer McInnis and Pte. George Griffiths, the latter two badly wounded.

None of the captured RCR infantrymen was blindfolded; they were spirited underground from one bunker to another. Each of the men remembers the elaborate network of tunnels buried deep in the hills behind Chinese lines, where not even the most powerful UN bombing could inflict damage. The Canadians were hurried through a virtual honeycomb of kitchens, supply rooms and sleeping quarters of the Chinese armies. All rooms and passageways were shored with wooden beams and log roofs much like mine shafts. There were so many soldiers moving back and forth that people had to be directed like traffic. While underground, Pte. Dawe and two other RCR prisoners were forced to re-enact their capture in front of still and movie cameras. They were threatened with severe punishment or execution if they did not cooperate.

At this stage, Chinese interrogators also pressed the Canadians to reveal their service histories. Questions focused on the RCR's service on Koje-do, the island where "B" Company had taken part in the forced relocation of communist POWs in May and June 1952. The interrogators wanted to know which RCR captives had participated in "the Koje Island massacre." L/Cpl. Fred Jollymore, L/Cpl. Bill Bell and Pte. Tom Allan had served on Koje-do and they were separated from the rest of the group. Koje-do preoccupied the interrogators so intensely in the days that followed, that most of the Royal Canadian Regiment POWs anticipated being shot. Jollymore smuggled a note to his mates asking them, should they ever be released, to explain to his family what had happened; he feared imminent execution.

Instead, the Chinese moved the RCR captives in vehicles to prison camps, some as far north as the bank of the Yalu River, the border between North Korea and China. The camps were not what the Canadians expected. Unlike the German stalags or the Japanese jungle prisons of the Second World War, the Chinese had no organized POW camp system in Korea. Theirs were ad hoc arrangements. L/Cpl. Paul Dugal, and others released in April 1953, described the camps as little more than Korean villages taken over by Chinese authorities. The mud and straw huts with ten-by-ten rooms, a wooden-framed door and windows with paper over them would hold about ten men. There were no lights, no tables, no chairs and no beds. An adjacent hut housed the kitchen, whose stove pumped smoke through a flue system into the floors and walls of the adjoining huts for heat. Some prisoners were issued a blanket and a set of Chinese worker's clothing.

Canadians were held in these evacuated villages that were often numbered camps (sometimes nicknamed by the inmates). Camp 5, where Jollymore, Bell and Allan were sent, had the worst reputation; its mortality rate was reportedly as high as 70 percent. Chinese interrogators at Camp 5 put L/Cpl. Bell into solitary confinement for seven months, six months in a hut by himself and one month in a makeshift hospital where he underwent primitive medical treatment for a shattered left leg. However, in general, the camps were not heavily fortified nor bristling with machine-gun turrets. There was little, if any, barbed wire strung around their perimeters. Guards were present but not in overwhelming numbers.

What made these villages prisons was their environment. Most were located hundreds of kilometres from United Nations lines. No neutral states were nearby to offer refuge. Any escapee would be instantly identifiable, if not by prison dress, certainly by his Western language and physical appearance. The countryside was inhospitable and the population hostile; because many North Korean villages had long been targets for UN fighter jets and bombers, villagers would have very little sympathy for Westerners on the loose in their communities. None of these factors, however, prevented escape attempts.

The key to a successful escape, George Griffiths and Ron "Butch" Watson figured, was packing enough food to remain underground and out of sight until a small group of POWs could make it to the North China Sea. Then, afloat on logs or a raft on the ocean, they might be picked up by friendly merchant navy men. Fortunately, RCR prisoner-of-war Don Orson had worked his way into becoming a cook at Camp 3, where most of the RCR prisoners were being held. The escape attempt hinged specifically on the night Orson could inconspicuously provide the eight POWs with a supply of cabbage and potato-filled turnovers as escapee provisions.

"Some Puerto Ricans, who were in on the plan, began singing songs as loud as they could," remembered Griffiths the night the escape began. "And the guards stopped what they were doing to watch and listen.

"[Meanwhile,] we crawled on our bellies through a guard line and then along behind some houses to the outskirts of the camp. There was no fence. But at the end of the village there was a schoolyard and a teacher's house. We had to tunnel through. And as we tunneled through, [the guards] caught a couple of the Americans in our group.

"All hell broke loose. There were bugles going off. Guards running everywhere. So, Butch and I worked our way back, just in time for a roll-call, to see if anybody was gone. Fortunately, they started counting in the front ranks, while I was passing the food I had packed to guys in the back ranks. And they were quickly eating it to get rid of the evidence. [The Chinese] knew there were Canadians involved in the attempted breakout, but they didn't know who, The ones they caught were put in the hole."

"The hole" wasn't a hole in the ground, but a gap between two village buildings. It may have been thirty feet long, but only two feet wide. It had no shelter from the elements. It had no toilet. The occupant was forced to defecate at the entrance to the narrow alleyway. And it was through the same entrance that his daily ration of food and water would be passed. Then he would retreat to the opposite end of the space to eat and find what little warmth a blanket and the building walls might provide.

Other forms of solitary confinement befell prisoners who resisted indoctrination or who showed "deviant" leadership qualities among the general POW population. These men were considered "reactionaries" and were therefore not entitled to the same "lenient treatment" policies as the rest. At Camp 5, for their perceived crimes against the Chinese people, L/Cpl. Gerald McKinney, a medic captured in October 1952, and L/Cpl. Bill Bell were beaten and confined in either latrine pits or "sweat boxes" without food and water for extended periods of time. Bill Bell's months of isolation meant sensory deprivation as well as life in rat- and lice-infested quarters. The young infantryman attempted to keep his sanity by picking lice from his body, collecting them in a matchbox and keeping an accurate daily count. The food ration at Camp 5 was a minimal diet of water, half a cup of rice and an occasional portion of potato, turnip or cabbage.

Though few POWs knew it at the time, the inauguration of a new US president in early 1953 improved their prospects for release. The incoming administration of President Dwight D. Eisenhower turned from the Truman hard-line to power diplomacy, or what journalists of the day called "brinksmanship." Eisenhower and his new secretary of state, John Foster Dulles, de-emphasized threats of invasion of communist China by Chiang Kai-shek and the Nationalist Chinese. They also stopped hinting that if the deadlock in peace talks was not soon broken, the US might not confine the war to Korea and could resort to using atomic bombs in Asia. The US approach in Panmunjom was suddenly more conciliatory.

Another stroke of fate was the sudden death of Joseph Stalin in March 1953. Within two weeks, the new Soviet chief, Georgi Malenkov, announced in a speech that there was no existing dispute between Moscow and Washington that "cannot be decided by peaceful means." Whereupon Red China's foreign minister Chou En-lai and North Korea's Premier Kim Il Sung appeared to soften their opposition to voluntary repatriation of communist POWs; instead, they favoured an earlier proposal to allow a neutral state, such as Switzerland, to supervise the exchange and interview of communist prisoners who might refuse repatriation.

Operation Little Switch, the swap of sick and wounded POWs, resulted. In addition to repatriating L/Cpl. Paul Dugal of the Vandoos, the swap brought home Pte. Arthur Baker from the 2nd Battalion of the Royal 22e Régiment; he and two other privates had been captured during the Vandoos' heroic stand at the base of Hill 355 in November 1951. However, on May 3, the day that Operation Little Switch was completed, Chinese forces overran "C" Company of the 3rd Battalion of the RCR on Hill 187. Seven new Canadian prisoners found themselves behind Chinese lines and en route to POW camps in North Korea.

During the first hours and days of his captivity, sniper Jim Gunn felt more afraid of UN weaponry than of its Chinese counterpart. Captured in the attack on Hill 187, he was prodded and marched by Chinese soldiers through what he knew was a Canadian minefield; fortunately, none was triggered by his footsteps. En route to Camp 2, beyond the Chinese-held hills, the POW column faced the wrath of UN jet fighters and bombers. Their crews regularly unloaded excess bombs or strafed North Korean "targets of opportunity" as they returned to their bases. Even when he reached his POW camp, Gunn discovered that so-called "friendly fire" was sometimes a greater threat than solitary confinement.

"The Chinese claimed that the camp was properly identified as per the Geneva Convention," Gunn said. "The bombing raids were exploited by the Chinese in their quest to have us sign petitions . . . addressed to such personages as the Secretary-General of the United Nations, the President of the International Red Cross and the presidents or prime ministers of the various NATO countries [to stop bombing a neutral site].

"And on a couple of occasions the gates were closed as the planes swept down, so that prisoners couldn't get into the tunnel shelters. A few prisoners were hit. This brought more petitions for us to sign, claiming that our planes were trying to kill us. They suggested if we signed, it would put an end to the bombing."

"They wanted us to sign declarations," Pte. George Griffiths said. When the Chinese interrogators failed to persuade the Canadian POWs to denounce the war per se, they tried a daily program of social studies lectures "to get us to admit the UN was using germ warfare."

"We were given a notebook and given history lessons," recalled L/Cpl. Len Badowich, also captured on Hill 187 on the night of May 2/3. "They told us that there was a cholera epidemic going on in Korea and northern China . . . and they blamed the epidemic on [the UN] for dropping germ bombs . . . But we did not sign any of the statements."

As desperately as the Chinese interrogators wanted Len Badowich's signature on the germ warfare declarations, they suddenly discovered the young soldier possessed something even more valuable. Not long after the new crop of prisoners arrived behind the Chinese lines, one of the South Korean POWs revealed to interrogators that Badowich had trained Katcom (Korean Augmentation to Commonwealth) soldiers for the Canadian Army. Badowich immediately found himself being squeezed for information on South Korean participation in the war.

"When is the South Korean army going to take over from the Canadian Army?" an interrogator asked.

Badowich thought, "How the hell would I know that? I'm nineteen years old, a lance-corporal and they want to know about military strategy?" He shrugged.

"You are training Koreans," persisted the interrogator. "When do they take over?"

Badowich played dumb.

"What rank do you hold?"

"I'm a lance-corporal," Badowich replied. He wasn't aware that the Chinese only knew American army ranks and lance corporal was new to them.

"What's that?" the interrogator said. He was getting frustrated.

Badowich tried to use terminology the Chinese understood, and offered, "I'm a squad leader."

"No. No. You're higher rank than that," the man shouted. "You train Koreans!"

For three days the Chinese pressed Badowich for his Katcom experience. But they got nowhere. Badowich and the others had few weapons against their interrogators except their own resistance to giving the Chinese information. However, when they had the energy to fight back, Canadian, American and Australian POWs christened their social studies lecturers, or "instructors," with nicknames. One instructor who always referred to camp duties as "glorious work," became "Comrade Glorious." The camp commander, who once paraded prisoners past civilian bodies allegedly killed in a UN air raid, and who then claimed POWs had "Korean and Chinese blood on your hands," became "Commandant Bloody Hands."

The psychological warfare at Camps 2 and 3 continued.

Next, Chinese instructors introduced motion pictures to their indoctrination lectures. One of the primitive movies depicted a US Superfortress B-29 bomber flying over Korea. There was a close-up of the bomb-bay doors opening. A canister fell from the plane. A parachute opened and the package floated to earth. Despite the Chinese narration on the film, the English-speaking instructor delivered a live commentary.

"Here, American planes release germ bombs on Korea," the instructor explained. "Now, the international scientific group arrives."

On screen, the surface of the ground was white, and a group of Asians in surgical masks scurried around the site picking up supposedly germ-infected grasshoppers and placing them in paper bags.

"Do you believe, now, that Americans are dropping germ bombs?" the instructor asked rhetorically.

"Comrade instructor," piped up an American POW in the lecture. "I have a question, sir."

"Yes?"

"How do grasshoppers survive in snow?" he asked. It was clear, for expediency, that the Chinese producers of the movie had shot the entire episode in winter. "Americans wouldn't be so stupid, would they, to drop these creatures in cold weather?"

The POWs laughed at the instructor's expense. For his trouble, however, the American GI was quickly grabbed by guards and escorted out of the classroom for a visit to the hole. Soon after, Camp 2 was plagued by dysentery. The Chinese attributed the problem to flies introduced to North Korea by UN germ warfare. As a consequence, POWs were issued fly swatters and told it was their responsibility to clean up the flies.

"Every prisoner had to kill a quota of a hundred flies," Jim Gunn said. "And each morning at roll call, we each had to show our quota of dead flies, or else we wouldn't get full food rations for the day."

"So there are 500 POWs running around killing flies and putting them in paper bags," Len Badowich added. "And pretty soon, the flies became scarce. So we began breaking them into pieces. Each day the guards counted the flies you caught. And at night we'd play poker using flies for chips. It got pretty comical."

The fly-swatting episode wasn't the last in the battle of wits between POWs and Comrade Instructors. Lt. Gordon Owen, captured with the others on Hill 187, recalled countless boring lectures on bug warfare in the camp. Then, "some of the prisoners hit upon a plan to help the Chinese produce 'evidence,'" Owen wrote. "A mouse was caught and fitted with a miniature parachute and harness. Then it was hung in a tree.

"When the guards discovered the 'para-mouse', all hell broke loose. Camp officials, photographers and guards swarmed over the area to record the latest event in the germ war. And the pictures served as evidence for many future lectures. To my knowledge, the Reds never did catch on."

Prisoners at Camp 5 found little to laugh about. It was here that L/Cpl. Bill Bell endured seven months of solitary confinement amid the rats and lice. It was here that L/Cpl. Gerald McKinney survived time in sweat boxes without food or water. And it was here that another captive from the May 2/3 assault on Hill 187 arrived on May 22, 1953. Suffering wounds in the right arm and both legs, RCR

Cpl. James Pelletier spent his first night in a chicken coop and the next in a makeshift hospital where the mentally disturbed, those with chronic tuberculosis and surgical cases were all housed together. Here "a prisoner captured in 1950 told me that the Koreans had no medical supplies or facilities at that time, and a chaplain told them they could use the pages of their pocket bibles to make marijuana cigarettes to smoke for the relief of their pain. He described how many of these early prisoners had died and were buried on an island in the Yalu. There had been no medical aid for them. They told of a death march during the winter of 1950–51 when those POWs dropping out were bayonetted."

Even in 1953, when the Chinese took over the POW camps, medical methods were basic at best and Cpl. Pelletier underwent a series of primitive operations to save his badly injured legs. A captured American doctor, with no medicine on hand, used natural remedies on injured prisoners. In one case, "the doctor led a prisoner who had an infected open shrapnel wound to the washroom and allowed flies to land on the wound. The doctor immediately bandaged up the wound. A week later, the doctor removed the bandage, and the wound was covered with lice. The doctor scraped away the lice and the arm was free of infection."

The battle for sanity in the prison camps was gruelling and unending. As a group, the Canadian POWs resorted to the counter-propaganda tactics such as nicknaming the instructors and planting the para-mouse and planning escapes. Ultimately, each POW depended on his own internal resolve and coping techniques for survival. Cpl. Pelletier was stripped of his RCR uniform and identity in the camps, but managed to hide his regimental scarf throughout his internment. For critically injured Paul Dugal, salvation was his secret diary. French-speaking POWs Joseph Allain and Joseph Belle-feuille relied on their religious faith and the language barrier to survive indoctrination. Bill Bell had no control over his long-term fate, so he controlled his immediate world of solitary confinement by counting lice collected from his body. George Griffiths salvaged cigarette papers and on them he recorded the names and addresses of his fellow inmates. To keep himself from going over the edge, Jim Gunn had his friendship with Ernie Taylor.

Cpl. Taylor's military record was short and inglorious. Soon after being posted to Europe during the Second World War, he was shot in the arm and taken out of action. As a member of the 3rd Battalion of the Royal Canadian Regiment in 1953, he wasn't in Korea a week before being captured on May 2/3 at Hill 187. Nevertheless, he was always interested in the welfare of his comrades-in-arms and the stories they had to tell. In fact, whenever new prisoners arrived at Camp 2, Ernie "Scoop" Taylor was usually the first at the gate to sponge up what new information they had about the war and the latest from the peace talks. Whenever Taylor met Jim Gunn in the POW camp, he'd ask about their possible release, "How long do you think, Gunner?"

"Two or three months," Gunn would guess.

"Nah," Taylor scorned. "Two or three years!"

The next time they'd meet, Gunn would suggest "two or three years" and Taylor would contradict him and say, "two or three months."

When word about progress at the peace talks suggested they might be home by Christmas, the Americans in the camp began chanting, "Trim the tree in '53!"

To which, Ernie Taylor replied, "See the Golden Gate in '58!"

"I don't know whether Ernie was an optimist or a pessimist," Jim Gunn said, "but he sure made the time pass easier for me."

POW Andy Mackenzie had no Ernie Taylor, no hidden regimental scarf and no crippling wound or language barrier to hide behind. For a time he had neither amenities nor any human contact on the other side of the hill, and when the Chinese raised the subject of warfare, they not only wanted a declaration, they wanted a confession too.

Squadron Leader A. R. Mackenzie was an RCAF pilot on loan to the Americans in Korea, flying F-86 Sabre jet fighters with 139 Squadron, 51 Wing, in the US 5th Air Force. It was just after noon, on December 5, 1952, during his fifth mission—a patrol south of the Yalu River. At 42,000 feet, the main hydraulic control system in

Mackenzie's Sabre failed. Coincidentally, the squadron encountered about 20 MIGS. Mackenzie switched to his battery-operated control system and began to engage the MIGS. In the dogfight, Mackenzie's jet took shells through the right aileron, fuselage and control panel (later revealed to be shots mistakenly fired by another UN jet). In an uncontrollable roll and descent at 780 mph, Mackenzie ejected.

"It took me thirty-seven minutes to get down to the ground," Mackenzie said. The velocity of his ejection and accompanying turbulence had ripped helmet, mask, gloves, rings, watch and other clothing from his body, but he landed with his boots on "on the side of a mountain. About six feet away from me was an old woman gathering sticks and grass for fuel. She looked up, but the expression didn't change on her face and she went right on picking up sticks. You'd have thought somebody parachuted down beside her every day of her life. Amazing creature she was."

Mackenzie was pursued up the mountain by thirty armed soldiers and captured right there, ten miles south of the Chinese border with North Korea. He spent the next three months in a tiny room in which he could not stand up, but was forced to stay reclined among "millions of body lice," which drove him to attempt an escape, and then attempt it a second time. When he was handcuffed, put under a tarpaulin and tossed into a jeep, Mackenzie expected he would be executed. Instead, he was moved to a prison cell in China, where he remained for the next twenty-one months. The Canadian was incarcerated for 750 days, most of them in solitary confinement.

When Mackenzie was interrogated, it was as if he had bailed out over China, not North Korea.

"Why am I in China," Mackenzie would ask, "when I was shot down in Korea?"

"You weren't shot down in Korea," they would say.

Mackenzie would try to correct them.

"Why would you be in China now, if you were shot down in Korea?" they would say.

The frustrated pilot began to realize that they wanted a confession for a combat flight over China. While he hadn't been trained in anti-interrogation techniques, Mackenzie determined he should resist the temptation to give in and earn a release. He decided he had to stand up to his captors in order to survive. He suspected that "if I told them everything they wanted to know, the next day I would be killed. So I didn't interrogate properly." (Ironically, within a week of Mackenzie's capture, all American forces were instructed not to resist. Intelligence from Chinese POW camps revealed that all downed pilots should tell the Chinese anything they wanted to know, since there was nothing an individual soldier knew that could help the Chinese.)

Near the end of his stay in the Mukden prison, in late 1953, the Canadian flyer discovered that there were three American pilots being held there too. It was American airman Hal Fischer who tapped a message to Mackenzie through his cell wall that the war had ended that summer.

"Didn't they tell you the war was over?" Fischer asked through the wall.

"No," Mackenzie answered. He remembered what the interrogators were always saying: "Because you have penetrated the sacred skies of China, you will be in China for the rest of your life."

The Canadian pilot began to believe it "and eventually I was able to understand that the truth they wanted me to tell them was not my truth, but what they wanted to hear." He started a six-month process of fashioning a statement of his mission that would be acceptable to his Chinese captors. Each draft he guessed what they wanted to hear and signed it. Each time it was rejected. Each statement became a process of trial and error as he admitted penetrating Chinese airspace. Then how far? Five miles? Ten miles? His figures would be circled in red ink as if he were being marked on an exam. The truth they wanted to hear was fifty miles. At times, frustrated, he would tear up the parchment he was writing on, and he was told he would pay. His release home—to his wife and four children—would be further delayed.

Helene Liston was at home in Ottawa in August 1952 when a young man arrived at the door with a telegram containing news about her husband in Korea.

"Are you Mrs. Joe Liston?" the boy asked.

"I'm Mrs. Liston," she said.

"Is there someone here?"

"Is the telegram for me?" Mrs. Liston asked.

"Yes," he said. "But there should be someone else." The boy was trying to follow the rules of delivering such news, but was embarrassed at the awkwardness of the situation.

Mrs. Liston insisted the boy give her the telegram. She never thought for a moment that anything had happened to her husband. When she read the message, she was traumatized.

Captain Joe Liston was the highest-ranking member of the Canadian forces captured in Korea. Like Andy Mackenzie, Joe Liston was early in his tour of duty, flying only his thirteenth mission in August 1952. However, Liston was not a fighter or bomber pilot. He was an artillery observer with the 1st Field Regiment of the Royal Canadian Horse Artillery and piloting an Auster—a single-engine reconnaissance aircraft used to direct UN artillery fire. Flying at 7,000 feet, about a mile behind Chinese lines, he was surprised by a direct hit from ground anti-aircraft fire. The blast separated the small plane's tail section from the fuselage and it was all Liston could do to escape the plummeting aircraft and parachute to the ground, where "a real large reception party" awaited.

"They marched me off the hill," Liston said. "And when I sat down they gave me a couple of cigarettes. It was after I'd finished the second cigarette that I realized I must be in shock, because I don't smoke."

Liston's captors had some trouble beginning the interrogation process. None spoke English, so they hustled him from bunker to bunker until they found a bilingual officer on the reverse slope of a Chinese position. The man demanded Liston explain how the UN engaged targets from the air. When he refused, the Chinese officer threatened the Canadian with the Very pistol retrieved from Liston's downed Auster, not realizing the gun fired flares not bullets. However, Liston did meet his intellectual match at an interim interrogation camp farther behind the lines.

The interrogator first tried to engage him in a discussion of Canadian politics. Liston faked broken English, suggesting he was French Canadian, whereupon the Chinese interrogator came right back at him in perfect French. Eventually, Liston admitted his mother tongue was English and the interrogator told him to start pointing out UN artillery locations and demarcation lines between infantry regiments or he'd be put on public trial. Liston balked. The threat was a bluff.

The Canadian artillery officer was handed off from one prison camp to another. Along the way he encountered another Canadian POW who "was paralyzed completely up one side, so when he had to go outside I was first in line to help him . . . to get a chance to talk." It must have been L/Cpl. Paul Dugal, because Capt. Liston's name appeared on Dugal's secret diary list when he was released during Operation Little Switch in April 1953. At Liston's POW camp—a valley prison where about forty aircrew were gathered in a hut—he was senior officer and set an example for the rest.

On his arrival, Liston was told by his captors to increase the height of the fence around the prison.

"I'm sorry," Capt. Liston replied. "We're not allowed to do that kind of work."

"Why not?" the Chinese asked.

"Why should we help imprison ourselves?" said Liston.

"No. No. It's to keep the unfriendly Koreans from throwing grenades in."

"Well, if they can throw a grenade over the top, they can hit any of us." Liston also knew, in their weakened condition, the UN POWs would have taken weeks to finish the fence. However, it appeared that the Chinese were as fearful of a Korean backlash as the POWs; the Chinese put up the fence that night.

Later, in an attempt to get at Liston via his emotions, a Chinese interrogator tried to persuade Liston to keep a written record of his imprisonment, on the pretext it would be sent home to his family. Liston refused and surprised them by saying, "I hope my wife thinks I'm dead. Maybe she'll get remarried."

Helene and Joe Liston would not be reunited for nearly thirteen months.

In spite of the diplomatic success of Little Switch—684 UN prisoners were swapped for 6,670 Chinese and North Korean POWs in April 1953—delegates at Panmunjom could not agree on which neutral nations would supervise the repatriation of the remaining POWs. Talks broke off again. Hawkish elements on both sides again got the upper hand. On May 2/3, 1953, the Chinese attacked Canadian forces on Hill 187. On May 13, UN bombers began blasting North Korean irrigation dams in order to wipe out the North Korean rice crop and "starve the communists into submission." In retaliation, Chinese forces launched massive offensives in US Army and Republic of Korea Army sectors, pushing UN troops off hilltops east of Panmunjom.

In the midst of all this re-escalation, President Syngman Rhee declared that no matter what the talks at Panmunjom accomplished, South Korea would continue to fight the war alone. He insisted that no concessions be made to the communists and he disavowed his allegiance to UN Command. In an attempt to sabotage the proposed peace plan, he instructed ROK guards to release all North Korean People's Army prisoners who did not wish to be repatriated. One night in early June, 25,000 POWs stripped off their uniforms, ran through the open prison gates and disappeared into the South Korean population.

Nevertheless, senior delegates at Panmunjom itself pressed on. By June 4, both sides agreed on the mechanics of exchanging the rest of the POWs. Most of the details of the armistice were worked out, and four days later delegates signed a repatriation agreement that removed the one issue that had deadlocked talks for a year and a half.

Within hours of the signing of the armistice on July 27, Albert Batten travelled to Panmunjom to assist in the exchange of POWs—Operation Big Switch. He was the lone Canadian on the United Nations Joint Red Cross team assigned to supervise the release of

UN POWs from North Korean prison camps. His trip north to the Yalu passed paddies, villages, bridges and roads and "as far as the eye could see, the place was flattened" by years of war. When he arrived on the doorstep of the camps, his work was "frustrated by the delaying tactics employed by the communists.

"The Commandant invariably gave a lengthy lecture," Batten wrote. "Every word had to be translated . . . which took much valuable time. The next step allowed us to interview the Prisoner of War Committee, a hand-picked group who we could not speak to individually or in private."

By the time the POW Committee interviews were over, the Chinese had already loaded the prisoners into trucks. Red Cross officials were deliberately kept away from prisoners until the last minute. No representative was allowed to stray into the camp unguarded "even to visit the latrine" and nobody saw anything he wasn't supposed to. When Albert Batten was permitted inside a hospital, he found beds, night tables, chairs and whitewashed walls. Later, a POW hospitalized during his captivity revealed "he had never seen a bed. He and the other patients slept on rice mats on the dirt floor. The operating room, the laboratory and dental office had been installed for our inspection. One building was so new the paint wasn't dry."

For some POWs the trucks began arriving right after the armistice. However, the authorities at Cpl. James Pelletier's camp decided to stage one last propaganda event—a special feast of food on tables covered in white cloth—to be photographed by the Chinese. When the prisoners were led into the courtyard to eat, they all sat down stoically with heads erect "so we wouldn't give an impression that we were saying grace with heads bowed." The POWs were eventually ordered back to their cells.

"On August 3, we were . . . taken to a railyard, where we were put in box cars," Pelletier wrote. "It was crowded and we had to find a comfortable spot on the bare wooden floor . . . We travelled overnight and the next day off-loaded at a tented camp. The Australian Red Cross provided a parcel with a towel, soap, razor, tooth brush and tooth paste . . . On August 5 we were again loaded on trucks and taken to 'Freedom Village' where we were released."

When Cpl. Pelletier emerged from the back of the Russian truck at Panmunjom, he was the first Canadian since L/Cpl. Paul Dugal to cross into Freedom Village. Pelletier sported his regimental scarf, hidden from the Chinese since the day he was captured three months before.

The day he headed for Panmunjom, Lt. Gordon Owen—being the senior UN officer—was put in charge of the convoy of Soviet Molotov ambulances. Each was loaded with sick and wounded UN prisoners-of-war. However, when Owen's lead ambulance reached the checkpoint at Panmunjom, he was stopped by an American sentry; after all, Owen was dressed like the Chinese truck drivers in blue cotton uniform and blue cap.

"There isn't anyone due on this road until tomorrow," the American said.

"Open the gate or I'll drive through it," Owen threatened.

"I'll have to shoot!"

Owen's Chinese driver understood English and was alarmed by the sentry's warning.

"Go ahead!" Owen ordered the driver. "Drive on through!"

There was no way Lt. Owen wasn't going through. With all the ambulances rolling, the sentry had little choice but to open the gate and allow them to pass. When Owen (an American in the Canadian Army) and the rest of the Canadian POWs arrived at Freedom Village, most of the former prisoners had to be helped down from the high tailgates of the trucks. US Marines began reading a roll call. There were long pauses between names. Many calls were answered with, "He's in the ambulance, sir."

At POW Camp 2, the Chinese were vague about when and how many prisoners would be released. Suddenly in late August, they told all the POWs to pack up for departure. Even then, "Scoop" Taylor expected the worst. He complained to his buddy, "I don't like it, Gunner. We're not getting out of here."

Two days later they were loaded into trucks and shipped out of Camp 2 to be patriated. But Taylor was still skeptical, saying, "They're taking us over the Yalu into China."

"I don't think so," Jim Gunn said.

"I bet these guys aren't going to Panmunjom at all, Gunner."

This time Cpl. Taylor was wrong. The trucks rolled into Freedom Village with the majority of Canadian POWs between August 22 and 25, 1953. There to greet them was a young Red Cross volunteer from Canada, Ina McGregor. She worked at the Canadian Advanced Dressing Station closest to Panmunjom and recalls vividly that "when the trucks came into the camp . . . some of the men weren't in good shape . . . pretty frail . . . But as they stepped out, the Argyll and Sutherland Highlanders played the pipes. It sounded wonderful."

On September 3, one more Canadian emerged from the camps—artillery observer Joe Liston. As he watched one group after another leave for the Freedom Village border crossing, he sensed his turn would come and he felt "exhilaration at seeing the move out each night. You figure even though they have deceived you at every turn in the past, it looks like you're on the move . . . I had convinced myself for some time that it was real, I was getting out."

Waiting for all of the prisoners was the delousing process—spraying to be disinfected. Then the POWs got re-kitted with proper uniforms. Most were invited to enjoy a meal of steak and eggs, beer and ice cream or chocolate for dessert. Jim Gunn got the greatest pleasure from drinking a glass of cold milk. George Griffiths had his foot operated on again, this time in a real hospital with real anaesthetic, not opium seeds. But Len Badowich remembered "being interrogated yet again, this time by our own Intelligence Officers.

"The first thing they did was have us swear allegiance to the Queen, because the King had died while we were in prison . . . Then they asked, 'Why didn't you escape?' How the hell do you escape in Korea, where the place is full of Orientals? You're white. Where do you go? Nobody could have escaped. These assholes made us feel like we had committed a crime. Or deserted."

Thirty-three Canadians had been POWs in Korea. Several did try to escape and had paid dearly in solitary confinement. Two prisoners—Allain and Bellefeuille—"acknowledged that they signed a communist petition in June 1952 petitioning Lord Alexander, British defence minister, to stop the imperialist war," but no Canadian POWs wrote declarations against the United Nations Command. There is no definitive evidence of Canadians in North Korean prison camps collaborating with their captors. Indeed, there is every reason to believe that the thirty-three Canadians imprisoned there resisted interrogation and indoctrination and that they sabotaged Chinese "brainwashing" attempts to a man.

Still, after debriefing the POWs, Canadian intelligence officers issued them grades for their performance during internment in North Korea. A "white grade" meant undistinguished performance with satisfactory resistance. A "light gray grade" meant low resistance. A "black grade" indicated low resistance and suspicion of collaboration with the enemy. Eleven Canadians were graded "light gray," nineteen POWs were graded "white," one got "black" and the last two were not graded. In other words, Canadian officials graded the majority of Canadian POWs' performance in Korea between satisfactory and undistinguished. None was considered better than average in the service of his country while in military prison.

Early in the afternoon of December 5, 1954, a year and a half after the armistice, fighter pilot Andy Mackenzie was released from imprisonment in China. He had finally regurgitated the truth about being shot down the way they wanted it. For his crime he had endured 465 days of solitary confinement. He weighed 130 pounds (70 pounds less than the day he was captured). He had been shipped cross-country to Canton. On that afternoon, he left behind five armed Chinese soldiers on the communist side of a border trestle, and he walked 200 yards toward five Hong Kong police at the other end of the bridge.

"They made me wait till exactly 1 o'clock on their watches," Mackenzie recalled. "I was never put on trial. I was never sentenced.

But I was detained in China for exactly two years to the minute from [December 5, 1952] when I was shot down . . .

"I think I set the world record going across that bridge, jumping ties four or five at a time . . . I had seen Don Skeen, my brother-in-law, and Mr. Fraser [Canadian trade commissioner] waiting for me on the other side. I fell into their arms, so happy to be free again."

THE WAR THAT
HISTORY FORGOT

I T WAS just over a month after the armistice in Korea—August 30, 1953—when eleven former inmates of communist Chinese prison camps stepped off the airplane that had brought them home to Canada. Canadian Press reporter Joe MacSween was in Vancouver to meet them. He directed questions to a few of the men and just noted the behaviour of others. He described Pte. Bernard Jewer as "outwardly laconic." He watched as Lt. Gordon Owen "gathered his family into his arms." And he noted that returning with the men was war correspondent Bill Boss, who said the soldiers shied away from publicity because "their communist captors had photographed them at intervals for propaganda purposes, leaving an unpleasant association with the men."

In contrast to the subdued demeanor of some, former POWs Pte. Donald Orson and Pte. Ronald Watson kibitzed with other soldiers, reporters and family members as they milled about the lawn in front of the Sea Island airport reception building.

"Did it happen?" Orson said, repeating MacSween's question about his Korean experience. He didn't answer. He just raised his arm and swept it over the gathering, referring to the gaiety of the occasion.

"No, it never happened," Butch Watson said. "Let's forget it ever happened."

Prophetic words, because without being encouraged, most Canadians did exactly that. They forgot, or in many cases, never even acknowledged the Korean War had taken place. The country was preoccupied with seemingly more important matters. A national pipeline would soon bring Alberta oil to Sarnia, Ontario. A canal system up the St. Lawrence would soon give Atlantic Ocean freighters access to the Great Lakes. Old-age security cheques were a reality and some hospitals were fighting cancer with a new radiation therapy called cobalt 60. Canadian television would soon air nightly national newscasts, "The Wayne and Shuster Show" and "The Adventures of Ozzie and Harriet." And after winning the 1952–53 Stanley Cup, the Montreal Canadiens had signed a rookie named Jean Beliveau. Would the Flying Frenchmen from Montreal ever lose?

Even if newspapers, radio and television hadn't been full of the Yankees' pursuit of a fifth straight World Series or Senator Joseph McCarthy's latest charges of communist spies operating in the US, Canadians had little appetite for stories of returning veterans of the Korean War. The *Hamilton Spectator* telephoned Jim Cruden's home the day he got back from Korea that summer of 1953. Because he had a broken leg, Cpl. Cruden had been flown home, and since he'd been with the 3rd Battalion of the Royal Canadian Regiment when the Chinese overran Hill 187 on May 2/3, a reporter thought Cruden would be worth an interview. He asked Cruden to be home for the story and pictures the next day; Cruden was home but nobody from the *Spectator* came.

"This guy's been away for thirteen months," shouted Cruden's brother over the phone to the newspaper. "He comes home. And on his first day back, you don't show up!"

"We'll come tomorrow," the newspaper representative said.

"Don't bother!" and he hung up.

Few Canadian veterans back from Korea received a hero's welcome. No ticker-tape parades. No brass bands. No civic receptions. No passionate kisses in the middle of downtown streets from women they didn't know. There were some exceptions. Upon its return, the

1st Battalion of the Royal Canadian Regiment was paraded through downtown Ottawa and received by Prime Minister Louis St. Laurent on Parliament Hill. At the docks in Seattle, the 2nd Battalion RCR was greeted by a band and girls in hula skirts, but that was because the troopship was mostly filled with returning Americans. By the time most Korean War veterans came home to Saskatoon or Timmins or Chicoutimi, nobody noticed and nobody cared. In the words of one returning platoon commander, most Korea veterans were considered little more than "an administrative problem to the processing staff."

Bill Jackson arrived home on the prairies nine months before the Panmunjom armistice. By October 1952, he had served his voluntary tour of duty with the Princess Patricia's Canadian Light Infantry and had witnessed his share of warfare and war zones. On the way in, his troop train north from Pusan killed dozens of civilians on the track in Taegu. His first night on the Jamestown Line he had to bury dead Chinese soldiers near his slit trench. During Operation Pepperpot north of the Imjin, one of his friends was blown to pieces by a mortar bomb. And many nights in his bunker, "I'd wake up with the nose of a rat inches from my face."

The night he came home to Brooks, Alberta, the platform was empty. He had to phone long-distance to the family farm for someone to pick him up. About a month later, Jackson attended an Armistice Day observance and then joined an evening smoker at the local Legion Hall. No women. Just forty or fifty veterans sitting, drinking and telling war stories. At one point, a friend of the Jackson family rose to address the gathering. He and Jackson's father had served in the First World War together.

"Hold it. Hold it," the veteran said.

The chatter in the room quieted down.

"We've got a guy just back from the trenches in Korea," he said. "And we'd like to welcome him . . ."

Bill Jackson felt a little embarrassed.

"Go ahead," encouraged Jackson's father. "Stand up and say something."

Jackson slowly got to his feet, but before he could utter a word, a voice boomed from the back of the Legion Hall, "Sit down, you ass-hole. So you were in Korea. So what?"

Royal Canadian Horse Artillery veteran Doug Walton received a similar welcome. His outfit, the 2nd Regiment of the RCHA, was the one decimated by the train wreck at Canoe River, B.C., in the fall of 1950. In fact, most of Walton's comrades in "E" Battery were among the 21 dead and 58 injured in the crash. Eventually, Walton recovered from his injuries and made it overseas to Korea. Nevertheless, some years later, when he attended a Vimy supper at a Legion Hall in Ontario, Walton heard a speaker pay tribute to "veterans of the First World War, the Second World War . . . and other skirmishes." Walton got up, left and handed in his Legion membership.

Don Flieger's treatment at home was even worse. While he was on duty at Kimpo Airfield, near Seoul, in February 1952, the Service Corps private had contracted haemorrhagic fever. En route home to Saint John, New Brunswick, Flieger underwent eight transfusions. Months of convalescing at the Lancaster Military Hospital followed.

"When I got out of hospital," Flieger said, "I went back up to Fredericton, my home depot. That night, I went to the Legion. I was in uniform. But they wouldn't let me in. Said I wasn't a veteran. I told them my story, but they said, 'That doesn't cut it here.'"

"Korea . . . so what?" "A skirmish." "Doesn't cut it." To a certain extent these attitudes were not surprising. They represented an inevitable chauvinism that could be expected between generations of soldiers or military units. No Korea veteran disputes the scope and importance of two world wars compared with what happened in Korea. No Korea veteran has ever said that the survival of the free world depended on him, although some honestly believed the war was necessary "to stem the flow of communism." Nor were Canadian shores and streets under threat of invasion by the armies of North Korea or China. But characterizing the volunteer service of nearly 30,000 Canadians in Korea as a "skirmish" was unjust as well as untrue.

It's a fact that United Nations delegates, as well as political leaders of the sixteen-member nations that contributed troops, described Korea as a "police action." In the strictest sense of the founding UN principle—"the maintenance of international peace and security"—the servicemen sent to Korea were enforcing that principle. However, no one on the peninsula in the first days, when the city of Seoul fell five times, ever called it policing; and no one in the trenches north of the Imjin River from 1951 until the armistice ever considered it enforcement of anything less than a war of attrition. From the very beginning, UN Secretary General Trygve Lie described North Korea's move across the 38th parallel as "war against the United Nations."

As early as the fall of 1951, the fighting in Korea appeared to be an overlooked phenomenon. When he returned to Canada from a visit to the Korean front lines, the Archbishop of Edmonton warned there was "ominous danger" that Canadian troops might "become infected with the feeling that Canadians at home have relegated the Korean War to a position of unimportance." Reverend W. F. Barfoot said he was afraid that the efforts of Canadian soldiers were little more than "a forgotten war." Years later, in his book *Korea: Canada's Forgotten War*, author John Melady echoed that sentiment. In attending Remembrance Day ceremonies at the National War Memorial in Ottawa he lamented that "the young Canadians who died during the Korean campaign were barely mentioned."

In South Korea, exactly the opposite was true. Beginning in January 1951, Canadians killed in the war were carried to a permanent cemetery at Daeyon-dong, near Pusan. There, about fifteen hectares of land were offered in tribute to the UN war dead by the Republic of Korea. Like the military cemeteries in Normandy and Holland, children regularly tend the graves of Canadian soldiers in South Korea. While the bodies of 11,000 service personnel killed in Korea were repatriated to Belgium, Colombia, Ethiopia, Greece, India, the Philippines, Thailand and some to France and Norway, most Canadian war dead were interred at Daeyon-dong. There were 378 buried there.

The remaining 138 Canadian fatalities included 16 with no known grave; 24 buried in Yokohama, Japan; 93 buried in Canada; and 5 missing at sea. A total of 516 Canadians died in the war.

In 1992, Korean War veteran Bill Allan and his wife travelled to South Korea on a re-visit. The trip proved to be an emotional roller coaster for the former RCR private in the 3rd Battalion. A return to the United Nations Cemetery in Pusan affected him most. As he walked, Allan snapped pictures of the crosses and markers of some of his fallen comrades, including that of his Maritime friend, Bernard "Tunny" MacDonald, killed on patrol January 8, 1953.

Back in Canada, Bill Allan turned the photographs over to fellow RCR veteran George Mannion, past-president of Unit 57 of the Korea Veterans Association (KVA) in Mississauga, Ontario. The day Mannion was sorting through Allan's re-visit shots, the phone rang and a soft female voice on the line identified herself as Mary Robertson of Don Mills, Ontario. She said, "I'm looking for someone who may have known my brother in Korea."

"What's your brother's name?"

"Tunny MacDonald," she said in a whispery voice. "He was killed over there."

Coincidentally, Mannion was holding the photograph Bill Allan had taken of MacDonald's grave site in Pusan. He told Mary.

"I've never seen the grave," Mary said.

"I'm sure Bill Allan would be glad to make you a copy."

Mary Robertson's inquiry, or as her sister describes it, "Mary's whisper," began a process that would bring together thousands of veterans, physically and spiritually, for the first time since they had come home from Korea. It would also give the war that history forgot a permanent resting place. Between them, Mary Robertson and Bill Allan hatched the idea of fashioning a Korean War memorial for Canadians. At first, it was envisaged as a portable collection of photographs of the grave markers in Pusan and Yokohama. The concept expanded to a plan for a permanent monument built of stone with

516 bronze replicas of the Pusan grave markers mounted on "a wall of remembrance."

A Wall Committee—including Bill Allan, George Mannion, Len Pelletier, Ben Mathers and Don Williams of Unit 57 of the KVA, as well as Dave Davidson, Don Flieger, Sam Carr and Clyde Bougie, a KVA founding member—began planning the memorial and raising funds for its construction. "That was the toughest part," admitted Allan, who began raising awareness and money for the project. "I spoke to city councils and corporations. A lot of these people were forty years old. They weren't even born when the war was on. Getting them to connect the Korean War with Canada was very difficult."

Of the $300,000 the committee raised, donations came from Legion branches and other military associations. They came from trusts, corporations and individual businesses. Funds arrived from service clubs, community organizations and Korean-Canadian groups. Individual politicians donated, as did scores of Canadian cities and towns, from Altona, Manitoba, to Whitehorse, Yukon. However, no provincial or federal funding was offered. By far the largest portion of the Wall Fund was raised by the Canadian veterans of the Korean War themselves. Typical was Jack LaChance, a former lance corporal in the 2nd Battalion of the PPCLI.

"When I received my notice in the mail asking for a donation," LaChance said, "I couldn't believe somebody was finally doing something. I had shut my Korean experiences out of my life." He had never even talked to his family about them. He shut out the image of carrying out the body of his friend Patty Patterson, killed in an artillery barrage in October 1951. He blanked out the faces of Chinese soldiers his unit captured; they were as young and scared as he was. He erased memories of coming home with malaria that hospitalized and nearly killed him. "But when I received that package from the KVA . . . all the faces, all the memories came back."

As the recollections filled his head, LaChance began jotting them down. He wrote personal anecdotes about Korea, stories for veterans' periodicals and he began an autobiography. The day he received the Wall donation request, as part of his own cathartic process, Jack

LaChance also sat down and composed a poem—"The Korea Veterans' Wall"—and sent it to the Wall Committee. Five months later they informed him it would be engraved in the Wall of Remembrance.

The Korea Veterans' Wall

Each uniquely mounted nameplate
On this Korea Veterans' Wall
Tells the story of a person
Who rallied to their country's call.

With courage and with vigor
They trained and went to war
And shielded us from danger
On the South Korean shores.

They gave their lives for freedom
That we all share today
In a far-off foreign country
Where most of their bodies lay.

We still hear the bugler sounding
Each stirring note of his "Last Call,"
While viewing all the nameplates
On this Korea Veterans' Wall.

The forty-fourth anniversary of the Korean War armistice—Sunday, July 27, 1997—dawned sunny and warm at the Meadowvale Cemetery near Brampton, Ontario. There, nestled into a natural bowl in the veterans' section of the grounds, the 200-foot-long, two-foot-high wall of grey granite sat shrouded in a green cloth. Canopies had been erected on the rise behind the wall for Korea veterans' families. All week they'd been arriving by the hundreds from across the country to witness the unveiling of a new national war monument.

By 9 o'clock, a convoy of buses began unloading the first of nearly 1,600 people for the dedication ceremony. Seated on one transit bus was Georgette Milliere. She was anxious to see the plaque bearing her brother's name, regiment and date of death—Leo Paul Gladu, PPCLI, April 3, 1951; much of her family came with her to share the moment. Also on the bus was former RCN stoker Lorne Barton, from the destroyer HMCS *Nootka*; he cut short a fishing trip in northern Ontario to see the plaque of a crew mate, Leon Armand Gauthier, who was washed overboard off Korea on January 11, 1951. Above and around the wall, army cadets stood at attention, reporters and videographers sought out the best vantage points and master of ceremonies, Korea veteran Herb Pitts, counted heads of arriving dignitaries; the South Korean ambassador was overdue. The Queen's Own Rifles of Canada band played a ceremonial piece until everyone was in place.

A few minutes later, the colours were presented, the dignitaries' speeches were delivered and the scripture readings offered. In the distance, the Lorne Scots Pipes and Drums were heard. Behind them, nearly 600 Korea veterans paraded to a semicircular roadway in front of the wall. Among them was Vern Roy; he of the *Sudbury Daily Star* photo in August 1950, when he and several buddies were on their way to join the Special Force for Korea. Former Vandoos corporal Roland Pearce marched in the parade; the way was far safer than the one he walked on the night of October 8, 1952, when he helped carry dead and wounded from a minefield in front of Hill 355. Keeping step en route to the wall was PPCLI veteran, now poet, Jack LaChance, who'd been "training for three months so that I could march in this parade."

Just before noon, Bill Allan, the Korea veteran who started the project five years before, with a snapshot of his friend Tunny MacDonald's grave in Pusan, unveiled the wall. For Allan, who claimed before the war, "I had nothing to look forward to in life, nothing in my future," this was a dream come true. A few minutes later, Tunny MacDonald's sister, Mary Robertson, representing deceased veterans' families, laid a wreath before the wall. Although they had been the co-inspiration for the monument, Bill Allan and Mary Robertson met face-to-face for the first time at the dedication.

"It brought me close to [Tunny] again," said Mary about the sense of closure at the wall. "Tunny was buried in Korea, but we could never go there to see him. But touching the wall, I felt he wasn't in Korea anymore. We have brought their spirits home."

The minutes that followed gave closure for many more. As soon as the dedication of the wall was complete, the veterans in the parade broke ranks and removed the poppies they'd been wearing, pinning them on the wall. Some of the men bowed their heads before the plaques. Some saluted smartly. Others embraced surviving comrades. And many wept openly. But then, in spontaneous response to the veterans' individual and collective grieving, many of the family members and veterans standing nearby joined the men from the parade at the wall.

In front of the plaque inscribed "Cpl. C. E. Bignucolo, Royal Canadian Regiment, 17th Oct. 1952, Age 23," three of his ten brothers and sisters joined the veterans. Ernest Bignucolo was the battle school instructor who Eddie Nieckarz saw blown up by a mortar bomb during training at Haramura, Japan. The family shared childhood memories of a brother who played music and hockey and was due to come home from Korea when the training accident occurred.

Walter Mann, who spent a year as a Roman Catholic chaplain in Korea, walked along the wall and "I realized that I had attended eight of the men commemorated on those plaques." Jack LaChance found the name G. L. Patterson on the wall, and as he put his poppy above the plaque, tears welled up as "I remembered the four of us carrying him out." At the spot in the wall where Tunny MacDonald's name was inscribed, his two sisters—Mary Robertson and Helen Arndt—stopped and reflected. A veteran gave the women each a poppy to place on Tunny's plaque, but when Helen saw that the plaque below Tunny's had no poppy, she placed it next to "that MacDonald's name, in case maybe his family didn't have the chance to be there."

Among the plaques was the name Gnr. William David Wright. Fellow RCHA gunner Doug Walton realized it was the name of one of his battery mates killed in the Canoe River train wreck in 1950. After the crash, Walton had been given Wright's greatcoat to keep him warm in the makeshift hospital car at the back of the train. At the wall, Walton paid his respects by pinning a poppy above Wright's plaque.

Also in the press to the wall were Barbara Differ and Hazel Regan. Hazel carried a framed photograph of their brother Bill. The two middle-aged women held each other for emotional support as they knelt before the plaque commemorating their brother. Presently, a veteran quietly emerged from the crowd and introduced himself as Clyde Pryor. He was in Bill Regan's section in Korea. For the first time, Barbara and Hazel learned how their brother was killed. On July 14, 1953, the 3rd Battalion of the Royal Canadian Regiment was forward at Hill 187. As usual on that position, nighttime Chinese shelling had broken ground-laid communication lines. A volunteer patrol was assembled to go out and repair the lines. Regan and Pryor flipped a coin to see who would go and Regan lost. During the operation, Chinese shelling resumed and Pte. Regan was wounded by shrapnel. He died at a MASH unit on July 17—ten days before the armistice at Panmunjom.

"In 1991 we went to Korea," Hazel explained. Of Bill Regan's six sisters, five went on that trip "expecting to meet someone who knew my brother. We found nothing. . . . In my heart I always knew someday we would meet someone.

"Just for us to know that [Clyde Pryor] was the man who had been with our brother," Barbara said, "that this was the last person he had talked to, had contact with, it touched us."

Following the day's dedication, Bill Regan's sister, Mavis Gergen, concluded, "Now we know where we're going to go for Remembrance Day services."

Terri O'Connor was four when her father, Patrick, was killed at the battle of Chail-li and Kahkul-bong on May 30, 1951. She grew up feeling "I only had a father on Remembrance Day" and later pursued legal channels to have his remains brought back to Canada. Hearing other veterans say that her father's body belonged where he had fought, helped her "accept that he's where he's supposed to be and we can come here to the monument.

"It's beautiful," Terri continued. "It's not on the scale of the Vietnam Memorial, but I think it's very Canadian. Sturdy, understated and peaceful."

Like the Vietnam Veterans' Memorial in Washington, D.C., the Wall of Remembrance tells only part of the veterans' story. Whether it's engravings in black granite listing 58,000 dead and missing in an unpopular Vietnam War, or the 516 bronze plaques commemorating those killed in a too-soon-forgotten Korean War, there is much a stone memorial doesn't describe in the aftermath of the war.

The physical and mental toll on survivors of the Korean War was only barely assessed, much less compensated. When Canadian POWs were released in the weeks and months after the armistice, the army conducted medical and psychiatric tests. All ex-prisoners suffered from malnutrition. Most had intestinal parasites. Some suffered from something called "photophobia," a dread of, or shrinking from, light. On the psychological side, doctors found (particularly among soldiers captured between 1951–52) moodiness, and some acute depression bordering on severe personality trauma and paranoia. However, Canadian army policy dictated that psychiatric counselling and treatment were voluntary. There was no scheme to handle long-term medical or psychological after-effects. Both Pte. Elmer McInnis and L/Cpl. Paul Dugal suffered epileptic seizures as a result of injuries compounded in Chinese POW camps. Neither man was admitted for long-term veterans' care. The army discharged them and gave them minimal disability benefits.

Elsewhere, Canadian veterans of the Korean War suffered everything from skin irritations to shell-shock or battle fatigue (post-traumatic stress disorder was not yet in the army medical lexicon). Few received medical, psychiatric or financial assistance to deal with their problems. Before he went overseas as a reinforcement with the 2nd Battalion of the PPCLI, Art Marion was not a public smoker or drinker. After a year of days sleeping in snake-infested bunkers and nights when his ears and nose bled from the concussion of exploding shells around his front-line position, Pte. Marion came home a changed man.

"I was a nervous wreck," Marion said. "If Mum dropped a spoon on the floor I was down under the table in a second. I'd never smoked when I was home. And I was becoming an alcoholic . . . You know, the army never really prepared us to go into that war. I was only nineteen. We knew what to do. Physically we were ready, but mentally we weren't." In 1991, after a long fight with the Department of Veterans Affairs, "I was awarded a hearing pension . . . But I still wake up at night, moaning and groaning. I'm still fighting that war."

Margaret Cripps married Korea veteran Luther Ferguson in 1962. Her husband had served with the 3rd Battalion of the RCR on the Hook and then at Hill 187 when the Chinese overran Charlie Company. Margaret recalled, "the first time I shook him to wake him up, he was up from a dead sleep in an instant, fists at the ready . . . And one time my kid sister threw a pet squirrel at him. It was a joke. But not for him. It brought back memories of rats in the trenches."

During his tour of duty in Korea, Ted Zuber's skills as a marksman were employed in an RCR scout and sniper section, and because the army had very few cameras at the front, Zuber's talent for sketching was also put to work. He made dozens of field drawings of Chinese positions and bunkers for the Canadian Intelligence Section. For himself, he drew soldiers washing, writing letters or waiting. And he tucked them away.

"Years later, when I decided to commit myself to putting my memoirs of the Korean War on canvas," Zuber said, "I looked at the sketches and realized they were emotionless. They were about as interesting as a topographical map . . . Every single face was absolutely dead, lifeless, no expression whatsoever," so when he eventually began to paint from memory, "the one thing I had to inject later was the emotion."

The Korea experience left invisible scars on Jim McKinny too. When his outfit, the Royal Canadian Horse Artillery, disembarked the train at Winnipeg, L/Bdr. McKinny recalls being formed up in the railway station and marched downtown to the cenotaph. The young gunnery veteran felt a genuine excitement knowing that his parents and girlfriend had come in from western Manitoba to welcome him home.

"But I couldn't face [my girlfriend] for nearly a month, McKinny said. "We only lived twenty-three miles apart, but I just couldn't handle people anymore. I had written to her every day I was away, but I just couldn't put my feelings into words. I was literally bushed. Korea made me a social misfit."

While he eventually broke the ice with his girlfriend, Lee (whom he later married), McKinny locked away everything that had happened in Korea. He never spoke to family or friends about the experience. He made no effort to find fellow veterans. It was the chapter of his life he was determined to forget. In 1991, when he and Lee decided to attend a Saskatoon Legion dance, McKinny dropped by the branch to buy the tickets. He was asked to fill out a form, on which he included his overseas service in 1952–53.

"Oh," the Legion official said. "You're a Korea veteran?"

"Yeah," McKinny answered. He paused and added, "Can't we join?"

"Oh, sure," the man said. "I was just curious because your group meets here once a month downstairs."

"What group?"

"The Korea Veterans Association," the Legion man said.

The Korea Veterans Association of Canada had its beginnings in a small reunion at Camp Borden in the summer of 1973. About 130 veterans and their wives gathered for the initial event, and a year later they formed the association with Clyde Bougie as president. When Jim McKinny joined Unit 46, the Saskatoon branch, in 1991, he found kindred spirits among fellow veterans. Finally, after nearly forty years, he began dealing with his thirteen months of service in Korea. Moreover, McKinny began campaigning to have local cenotaphs around Saskatchewan re-dedicated to include recognition of the Korean War and its veterans, because "it should have been done a long time ago!"

"That's what this association is all about," David Graham added. When he was a boy on Manitoulin Island in Ontario, Graham dreamed of being a locomotive engineer. He left the CPR to serve with the 2nd Battalion RCR in Korea. Then, as a member of the Korea Veterans Association, his wish was to "make sure there is a Korea War plaque on every cenotaph across northern Ontario." Since 1993, the KVA's Roy Borsholt and his memorials committee, including David Graham, have located twenty-eight cenotaphs in northern Ontario: "We've helped get civic officials and Legions to place Korea plaques where they never were before . . . It wasn't the Canadian Government doing this, just Korea veterans. It shows you what men can do."

Don Flieger joined the veteran's association after spotting a man in a KVA T-shirt in 1985. His rejection by the Legion was still fresh in Flieger's memory, so being welcomed into a brotherhood of Korea veterans was a welcome change. Flieger joined the local and in 1996 became national president. While the memorials committee worked on cenotaph re-dedications, Flieger worked on a committee representing Korea veterans whose applications for disability pension to the Department of Veterans Affairs had been turned down.

Among the cases was that of James Cotter, an RCHA gunner who claimed his exposure to the pesticide DDT in Korea left him with a chronic respiratory illness. In its meeting with Veterans Affairs, the KVA didn't so much argue Cotter's case as it briefed the review board about environmental conditions Canadian soldiers faced in Korea. Among other scenarios, the KVA described "DDT used in Korea for 'fogging' for spraying of heads, necks and bodies, for spraying camps, trenches, fire pits, underground bunkers, toilets, urinals, tents, kitchens and the troops' living environment from the air, from jeeps and trailers, from backpack sprayers, from hand-held 'swingfogging' machines and for dipping and soaking clothing and sleeping bags in accordance with the Handbook of Army Health 1950."

Testimony the KVA presented included the assessment of an Australian medical officer who wrote, "If the Australian army wanted to choose a country in the world, in the early 1950s, that would expose their troops to the greatest short and long term health risks, Korea would have headed the list."

Based on the scope of the evidence presented (by the KVA and the Royal Canadian Legion) and testimony that James Cotter's exposure to DDT had occurred during his service in Korea and that the resulting health complications had been chronic, Cotter eventually received a 60 percent disability pension. However, the history of Korea veterans applying for and winning service-related pensions is short. Most never bothered claiming or were met with the bureaucratic response: "Korea doesn't qualify." Between 1990 and 1995, a period during which the KVA stepped up its representations to the Veterans Review and Appeal Board, 164 Korea vets died of cancer, heart disease and other respiratory illness. Perhaps more telling is that of the 378 Canadians buried at the United Nations Cemetery in Pusan during the war, 25 died of disease.

Most of the men who volunteered for service in Korea did so in an instant. Whether regular army, Special Force troops or reinforcements, it took them months to train, weeks to cross the Pacific and a year or more to fulfill the commitment in Korea. It took their Canadian government nearly forty years to recognize that voluntary act. Immediately after the war, a group known as the Battle Honours Committee was established to review claims by military units for recognition of certain battle sites. In the late 1950s, the committee reviewed honours claims for the Second World War and what it called "the United Nations Operations—Korea." The committee (composed mostly of Second World War vets) felt that "to award a multiplicity of honours"—that is, to include battles in Korea— might diminish the importance of the award. Korea veterans, even to their fellow soldiers, appeared to be second-class citizens.

"When we came home," Korea veteran Harley Welsh said, "we weren't officially allowed to wear the blue square and gold laureate," of the US Presidential Distinguished Unit Citation for the Princess Patricias' stand at Kap'yong. "And the Canadian government had a problem with the Syngman Rhee [South Korea] volunteer medal too. It still hasn't decided whether we can wear it."

Even more mystifying was their country's long delay in awarding the Canadian Volunteer Service Medal for Korea. It had taken the KVA several years of lobbying government officials to convince them that Korea was not a "conflict," but a "war." Ironically, it was perhaps the presentation of volunteer medals to Canadian service men and women returning from the Persian Gulf War in 1991 that turned the tide. Korean War veterans were finally recognized in 1992 (although most of the medals were mailed to their recipients).

"My brother was in REME [Royal Electrical and Mechanical Engineers] corps in Korea," said RCAF transport pilot Rowly Lloyd, who, like most, got medals from the United Nations and the Commonwealth for service in Korea, "but my brother died about a year before the Canadian medal was awarded. He had always wondered about it."

Tom Boutillier still wonders. A member of Fox Battery in the 2nd RCHA, "Boots" had survived the Canoe River train wreck in 1950 and had gone on to do his full tour in Korea. L/Bdr. Boutillier was dumbfounded to learn that his seventeen comrades killed in the crash did not receive the Canadian Volunteer Service Medal posthumously.

"These people volunteered for service in Korea," Boutillier insisted. He has spent many days of his retirement writing letters to generals, journalists and politicians to convince them his gunnery mates "were killed on active duty on a troop train going to a theatre of war. But they don't get the medal because they didn't spend a day in Korea."

The Canadian Brigade remained operational along the DMZ (demilitarized zone) in South Korea until November 1954. The last Canadian unit to depart was the Medical Detachment, which ceased to exist on June 25, 1957, seven years from the day the war broke out.

The war that was not a war, but a police action, was over; and the peace that was not a peace, just an armistice, settled in Korea. At the time of the armistice, Lester Pearson, then president of the UN General Assembly, said it was "the end of one chapter of bloodshed and fighting. But it is only the beginning of a new and difficult one—the making of peace." Ahead lay years of rebuilding, political turmoil, student protests, an Olympic Games and no fewer than 440 fruitless sessions to find a permanent peace. At this writing, the two Koreas are still technically at war.

For some Korea veterans a subtle state of war persisted well into their repatriation to Canada. It took thirty-nine years for the government to recognize their volunteer service. It has taken the creation of the Korea Veterans Association to secure many overdue disability pensions. The re-dedication of all Canadian cenotaphs to include "Korea 1950–1953" goes on. And the creation of a national monument—the Wall of Remembrance—to honour Canadian war dead in Korea, would never have happened if not for the veterans' initiative.

Individually, coming to terms with the war and participation in it has been equally difficult and long in coming for Korea veterans. No medal, no pension, no national monument would ever give complete closure. When the war ended, Rose Marie Stumpf, the Alberta high school girl who wrote hundreds of letters to soldiers of the Princess Patricias overseas, moved away and never corresponded with the men again. "The sweetheart of the PPCLI" lost touch with Len Peterson, the PPCLI private who sent the first letter inviting Rose Marie to write other members of his platoon.

"Len Peterson was handsome and shy and sweet," she wrote later. "The war changed him. Although I never saw him after his return from Korea, the word was that 'he drank too much' and one night a car accident ended his young life."

It took many years for Don Nelson's family to come to terms with his Korea experience. In the winter of 1952, when he was sixteen, Nelson left home in New Brunswick and crossed the international border into Maine. A friend of the family, Gerard White, had just been drafted into the US Army and Nelson had decided to see him off at the training camp of the US 82nd Airborne Division in Calais, Maine. Somehow, the glamour of joining an airborne unit got to Nelson and he decided to join up too. He lied about his age. He lied about his nationality. He even used the name of one of his friends in Saint John, Charles Morell, to get in.

Before he knew it, Nelson had graduated from paratroop training, was airlifted to Korea and, under cover of darkness, was sent north of the 38th parallel. Pte. Chuck Morell was now part of a nine-man commando unit of the 82nd Airborne operating behind Chinese and North Korean lines. His job was to radio back Chinese military activity, blow up communist ammunition, fuel and military equipment, disrupt their communications and bury any evidence of his activity. He wore no uniform, just khakis without unit or rank identification. He understood, if he were ever captured, his existence would be denied. His unit worked at night, leaving its dog tags and tommy-guns in a mountain hideout. His only weapon was a Bowie knife.

"When I arrived home there were lots of hugs and kisses," Nelson said, "but when I dropped my knapsack the Bowie knife fell out, and my father just looked at me . . . As far as he was concerned, I had dishonoured him, my mother and my brothers and sisters . . . I was told never to talk about what I had done." Later, Don even presented the knife to his father as a peace offering, but it was refused. It was only following his father's funeral in 1973 that Don's mother told him, "We buried it with your father."

"Buried what?" asked Don.

"The thing that disgusted him more than anything else."

Don Nelson understood then that his mother had quietly placed the Bowie knife in Daniel Nelson's coffin. It was only in death that father and son could be reconciled. It was only at that moment that Don's experience in Korea could be acknowledged. However, the whole episode was just as quickly buried. It wasn't until the winter of 1998, on the eve of his sixty-first birthday, that Don Nelson permitted himself to recall his Korean War record, but "I have always looked at that experience as never having happened."

When he got home, medic Don Leier found out his service in Korea wasn't worth a dollar. In 1950, he'd left the Saskatchewan family farm to make room for his eight brothers. He'd learned to administer needles, tourniquets and first aid. In 1952 he served with the RCAMC attending Princess Patricias at an Advanced Dressing Station. In the early 1960s, back in Saskatoon, Leier went to a veterans' loans officer to get a down payment for his first house. The man refused him, saying, "Korea was no war, just a police action. Here's fifty cents. That's all you're getting."

With that, Leier pretty much dismissed his Korea service for good. In 1982, Leier's ten-year-old daughter, Lisa, interviewed her dad for a social studies project on war. The Grade 6 student wrote some poetry and a short story based on her father's reminiscences. She borrowed his nearly forgotten photographs and she transcribed an interview with him.

"What unit did you serve in?" she asked.

"The 37th Field Ambulance, Royal Canadian Army Medical Corps," Leier said.

"What exactly was your job?"

"I worked in the advanced first-aid station."

It was the first time since the veterans' loan incident that Don Leier had thought about his service in Korea and the first time he cared to talk about it. The interview had both light and sober moments, such as when Lisa asked him: "Is the TV show 'M*A*S*H' realistic?"

"Just the medical stuff," Leier said. "Not the pranks they played."

"Were you ever scared?" she asked finally.

"Yup," Leier said, "I was scared."

Like Don Leier, former prisoner-of-war George Griffiths faced rejection when he applied for a housing loan in Kingston after the war. Only, Griffiths nearly throttled the loans representative who said Korea "wasn't officially a war." Eventually, Griffiths calmed down and he got a down payment, but that wasn't the last outburst borne out of his service or imprisonment in Korea. In 1982, when he worked as a prison guard at Ontario's Warkworth Penitentiary, there was an attempted escape in his part of the facility.

"I had one prisoner ahead of me and another behind," recalls Griffiths. Suddenly, he was back in North Korea in 1952 and a prisoner again himself, remembering the ten months of deprivation and brainwashing, reliving his own attempt to escape. "And I fired three times at the prisoner going by me. I wanted him dead . . . I wanted him killed the same way [the Chinese] killed a Canadian soldier and walked over him in Korea . . . You see, in my mind, I was surrounded again . . . I was still a prisoner."

Thousands of Canadian veterans have revisited Korea since 1953. They've marvelled at the metropolis that emerged from the ashes of war-ravaged Seoul. They've stood at Panmunjom on the edge of the demilitarized zone and realized that most of the hills they fought for or defended now lie in either the DMZ or North Korea. They've been wined and dined by the descendants of the displaced people they felt they were defending. They've cried at the Pusan cemetery for fallen comrades. But like George Griffiths, most of them have not yet closed this chapter in their lives.

It's not only the psychological aftermath Korea veterans are coming to terms with. Far too many remember feeling their country sent them to the ends of the earth ill informed and ill equipped. Veterans of the Special Force still resent being labelled "scruff" when the non-commissioned men in its ranks earned such battle honours as a US Presidential Citation as well as Military Medals and Mention In Dispatches. The survivors of Korean battlefields—on land, sea and air—knew that the Canadian public was tired of talk of war, but that shouldn't have diminished their voluntary service for their country. The Korean War had no days that seized the nation's attention, such that people remembered where they were "the day war was declared" or "the day the Canadians landed," but its veterans don't believe their contribution should be left off community cenotaphs or out of the pages of history books. There remains a gap in public perception that from 1950 to 1953 Canadians were at war in Korea. And their experience was unique.

More than three million people died in their war. Their war was the first ordered by the United Nations. Their war was the first between the communist East and the capitalist West, their shots the first in an extended Cold War. Their red badge of courage was a deadlock, a war fought to a draw. The fifty years since have left the Korean War behind, but the war has not left them.

Notes

The number at left is the page number on which the cited information appears. Unless otherwise indicated, quotations from participants in the Korean War are taken from taped interviews (which are listed as Sources).

CHAPTER ONE – THE WAR THAT WASN'T

page

2   "one of the occupants": Herbert Fairlie Wood, *Strange Battleground, Official History of the Canadian Army in Korea* (Ottawa: Queen's Printer, Department of National Defence, 1966), p. 207.

6   "similar to home": George Griffiths's letter to Dick Ogden, December 5, 1952.

CHAPTER TWO – SPECIAL FORCE

page

9   "Sextant": Winston Churchill, *The Second World War, Closing the Ring* (Cambridge, Massachusetts: Houghton Mifflin, 1951), p. 325.

9   "Korea shall become free": Kim Chum-kon, *The Korean War 1950–53* (Seoul, Korea: Kwangmyong Publishing, 1973), p. 14.

10 "an ideological battleground": Harry Truman, quoted in John Toland, *In Mortal Combat: Korea 1950–1953* (New York: William Morrow, 1991), p. 16.

12 "darkened today": Walter Sullivan, quoted in Bruce Cumings, *Korea's Place in the Sun: A Modern History* (New York: W.W. Norton, 1997), p. 244.

13 "I feel strongly": Syngman Rhee, quoted in Cumings, p. 252.

14 "People's Army": Kim Il Sung, quoted in Chum-kon, p. 54.

15 Casualty statistics, quoted in David Wallechinsky's *Twentieth Century* (Toronto: Little, Brown, 1995), p. 208.

16 "a meeting of the Security Council": Dean Acheson, quoted in Merle Miller, *Plain Speaking: An Oral Biography of Harry S. Truman* (New York: Berkley Medallion, 1973), p. 289.

16 "members of the United Nations": Security Council Official Records, Fifth Year, 474th Meeting, Resolution, June 27, 1950.

16 "an international police force": Harry Truman, quoted in Miller, p. 294.

17 "police action": Louis St. Laurent, Debates, House of Commons, 1950, IV, p. 4,253.

17 "at a given signal": Bruce Cumings, citing *New York Times*, July 21, 1950, p. 269.

18 "peace is endangered": Lester Pearson, quoted in newscast, July 14, 1950, CBC Radio archives, Toronto.

18 Canada would recruit: Broadcasts, August 7 and 8, 1950, CBC Radio archives, Toronto.

21 "2,075 men": Wood, pp. 27–28.

21 "They're off to enlist": *Sudbury Daily Star*, August 12, 1950.

24 "On-the-job-training": Brooke Claxton, Broadcasts, August 8, 1950, CBC Radio archives, Toronto.

CHAPTER THREE – A GALLON OF SWEAT

page

31 "chaotic": RCAF Number 426 Squadron Diary, quoted in Larry Milberry, *The Canadair North Star* (Toronto: CANAV Books, 1982), p. 143.

35 draw the Chinese into the war: Edward C. Meyers, *Thunder in the Morning Calm, The Royal Canadian Navy in Korea 1950–1955* (St. Catharines: Vanwell Publishing, 1992), p. 45.

35 first of 130,000 rounds: Tony German, *The Sea Is At Our Gates: The History of the Canadian Navy* (Toronto: McClelland & Stewart, 1990), p. 218.

36 "avalanche swiftness": *Time* magazine, October 9, 1950.

36 "a red maple leaf": R. C. K. Bob Peers, "Have No Fear . . . The Navy's Here" (Korea Veterans Association of Canada files).

36 "brought the sea": R. L. Lane "Under Enemy Shells Aboard HMCS *Cayuga*" (KVA files).

37 cost 303 men: Ted Ferguson, *Desperate Siege: The Battle For Hong Kong* (Toronto: Doubleday, 1980), p. 237.

37 "another Hong Kong": Victor Quelch, House of Commons Debates, September 4, 1950, p. 232.

37 "scruff' men": G. R. Stevens, *The Royal Canadian Regiment: Volume Two 1933–1966* (London: London Printing, 1967), p. 219.

38 "a couple of hunchbacks": Canadian Army official, quoted in Blair Fraser, "Clearing Up the Recruiting Mess," *Maclean's* magazine, August 1, 1951.

38 "only one on the draft": Reg McIlvenna, "First Korea Volunteer" (KVA files).

39 Of the 8,000: Wood, p. 31.

40 "A gallon of sweat": Robert S. Peacock, *Kim-Chi, Asahi and Rum: A Platoon Commander Remembers Korea, 1952–1953* (Lugus, 1994), p. 143.

41 "included the dogs": J. G. Tony Poulin, "The Vingt-Deux Descend Upon Wainwright" (KVA files).

41 "Brutal sun singed our hides": John Carson, "Don't Follow The Rules" (KVA files).

41 "brewing up": E. Ray Knight, "Hazards of the Training Area" (KVA files).

42 "the soldier evolved": Ron Trider, "Tales from 2RCR 1950–1952" (KVA files), p. 3.

43 "small token force": Wood, p. 42.

47 "the bodies of my friends": Bill Carbray, quoted in *Toronto Daily Star*, November 21, 1950.

48 "just ten seconds": Donald Duross, "Tragedy at Canoe River" (KVA files).

49 worst military train accident: Hugh A. Halliday, *Wreck! Canada's Worst Railway Accidents* (Toronto: Robin Brass, 1997), pp. 195–203.

49 "the feel of the battle": John Rockingham, quoted in Arthur Bishop, *Salute! Canada's Great Military Leaders* (Whitby: McGraw-Hill Ryerson, 1997), p. 214.

50 "a chilly version of British Columbia": *Korea* booklet (Ottawa: Bureau of Current Affairs, Department of National Defence, 1951).

51 "they're fighting men": John Rockingham, quoted in "Training at Fort Lewis" (KVA files).

52 "annihilate them": North Korean People's Army officer, quoted in Cumings, p. 279.

54 "'emergency' proportions": Thor Thorgrimsson and E. C. Russell, *Canadian Naval Operations in Korean Waters 1950–1955* (Ottawa: Queen's Printer, Department of National Defence, 1965), p. 31.

54 "black as the inside of a cow": Jeffry Brock, *Memoirs of a Sailor: The Dark Broad Seas, Volume 1, With Many Voices* (Toronto: McClelland & Stewart, 1981).

55 "most dangerous naval mission": Meyers, p. 95.

CHAPTER FOUR – LAND OF THE MORNING CALM

page

57 see the ship cast off: George Finlay, "Princess Pats Set Sail for Far Pacific Port" Canadian Press, November 27, 1950.

58 tubular steel: Trider (KVA files), p. 11.

61 "against my better judgement": Jim Stone, quoted in John Melady interview, October 10, 1981.

62 "land of the morning calm": Description of Korea from Choson dynasty in the 15th century; reference, quoted in James Scarth Gale, *History of the Korean People* (first published serially in 1920s by Seoul: Royal Asiatic Society, 1972).

63 "land of filth and poverty": Jim Stone, letter, quoted in Wood, p. 55.

63 "Glad you're here": Stone, quoted in Melady interview.

67 "In no time": Mel Canfield, "Memories of Korea: Part 1, Early Lessons," *Legion* magazine, Volume 73, Number 1, January/February 1998, p. 49.

67 "hunting guerrillas": *PPCLI War Diary*, January 1951.

68 "unlikely to become efficient": "Ten Percent Discharge Rate" Canadian Press, February 26, 1951.

68 Tommy Prince: D. Bruce Sealey and Peter Van de Vyvere in *Manitobans in Profile: Thomas George Prince* (Winnipeg: Peguis Publishers, 1981).

70 "all hell broke loose": Bill Boss, quoted in John Melady interview, June 20, 1982.

71 "Telling Canadians": Bill Boss, quoted in William Sparke, "I've Got the Best Job," *New Liberty* magazine, May, 1953, p. 31.

71 "about your story": Boss, quoted in Melady interview.

72 "earned the company's acclaim": Bill Boss, "Toronto Man Defies Reds to Attend Wounded Pats," Canadian Press, February 25, 1951.

73 beer issue: Jeffery Williams, *Princess Patricia's Canadian Light Infantry, 1914–1984: Seventy Years Service* (London, Leo Cooper, 1972), p. 82.

73 "campaign of vilification": Editorial, "The Censorship that Helps the Enemy," *Maclean's* magazine, October 15, 1951.

76 "Greetings-Congratulations-Alive!": Pierre Berton, "Milk Run to Korea," *Maclean's* magazine, May 15, 1951.

76 worst flying conditions: Les Peate, "The Korean War . . . The Other Airlift," *esprit de corps* magazine, Volume 4, Number 9, February 1995.

77 "bullets to broomsticks": Paul Lemeux, quoted in Peate, ibid.

CHAPTER FIVE – BLOODING OF THE BRIGADE

page

79 "A soldier's spirit": Young Sik Kim, *Eyewitness: A North Korean Remembers*, entry for November 1950 (Columbus, Ohio: Unpublished manuscript quoted with permission, 1995).

82 fighting their way: John Thompson, *The Battle of Kapyong* (Australia: Unpublished thesis quoted with permission, 1997).

83 "coming out of the hills": Roy Yalmer, quoted in Bill Boss, "Canuck Heroism Bared as Censorship Lifted," Canadian Press, May 11, 1951.

84 "well organized": C. V. Lilley, quoted in Wood, p. 77.

84 "fought extremely well at night": Stone, quoted in Melady interview.

84 "wonderful targets": Carl Deschamps, quoted in Boss, "Canuck Heroism . . ."

85 "[Chinese] bugle call": Jim Waniandy, quoted in Bill Boss, "Canadian Gun Cut Down 50 Glory-Happy Red Chinese," Canadian Press, May 12, 1951.

86 "stratagem was successful": *PPCLI War Diary*, April, 1951.

86 "strangers in hell": Kenneth Barwise, quoted in Boss, "Canadian Gun . . ."

87 "Flying Boxcars": George Cook, "The Battle of Kap'yong: A Personal Reminiscence" (KVA files).

89 "Patricias' epic stand": Trider, p. 13.

90 radioactive no-man's-land: Cumings, p. 291.

90 "a limited war": Harry Truman, quoted in *Ottawa Journal*, April 12, 1951.

92 "There were trenches": Trider, p. 20.

92 "a movement forward": Wood, p. 97.

96 "the rollicking air": Reg McIlvenna, "Splendour in the Mud" (KVA files).

96 "welcoming us to Chail-li": George Fuller, "Chail-li . . . A Very Busy Day" (KVA files).

97 "one platoon ahead of me": Don Stickland, "Up the Slippery Slopes of Mount Kakhul-bong" (KVA files).

98 "Maj. Boates's body": George Bickley, quoted in Marguerite McDonald interview on CBC Radio "Open House," September 2, 1991.

99 "ignoring the danger": Letter from Mr. and Mrs. H. Root family to Vera O'Connor, December 3, 1951.

100 "Blood On The Hills": Pat O'Connor poem (published with permission from Vera O'Connor).

101 "bearded farmers": John E. Dalrymple, "A Walk Through the Peaceful Valley" (KVA files).

103 "three liaison officers": Peking message, quoted in Clay Blair, *The Forgotten War: America in Korea 1950–1953* (New York: Random House, 1987), p. 937.

CHAPTER SIX — GOD KEEP ME FROM HEROES

page

106 "mountain freshet": Bill Boss, "Members of Princess Pats Enjoy First Canadian Beer," Canadian Press, May 26, 1951.

107 "Chinese Hussars": Peacock, p. 85.

109 bullet in his lung: Les Peate, "40 Years Ago . . . The Case of the Spurious Sawbones," *esprit de corps* magazine, Vol. 3, No. 5, Oct., 1993.

110 dean of philosophy: *Globe and Mail*, Toronto, June 9, 1982.

114 "pointless": "Claim 'Dear John' Letters Sapping Morale in Korea," Canadian Press, November 24, 1952.

115 "Set out early this morning": Fr. Walter Mann personal diary, published with permission, April 16, 1953.

115 "rice-burners": Les Peate, "A Salute to the Rice-Burners," *esprit de corps* magazine, Volume 5, Number 5, April 1996.

116 "so endeared himself": Bill Boss, "Houseboys with Canadians Make Korea Fight Easier," Canadian Press, May 16, 1951.

116 "a little boy of eight": Don Stickland, "Willie Royal, Son of a Thousand Fathers," (KVA files).

117 medical staff went without: John Clark, "The Magnificent Role of Canada's Nursing Sisters" (KVA files).

118 "Rochester General Construction Company": Bill Boss, "Sappers Everywhere in Korea," Canadian Press, July 6, 1951.

119 "short-take-off-and-landing": Sean Rossiter, *The Immortal Beaver* (Vancouver: Douglas & McIntyre, 1996), p. 91.

121 blew up four mines this way: Thorgrimsson and Russell, p. 19.

121 back in operation: Leonard Bailey, "Our Special Towing Service," (KVA files).

122 "Disaster was imminent": F. W. Chapman, "Recovery in Korea," *esprit de corps* magazine, Volume 3, Number 7, December 1993.

122 "no privacy": Trider, p. 32.

126 American MPs: Ken Campbell, quoted in Robert Hepenstall, *Find The Dragon: The Canadian Army in Korea 1950–1953* (Edmonton, Four Winds Publishing, 1995), p. 291.

126 "their leave expired": Trider, p. 43.

CHAPTER SEVEN – THE IRREMOVABLE DIGIT

page

134 "a new turn": Robert Clark, "A Young Corporal Earns His Stripes," (KVA files).

134 "aprons of barbed wire": Art Johnson, "An Exciting Beginning on Hill 187," (KVA files).

135 "good looking lot of men": Jeffery Williams correspondence, January 27, 1998, February 2 and 10, 1998.

138 "gallant FOO": *PPCLI War Diary*, October 23, 1951.

140 "waste of time and lives": Hepenstall, p. 123.

140 "utterly useless war": Blair; p. 950.

140 low number of infantry: Wood, p. 162.

141 "tightening of the heart": Charly Forbes, *Fantassin* (Sillery, Quebec: Septentrion, 1994), p. 293.

142 "No withdrawal": *2nd Bn R22eR War Diary*, November 22, 1951.

145 "worst since the Hochwald Forest": Rhéal Liboiron, quoted in Bill Boss, "Shelling Took Place During Their Epic Stand," Canadian Press, December 13, 1951.

145 "You get afraid": Denis LaPierre, quoted in Boss, ibid.

146 tossing it like an egg: Bill Boss, "Company Under Fire Five Days," Canadian Press, December 8, 1951.

146 "the irremovable digit": Tom Webb, quoted in Forbes, p. 312.

147 scaled several old parapets: Mario Côté, "No Withdrawal. No Platoons Overrun. No Panic . . ." (KVA files).

147 "down their throats": Ray MacDuff, quoted in Bill Boss, "Mount Kowang Stand," Canadian Press, December 10, 1951.

147 "buffaloes over a bridge": Ray MacDuff, quoted in Wood, p. 157.

148 "through the barbed wire": Rhéal Liboiron, quoted in Bill Boss, "Divisional Commander Praises D Co. Van Doos," Canadian Press, November 29, 1951.

148 "attacked by infantry": *R22eR War Diary*, November 1951.

149 "there to fight": Denis LaPierre, quoted in Bill Boss, "Company Under Fire Five Days," Canadian Press, December 8, 1951.

149 "mortar base plates": Forbes, pp. 317–318.

150 "deathly silence": René Lévesque, *Memoirs* (Toronto: McClelland & Stewart, 1986), p. 133.

CHAPTER EIGHT — AN UNHOLY MESS

page

152 "playing bingo": Bill Boss, "Canadians in Korea Play Military Bingo and Net a Prisoner," Canadian Press, January 5, 1952.

153 "if Chinese were captured": Pierre Berton, "This is the Enemy," *Maclean's* magazine, July 5, 1952.

154 "organize the hard-core communist POWs": Blair, pp. 966–967.

154 "Pro and anti-communist factions": Young Sik Kim, entry for October 25, 1951.

155 "an unholy mess": Haydon Boatner, quoted in Toland, p. 527.

158 US Army engineers: Bill Boss, "Canucks on Koje Island Get Wide Co-operation," Canadian Press, June 15, 1952.

159 "somebody escaping": Tom McKay, quoted in John Melady interview, August 18, 1982.

161 a few decent troops: Toland, p. 535.

161 "UN commitment": Wood, p. 193.

161 "misgivings": Douglas How, "Pearson's Koje Concern Vague," Canadian Press, May 28, 1952.

162 "Canadian Army organization": Bill Boss, "Canucks Surprised at Failure of Reds to Flee from Koje," Canadian Press, June 10, 1952.

162 "just ten minutes": Bill Boss, Canadian Press, June 13, 1952.

163 bridges that crossed the Imjin: Peter Worthington, *Looking for Trouble* (Toronto: Key Porter, 1984), p. 40.

164 T-6 Texan aircraft: Lea Peate, "The Korean War . . . Mosquitos Over the Imjin," *esprit de corps* magazine, Volume 3, Number 9, February, 1994.

165 Elmer Witten at the controls: J. P. R. Tremblay, "Sans pilote, au-dessus du no man's land," *Reader's Digest* July 1962 (KVA files, translated by J. G. Tony Poulin).

169 "debollockers": Les Peate, "Of Mines and Mayhem," *esprit de corps* magazine, Volume 6, Number 3, November, 1997.

172 littered with shrapnel: Bill Boss, "Walked Through Field of Mines to Lead His Comrades to Safety," Canadian Press, October 24, 1952.

CHAPTER NINE — IN THE KILLING ZONE

page

177 "positional warfare": Toland, p. 483.

178 "lessons for war from 1917": Peacock, p. 11.

178 "No patrol is ever routine": Peacock, pp. 62–63.

184 "irresistible traps": John E. Dalrymple, "Digging In," (KVA files).

186 "paludrine pills": Stevens, p. 248.

186 "eleven of fourteen bunkers": Peacock, pp. 21–22.

187 "heaviest casualties": Peacock, p. 11.

187 "The soldier sits in his dugout": Bill Boss, "Reports Reaction of UN Soldiers Under Shelling," Canadian Press, December 10, 1951.

190 "artificial moonlight": Joe York, "Assigned as Angels of Light," (KVA files).

190 "centre stage": Peacock, p. 79.

193 relief party: Andy King correspondence, April 16, 1998.

195 "less than an arm's length": Dan Loomis, quoted in Wood, p. 208.

198 "I am boxed in": Wood, p. 210.

199 "slightly the worse for wear": Stevens, p. 254.

199 a negotiated solution: Blair, pp. 970–971.

201 "unleashed poetic justice": *RCR War Diary*, January 26, 1953.

CHAPTER TEN — A BIT OF HOME

page

204 "something for the boys": Rose Marie Stumpf, quoted in "Canadian Pin-Up in Korea is Young Alberta Girl," *Calgary Herald*, August 8, 1953.

204 "conspicuous by its absence": Report by Lt.-Col. D. S. F. Bult-Francis on *Visit to Japan and Korea*, 1 July–4 August 1951.

205 department would provide: Brooke Claxton, *Debates House of Commons*, 1951, 2nd Session I, p. 1,081.

205 sports equipment: "Army Morale" Canadian Press, October 28, 1951.

208 "Frisco quake of 1908": Bob Hesketh, "News on Sport," *Toronto Telegram*, May 21, 1954.

208 "at every stop": Ken Charlton interviewed by Belle Charlton, November 1997.

208 "shaken hands": Bob Hesketh, "News on Sport," *Toronto Telegram*, May 27, 1954 and June 1, 1954.

209 "Saskatchewan's roads": Lloyd Saunders, guest-writing in Bob Hesketh, "News on Sport" *Toronto Telegram*, June 1954.

209 "joined the army": Maxwell "Duke" Poyntz, quoted in Bill Boss, "Duke's Donut Dive" Canadian Press, June 26, 1951.

210 "Peterson's Paradise is close enough": Bill Boss, "Peterson's Paradise Haven to Tired, Shaggy Canuck Soldiers," Canadian Press, December 7, 1951.

211 "the dawn stand-to": Trider, p. 51.

211 "a man enjoys": Jack Peterson, quoted in Boss, op. cit.

213 through Canadian positions: Bill Boss, "Danny Kaye, Canadians Make Movie," Canadian Press, November 5, 1951.

213 stole the show: Hepenstall, pp. 296–297.

213 "with the dessert": Lorraine McAllister, quoted in Bill Boss, "Vancouver Songstress Sang to Troops in Front Lines of Korea," Canadian Press, January 10, 1953.

214 "volunteered to go": Hank Snow, "Entertaining in Korea," (KVA files).

216 the first Canadian: Ted Barris and Alex Barris, *Days of Victory: Canadians Remember 1939–1945* (Toronto: Macmillan Canada, 1995), p. 146.

CHAPTER ELEVEN — THE LAST STATISTIC

page

234 "shells fired at our tank": Harry Pope, "Memories of War, Korea: Hill 159 in September 1952," *La Citadelle*, February 1989.

235 "Tony's Torches": Tony Poulin, "Linear Defence vs. Defense in Depth" (KVA files).

238 "the Victoria Cross": Terry Meagher, *True Canadian War Stories*, selected by Jane Dewar, *Legion* magazine (Toronto: Lester & Orpen Dennys, 1986), p. 280.

240 "concentration of shelling": Mann, personal diary, May 2/3, 1953.

241 "Lay down your arms": James Pelletier; "Observations On Life Among the Chinese," (KVA files).

242 fired 3,400 shells: George Ruffee, "Artillery Support for the Royals" (KVA files).

243 "filled with casualties": Ed Hollyer, quoted in Wood, p. 235.

245 "The Trainbusters Club": Meyers, p. 187.

249 inquiry into the grounding: Meyers, pp. 224–230.

250 "propaganda symbols": Toland, p. 575.

251 "a grandstand performance": Mann, personal diary, July 27, 1953.

251 "nervous laughter": Peacock, p. 138.

251 "few of us": Don Stickland, "That Night of Nights," (KVA files).

CHAPTER TWELVE — THE OTHER SIDE OF THE HILL

page

254 stripped of their boots: R. Bruce McIntyre, "The Forgotten Thirty-Three: An Examination of Canadian Prisoners of War of the Korean War" (thesis presented to the University of Waterloo, 1994), p. 33.

254 "United Nations prisoners": *Treatment of British Prisoners of War in Korea* (London: H. M. Stationery Office, 1955).

254 "victims of the ruling classes": McIntyre, p. 55.

258 "brinksmanship": Blair, p. 971.

259 "gates were closed": Jim Gunn, "A Sniper Disarmed" (KVA files).

262 "hit upon a plan": C. Gordon Owen, "Unscheduled Visit North" (KVA files).

263 "prisoner captured in 1950": James Pelletier, "Observations of Life Among the Chinese" (KVA files).

263 "doctor led a prisoner": Mike Dormer, Thames Television producer; "Korea: The Unknown War: Part V: The Battle For Minds" (Watertown, New York, WNPE-WNPI, November 9, 1990).

265 "thirty-seven minutes": Andy Mackenzie interviewed by Ron MacDonald at the RCAF Memorial Museum at CFB Trenton, Ontario, 1992.

266 "told them everything": Andy Mackenzie interviewed by John Melady, November 1, 1981.

266 at home in Ottawa: Helene Liston interviewed by John Melady, November 29, 1981.

267 "marched me": Joe Liston interviewed by John Melady, November 29, 1981.

270 "delaying tactics": Albert Batten, "The Prisoner-of-War Camps in North Korea" (KVA files).

270 one last propaganda event: James Pelletier, "Observations of Life Among the Chinese" (KVA files).

273 "communist petition": Bill Boss, "Eight Canadians To Be Freed, Reds Disclose," Canadian Press, August 24, 1953.

273 their performance: McIntyre, p. 504.

274 "world record": Andy Mackenzie, quoted in John Gardam, *Korea Volunteer: An Oral History From Those Who Were There* (Burnstown: General Store Publishing, 1994), p. 235.

CHAPTER THIRTEEN — THE WAR THAT HISTORY FORGOT

page

275 "outwardly laconic": Joe MacSween, "Lost Weight in Red Prison Camps, Freed Canadians Decline to Talk," Canadian Press, August 30, 1953.

277 "an administrative problem": Peacock, p. 540.

279 "ominous danger": Most Rev. W. F. Barfoot, quoted in "Korea Conflict 'Forgotten War'," Canadian Press, November 14, 1951.

279 "the young Canadians": John Melady, *Korea: Canada's Forgotten War* (Toronto: Macmillan Canada, 1983), p. vii.

282 "The Korea Veterans' Wall": poem published with permission from Jack LaChance.

286 "photophobia": McIntyre, pp. 107–108, 122–123.

289 "DDT used in Korea": *Handbook of Army Health*, 1950; and included in "16 Korean Veterans' Mortality and Health Study Research Papers" prepared by Col. Allan F. Limburg, CVO (RL), 1998.

292 "end of one chapter": Lester Pearson, quoted in Wood, p. 258.

292 "war changed him": Rose Marie (Stumpf) Thompson, correspondence, July 16, 1997.

294 project on war: Lisa Leier "War" project, 1982 (published with permission).

Sources

Bill Allan, Len Badowich, Charles Barker, Dave Baty, Ernest Beattie, Keith Besley, Bruce Best, Rev. George Bickley, Albert Bignucolo, Esther (Bignucolo) Chambers, Mary (Bignucolo) Forrester, George Black, Jim Boire, Clyde Bougie, Eugene Bourassa, Tom Boutillier, Dean Broadfoot, Art Browne, Bob Bunting, Rev. Bill Buxton, Mel Canfield, Larry Carpenter, Ken and Belle Charlton, John "Knobby" and May Clark, Herb Cloutier, Russ Cormier, Jim Cruden, Frank Cullen, Terry (Dale) Millar, Phil Daniel, Bill Davis, Jac de Bruijne, Bud Doucette, Bob Douglas, Larry Edmonds, Gerry Emon, Art Evoy, Leon Ferguson, Luther and Margaret (Cripps) Ferguson, Don and Kay Flieger, Pat Furlong, Leo Gallant, Eric Glustien, Neil and Marie Goodwill, Dave Graham, George and Barbara Griffiths, George Guertin, Jim Gunn, Roy Hardaker, Jack Henry, John Henshaw, Bob Hesketh, Don Hibbs, Al Hill, Ed Hollyer, Gil Hutton, Bill Jackson, Bill Johnson, Cosmo Kapitaniuk, Herb Kelly, Red Kelly, Deuk-Hwan Kim, Patrick Kimmitt, Andy King, Jack and Fran LaChance, Charlie LeBlanc, Chund Lee, Don Leier, Lew Lewis, Rowly Lloyd, Dan Loomis, Sophie Lucyk, Helen (MacDonald) Arndt, Mary (MacDonald) and Lloyd Robertson, Butch MacFarlane, Andy Mackenzie, Bentley MacLeod, Geoff Magee, Bob Mahar, Fr. Walter Mann, George "Scotty" Mannion, Art Marion, Jim "Scotty" Martin, Eric McClymont, Ina McGregor, John McKay, Jim McKinny, Don McNeil, Ken and June McOrmond, Terry Meagher, Hal Merrithew, Wayne Mitchell, Larry Moore, Larry Motiuk, Lea Muirhead, Don Nelson, Ed Nieckarz, Jack Noble, Terri and Vera O'Connor, Robert Peacock, Roland Pearce, Les Peate, Ed Pecarski, Claude Petit, Norris Petit, Bert Picotte, Desmond Piers, Les Pike, Bert and Nancy Pinnington, Herb and Marianne Pitts, Joe Pleau, Harry Pope, J. G. Tony Poulin, Phil Plouffe, Jackie Rae, Dani Regan, Hazel Regan, Jean (Regan) Campkin, Barbara (Regan) Differ, Mavis (Regan) Gergen, Ruth (Regan) McMann, John and Verna Rigo, Dal Richards, Paul Rochon, Vernon Roy, Ed Ryan, Ernest Sargeant, Frank Shuster, Earl (Simovitch) Simmons, Bob Somers, Ray Sorsdahl, Jean-Paul St-Aubin, Don Stickland, Jim Stone, Rose Marie (Stumpf) Thompson, Bill Tigges, John Tomlinson, Cy Torontow, Ron Trider, Bob Turner, Ralph Verge, Doug Walton, Harley Welsh, Jeffery Williams, Glenn and Eileen Wilberforce, Muriel (White) Yost, Peter Worthington, Ted Zuber

Index

Borsholt, Roy, 289.
Boss, Bill, 70-73, 86, 105, 106, 116, 149, 162, 187, 210, 275.
Bougie, Clyde, 281, 288.
Bougie, J.L., 145.
"bouncing Betty" ("bounding Betsy"), 168, 169, 173, 231.
Bourassa, Eugene, 250.
Boutillier, Tom, 44-47, 291.
Bovey, John, 245.
Bowen, Jerry, 235.
box barrage, 2
Boyle, Frank, 110.
Bradley, Omar, 90.
Bradshaw, E.F., 138.
Bren gun, 66, 84, 85, 87, 93, 98, 146, 147, 183, 190, 196, 235, 242.
Bridge of No Return, 6, 254.
British Navy, Army and Air Force Institute (NAAFI), 204.
British Commonwealth Air Training Plan (BCATP), 29.
British Commonwealth Hospital, 118.
British Empire Medal, 55, 254.
Britt, Elton, 212.
Broadfoot, Dean, 74-78.
Brock, Jeffry, 32, 53-55.
Bronze Star (US), 139, 191.
Browne, Art, 188.
Browning machine gun, 235.
Bruce, R.F., 178, 179.
Bunker Hill, 178.
Bunting, Bob, 197.
Burchett, Wilfred, 150.
Burma Star, 24.
burp-gun, 3, 87, 145, 238, 241, 242.
Butler, Red, 22.
Butt, Les, 195.
Buxton, Bill, 113, 114.

Cairo Conference, 9.
Caldwell, D.S., 199.
Campbell, K.L., 237.
Canadian Army Radio Show, 216, 217, 219.
Canadian Broadcasting Corporation (CBC), 18, 150, 204, 213, 216, 217.
Canadian Concert Party, 217-223.
Canadian Football League (CFL), 207.
Canadian National Exhibition (CNE), 251.
Canadian National Railway (CNR), 38, 45-49.
Canadian Pacific Airlines, 6, 207, 217.
Canadian Pacific Railway (CPR), 38, 93, 289.
Canadian Press, 71, 73, 149, 187, 275.
Canadian Volunteer Service Medal, 291.
Canfield, Mel, 19, 60, 63, 67, 86.
Canoe River, 45-49, 278, 285, 291.
carbine rifle, 86, 183, 239, 241.
Carbray, Bill, 47.
Carr, Carol, 213.

Carr, Maurice, 86.
Carr, Sam, 281.
Carson, John, 40.
Cassels, A.J.H., 146.
Casualty Clearing Station (CCS), 108, 109, 113, 240.
Central Intelligence Agency (CIA), 12, 156.
Centro, Vic, 217, 219.
Chaddock, Dale, 247.
Chail-li, 94-96, 98, 111, 139, 285.
Chapman, F.W., 122.
Charlton, Ken, 207, 208, 221.
Cheevers, Zena, 217, 218, 220.
Cheh Sang Sup, 145.
Chenoweth, R., 246, 249.
Chiang Kai-shek, 9, 13, 258.
Chicago Daily News, 250.
Childre, Doc Lou, 215, 216.
Chinnampo, 53-55, 62, 245.
Chipyong-ni, 72.
Cho Nam-Soum "Willie Royal", 116, 117.
Chonan, 17.
Chorley Park Personnel Depot (Toronto), 21, 90.
Ch'orwon, 94, 101, 105, 107, 108, 118, 132, 139.
Chosin Reservoir, 53.
Chou En-lai, 258.
Chuam-ni, 69, 70.
Ch'unch'on, 164.
Churchill, Winston, 9.
Clark, John, 195, 196, 198, 199.
Clark, Mark, 155.
Clark, Robert, 133, 134.
clergy, 102, 103, 113-115, 212, 240, 251, 263, 279, 284.
Claxton, Brooke, 19, 24, 26, 37, 42, 204-206.
Clooney, Rosemary, 214.
Cloutier, Herb, 156-163, 194, 196-199.
Cohen, E.L., 158, 197, 198.
Cole, C.H., 151, 152.
Collier, Andrew, 54, 55.
Colson, Charles, 155-160.
Companion of the British Empire, 42.
Compound 66, 159-162.
Compound 76, 155, 156, 160-162, 167.
Cook, George, 80, 85, 87.
Cormier, Russ, 188, 240, 251.
Coté, L.G., 232, 245.
Coté, Mario, 148.
Cotter, James, 289, 290.
C-Rations, 69, 106, 123, 168, 190, 234, 237.
Craig, Al, 175-177.
Craig, Bob, 45, 46.
Croix de Guerre, 42.
Crosby, Bing, 212.
Cruden, Jim, 240, 276.
Cullen, Frank, 107, 108.
Currie Barracks (Calgary), 39, 40, 187.